I0154770

BEYOND THE BLACK STUMP OF ETERNITY

A TOOLKIT FOR UNDERSTANDING THE DEEPER MEANING TO LIFE, ITS EXISTENCE AND GLOBAL ISSUES

DAVID SHAUN LARSEN

Copyright © 2017, by David Shaun Larsen

www.davidshaunlarsen.com

The opinions and suggestions expressed in this book are purely the author's own and do not necessarily reflect the official policy or position of any other agency, organisation, employer or company (unless directly referenced by a Government funded body whose role is to provide information and services for the community).

It is the reader's responsibility to verify their own facts.

No part of this book may be reproduced in any form or by any electronic or mechanical means, including information storage and retrieval systems, without written permission from the author, except for the use of brief quotations in a book review.

Requests to publish any work from this book can be emailed to:

davidsdm@yahoo.com

David Shaun Larsen

❀ Created with Vellum

CONTENTS

ACKNOWLEDGMENTS

- APPRECIATION AND THANKS FOR SHARING THE JOURNEY WITH ME

Writing this book wouldn't have been possible without my mum's valued love and support. Astrid has always provided a nurturing getaway for me to write; with so much belief and encouragement every step of the way. Also, I recently changed my surname from Murray to Larsen. Larsen is symbolic of embracing my mum's Norwegian heritage and privileged journey embarking on a possible career as a writer - a beholder of stories.

In addition, I'd like to acknowledge my dear friends and family, and various acquaintances I've met on my journey over the past year. They've had to brave many endless conversations about my book, which has also provided much validation for my writing. Nevertheless, I'd like to thank the following people for their contributions and support formally:

- Mark, Anthony, Maggie, Fran, Steph and Scotty for their valued love and support over the years.
- A special mention to Allister; Kevin and Hunter; Fran and Steph; Janet and Ralph; Gretel, and Mary, David, Declan, and Niamh for being there for me.
- Jamie, you've been an enormous support and always being there for me to the very end, I can't thank you enough.
- My dear friend Maggie your insights have always been treasured.
- Janet Murrell for her beautiful contribution - an Elogy for her son Wade who passed over 24/5/2008.

- My two dogs Gracie and Parker, you're always in my heart and life.
- Heather, a dear friend, and mentor who provided a very detailed review of some content and photographs from her time in the Kimberley Ranges, Western Australia.
- Kerrie Redgate, you have always encouraged and inspired me to write. And you have provided the most valuable advice and feedback; just when I have needed it the most. Her website: Kerrie Redgate: Living with Exceptional Purpose.
- Wil Groot for his contribution. **See Chapter 10: Humanitarianism** - *Our Global Responsibility for Humanity.* Willen & Doen, in English Will & Do. His website: Willen & Doen.
- Michael Wayne Garnam, Russell "Louie" Higgs and Frolance Besa thank you for teaching me about the true value and meaning of love.
- Ankush Rana, CEO at Creative3Studio for designing my website.
- Rob Williams, for book cover design Fiverr.com/cal5086.
- Cliff and Andrew for the privilege of using their property at Walligan to take the Black Stump photography.
- The Staff of the HIV Outreach Team in South Eastern Sydney Local Health District. You've been such a pleasure to work with and valuable support. Big thanks and hugs to Carol, Leo, Paul, Amanda, Julie, Althea, Mike, Alice, Dianne and Matt.
- Lastly, Ross and Dianne, you have been fantastic friends and mentors for me. I've enjoyed our many conversations; you are both such inspiring people!

All quotes and references are made with admiration and respect (without any particular permission) but with no intention of infringement of copyright.

And finally, special thanks to you the readers, for your openness, patience, and support. I hope this book provides something different and unique.

Dedicated with much love and blessings.

David

Visit me at: www.davidshaunlarsen.com

Email: davidsdm@yahoo.com

David Shaun Larsen

INTRODUCTION
- BEYOND THE BLACK STUMP OF ETERNITY

You may wonder what is so unique about this book compared to many other books on spirituality, self-development or societal and global issues for that matter. Firstly, I have always wanted to write a book but just not any book. It's been a life journey of immense challenges and discovery. I truly cherish and value, in the most heartfelt way, the responsibility to get this information out into the world; especially at a time when anyone can get media coverage or become published. Nevertheless, as this is my first self-published book, I'm also open to feedback about my writing content and style.

I've had my fair share of challenges over the past year i.e., recently left my job, sold my unit in Sydney and moved to Hervey Bay to be closer to mum. I had been vacillating about coming here for a good part of a year, which is the time it's taken me to write this book.

During this time, I took regular sabbaticals (from my former work) to visit mum and on every visit, I managed to do a significant amount of writing. I find Hervey Bay is a very creative place for writers, as it teems with tranquillity and life here is relaxed and peaceful. It's also a priceless piece of paradise in Australia; gateway to K'gari, as it known locally (or Fraser Island) and home to the Australian whale migration.

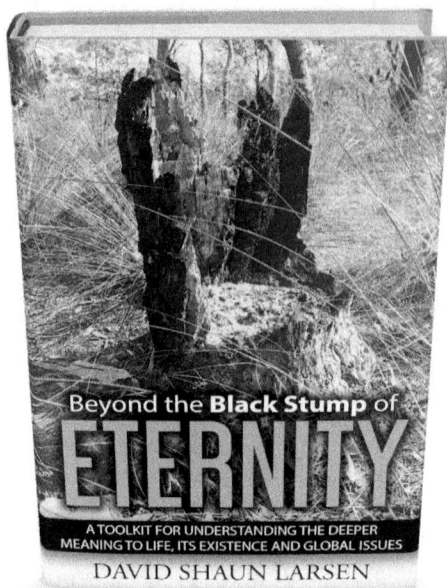

As an older person, I had also overcome the fear of writing that so inflicted me when I was younger. I would often wonder who would want to read anything that I have to say or write about with life. Last year at the age of 52, it all came together much like the stars aligning. Following a well overdue reunion with my Astrology teacher and mentor Kerrie Redgate; her encouragement and belief in me inspired me to write a book. Also, I'd also like to thank Gretel for her encouragement and support, I too am just a Zebra who lost its spots.

> It's a big job, but really worth it. Make that book shine!!
>
> — KERRIE REDGATE

This book is the first in a series of three books. Although it reflects some of my journey in life, it also describes the more profound mean-

ingfulness of my nature and the incredible experiences I have
witnessed, both joys and struggles.

> Run your fingers through my soul.
> For once, just once,
> feel exactly what I feel,
> believe what I believe,
> perceive as I perceive,
> look, experience, examine,
> and for once;
> just once,
> Understand...

It's intended to be an easy read that interweaves a mix of short, eclectic
stories and includes various ideas, concepts, and theories that have
formed over a lifetime of observation, logical reasoning and experience. Also as someone who has been on a spiritual path for as long as I
can remember; everything I write about is not a new concept or idea.
It's been influenced by many things; including the spiritual teachers I
have met; those who teach us about the meaning of gratitude and
loving-kindness; significant others who have come into my life (what I
call kindred spirits); transient periods of travel and the study of various
religious and spiritual philosophy.

'Beyond the Black Stump of Eternity' explores the deeper meaning to
life, its existence and global issues. How can one define Spirituality
without writing about their spiritual journey, at least over the earliest
years of life? Therefore, the first chapter: *'Beyond the Black Stump'*

tells the story of my early life until the age of 23 - what I call "the early script for my foundation in life". The next two chapters offer the reader what I call the spiritual essence or heart of the book, with *'Defining Spirituality'* and incorporates a chapter on a fundamental yet complex concept of *'Soul Evolution'* i.e., an idea that that tells a logical story about the evolution of our soul over many lifetimes. It represents a spectrum from the spiritual birth of the person, our most basic ego or 'Baby Soul' nature, to the most spiritually evolved souls (what some may call enlightened souls). This concept is not foreign to many of us, especially people on the spiritual path or those seeking to explore or Awakening to their spirituality.

The most exciting thing about this concept is once you dedicate or focus your life on the spiritual path - which is equivalent to lighting a candle for the first time - you start to develop greater intuition and experience more in-depth insights into life. For many people, this can be very unsettling or isolating, especially when they're younger. However, as you age you instinctively realise that the Universe has given you one of the most amazing and treasured gifts i.e., the gift of greater happiness and contentment. Once we understand that all life is impermanent - on a spiritual level - it affords us with a much more significant understanding of its illusory nature. Then and only then, can we truly transcend.

As an attempt to connect our understanding of soul evolution and other topics to everyday life; I've also included snippets of some of my favourite quotes and photography, poetry and writing. The use of photography is potent as it enhances the experience for the reader; especially in some chapters that may feel foreign to your world experience such as *'HIV'*, *'Dis-ability'*, *'Humanitarianism'* and *'Diversity in Life'*. Although this book is written uniquely for an Australian audience, it's also suited for broader global readership. It includes a chapter on *Australian Indigenous Culture* and also covers various other topics, such as:

- *Challenges for Humanity*

- *Gender Equality*
- *Politics*
- *The Environment*
- *Living, Loving, Ageing and Dying*
- *Mental Health and Substance Use*
- *Happiness and Wellbeing*

For those who are wanting to Awaken to the world or feel like life is forcing you to be out of your comfort zone, I offer up some guidance in a chapter called *'Awakening the Spirit'*. If by chance I haven't lost you as a reader and you're inquisitive for a bit of a futurist slant on the world, I write about when Australia becomes a Republic in the *'Republic of Australia',* most likely in early 2023. The aftermath of this time is when the next major global shift occurs in the world, this chapter is titled, *'Humanity and 2023/24'*.

Lastly, *'Our New Hope'*, offers a practical toolkit; essentially what Humanity needs for its survival. I write about a range of healing therapies and tools that people can use in their everyday life, framed around the concept of Universal Laws – a set of Universal Laws for our spiritual fulfilment and success. It gives the reader a range of tools, including things such as understanding the body, mind, and spirit; Astrology and working with energy; the meaning of the various Universal Laws; becoming what you are meant to become; meditations for receiving and incorporating other things into our lives such as flower essences, Traditional Chinese Medicine (TCM), and mindfulness practice.

I've explored, studied and used these various practices and tools over the past 25 years, and they represent a range of techniques that allow you to maintain good health, have a positive mind and provide a deeper intellectual insight and understanding around your life purpose, your choices, and roadmap. All I can ask is that you have an open mind and enjoy the journey.

1

BEYOND THE BLACK STUMP

- THE EARLY SCRIPT FOR MY FOUNDATION IN LIFE

> *Being born is probably one of the hardest things you will do; my childhood and family would influence everything.*
>
> *As challenging as it was, when I look back on this time it was a blessing in disguise. Woe is me; I didn't have the father I would've liked. That's life!*
>
> *Reframing the experience into a positive was the key; either way, I was blessed, maybe I chose this to be so. My father at least deserves compassion; perhaps he did not know any better.*
>
> — DAVID SHAUN LARSEN

HUMANS HAVE an innate need to find or search for the meaning of life. Some of us also search for the deeper meaning to life and its existence. My journey has often been offset by immense challenges but enriched with such amazing experiences. In many respects, it's been a personal journey with poignant themes around beliefs, courage, and hope.

"Beyond the Black Stump of Eternity" was an expression that I used later in life to express the contrast of growing up in an Australian mining town during the 1970s, set against the stark reality of where I was at that time in my life. For me, Mount Isa embodied the extreme of what I call, our "over masculinised" Australian culture. When I was growing up, it had one of the highest rates of alcohol abuse and domestic violence in the country. It's not something a nation should be proud of, yet it still permeates Australian culture and society even to this day.

My Earliest Memories

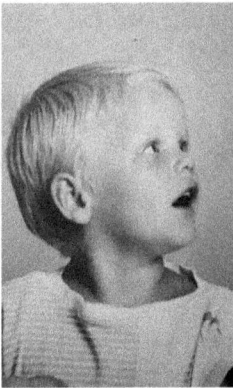

Me at age two.

My earliest memories as a child were mostly about my grandparents i.e., my Norwegian Grandfather Wilhelm (Grandad) and Australian Grandmother Margaret (Grandma) who lived in Adelaide, capital of South Australia. I loved my Grandparents very much, interestingly, my mother told me that Margaret means 'Pearl'; Grandma was without exception, a divine Pearl. Grandad was a striking man, of a big build, in many ways a real Viking warrior, however, he was a sailor and an engineer.

There is not a lot known about my Grandad's earliest life, but he was raised in Oslo and later worked as an engineer on a Norwegian shipping line, The 'Wilh. Wilhelmsen' and sailed on a ship called 'The Bramora'. He docked off in Melbourne in 1939 where he met Grandma, and they got married. She was a divorcee with four children, and the only child they had together was my mum or "Dolly" as her siblings called her. During the early years of their marriage, Grandma discovered that Grandad had left behind a wife and four daughters in Norway (he was a bigamist). I'm sure this would've been very upsetting for Grandma, but I won't dwell on the reasons why he left his family. I guess no one will ever know that story, but I do know that Grandad truly loved my Grandma. He also adored Dolly very much, but mum believes deep down that he would've preferred to have had a son. I think that's the Universe's way of teaching him a lesson in acceptance.

There is a positive side to this story. I managed to reconnect with my Norwegian family in 1992, and I'm blessed to still be in contact with them today. However, 'The Bramora' that my Grandad sailed on for most of his life was sunk by a Japanese submarine in 1943, towards the end of World War II. No crew survived. In some ways, I couldn't begin to imagine what personal distress (or torment) my Grandad went through, wondering about his wife and children in Norway but also losing his mates he had sailed

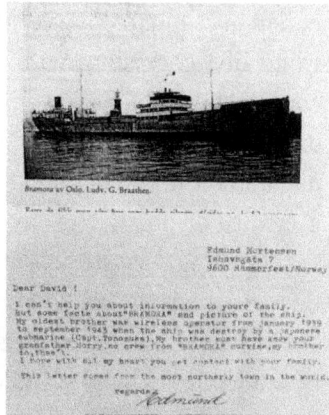

A photograph with documented evidence about the ship my Grandad sailed on, 'The Bramora'.

with for most of his life. How I discovered my Norwegian family is indeed another story or book in itself (I'm sure it would be a compelling script for a Hollywood movie or miniseries). Anyway, I touch on this briefly, later in the book. See **Chapter 15 - *Living, Loving, Ageing, and Dying*** - *The True Essence of Life.*

Grandma was diagnosed with breast cancer when I was merely a few years old and had undergone a radical mastectomy - the surgeon removed all of her breast, lymph nodes, and chest wall muscles. My earliest memory of Grandma is when she took me to the beach for the first time as a four-year-old, I'd ask her, "Grandma why do you have such a big hole in your chest?" and she replied that she got bitten by a shark. Hmm, I guess that was my Grandma's discreet way of not having to explain something so complicated and personal to a four-year-old. Though I must say, Grandma had no shame in wearing a one-piece swimsuit. This was the embodiment of her character. She was a very strong, down to earth woman who radiated love, warmth, and acceptance.

My parents had their set of marital conflict and issues in those earlier years. I'm sure my mum could write her own book on it, more on that later. What I remember so vividly about this period, was my untold belief in a higher power, force or something much greater than me. Ironically, coexisting with this; was an intense sexual nature which I could not explain however I kept it very private as I felt embarrassed. I discovered masturbation at the age of five, possibly something not too uncommon for any child at a young age. In many respects, this sets up a duality or polarity in my life at a very young age i.e., being a very sexual being, yet at the same time being very spiritual. In later years, this resulted in an internalised conflict and struggle that would contribute to a maze of questions, thus becoming the foundation of my life reflections, "how could these co-exist as a polarity?"

Another reflection forged at this time, was the search for a place to call home – the sense of not belonging - so in essence where was home? My father came from a wealthy Adelaide socialite family. Dad was very spoilt as a child and had everything he ever wanted including a private education, the finest clothes, motorbikes, and loans of money. Therefore, he had been gifted, with immense opportunity as a young man. For whatever personal reasons he became a professional gambler, namely horse racing, and poker. A few years after my parents got married, my father even gambled away the title/deed to our family house.

Astrid did the very best she could to keep the family together at this time of upheaval and instability. She took my siblings and me to live in Melbourne for a period of respite and recovery from the shame of being homeless i.e., my older brother Steven and younger sister

Natalie. My father's mother Nita even threatened her with a lawsuit to gain custody of Steven (her oldest grandchild). I guess when your father is also the perpetrator of domestic violence and used gambling, drinking and womanising as his escapisms; the future didn't bode well. It became a very down beaten path for Mum.

Living in the Black Stump

Living in the Black Stump refers to the time I lived in Mount Isa - a mining town in Queensland in the 1970s (at this time Sir "Joh" Beijlke Petersen was Premier). My family moved there when I was six years old, as Dad got employed working in the mines as a Ringfirer (a miner who drills the holes for detonating explosives). Dad's job was dangerous but paid well and apparently had its own set of stresses having to work underground in extreme heat and suffocating conditions. Around this time, my Grandma in Adelaide got sick with a recurrence of her breast cancer with metastases and was dying. Grandma's illness was also the first time I ever felt grief-stricken with the fear and possible pain of losing someone with whom I was very close. Knowing Grandma was dying caused a deep sense of loss, separation, and sadness. I couldn't end up going to see her and attend the funeral because mum could only afford for Natalie and her to fly to Adelaide.

From the age of six until sixteen, it was such a surreal experience growing up in Mount Isa. I always knew that I didn't belong there and that my life was meant to be somewhere else. "The Isa" as it was known, is listed in the Guinness Book of Records as the world's largest city in the area; its total civic area covers 43,310 sq. Km, which is bigger than Switzerland. Although quite a multicultural place at the time; it also had the highest divorce rate in Australia, second highest beer consumption after Darwin and deplorable racism towards our Indigenous people.

Here I was immersed in a town, far away from anywhere, oblivious to a childhood of dysfunction and superimposed with a Catholic education; it seemed extreme. In those years, Mum had to work to provide food and clothing for the kids because of Dad's gambling addiction. Even as a child, Dad did not allow the family to have a phone or any other comfort. Dad was hardly ever around, and when he wasn't working shifts in the mines, was either drinking and playing lawn bowls or just drinking at the pub with his mates. Invariably, Dad was drunk most of the time, and I often lived in fear of him, especially when he came home in drunken outbursts of violence. On the rare occasion, he would tell "us kids" that he loved us.

David at the age of 7 in Mount Isa (wearing his Dr Dolittle T-Shirt) with my brother, Steven, and sister, Natalie.

On The Brighter Side

On the brighter side, it was a childhood with responsibility, lots of freedom as any child of the 70s had, and I formed some great friendships; many of whom I have reconnected with, in recent years via Facebook. Although my parents were not religious, most Sundays I attended church on my own, played lots of sport outside of school, mainly basketball and hockey (the team sports) but in the 1970s these were seen as somewhat "girly" sports. The Christian Brother's College where I went to school only offered traditional sports such as cricket and rugby league. I was never really good at cricket or rugby, and I was always the last of the boys to be picked for the rugby team.

St Keiran's offered few positive memories, most often it exposed a hierarchy of brothers who used various brainwashing; verbal abuse and control techniques and caning in class. It embodied a terrible time with big bullies; both students, and teachers. I remember quite distinctly a gang of bullies led by a guy called Rory who once held me up behind the church threatening me with a Swiss knife. He got great pleasure out of forcing me to say swear words, "say fuck", followed by roars of laughter, "say cunt", more bursts of laughter, louder than before. Somewhere in that insoluble mess of antics, I made an escape and got on my bike and rode and rode as fast as I could. I managed to get to the Mount Isa Base Hospital where my mother worked; this was my magical escapism from their torment. They never tried that on me again but hey I got away from them, and maybe somehow they knew they crossed the line. I hope Rory is living the life he's meant to, as I hold no bad feelings.

Around this time, I also had this inherent desire to dance and used to dream about being a ballet dancer. When I asked my father, quite innocently at the age of 12 if I could learn ballet; Dad told me by no means, "No fucken poofter son of mine is going to be a ballet dancer". I guess at that moment, it kind of killed the dream, but it was the first time I felt something not so good about being a "poofter". It was also a pertinent reminder to any parent that it is not your role to stifle your child's creativity or expression. Upon reflection, being a parent is not something that should be "a right"; you sometimes wonder whether some people are genuinely fit to take on this responsibility. It's not your right as an adult to bring any child into this world without the intention to nurture, care and provide love for that beautiful soul.

Lesbian, Gay, Bisexual, Transgender, Queer, and Intersex (LGBTQI) people have the same right to have children as anyone else, although all of our society do not share this view. All I know is, if LGBTQI people choose to have or adopt children, it pretty much comes from a space of love, without judgment of what that child should be. The LGBTQI parents I know, have very well-adjusted kids who love their parents enormously. I'm yet to be proved wrong, but I've heard so many stories over the years of people who have come from so-called "straight" families and have had dreadful and traumatic childhood experiences of abuse, fear, and hate including torture, rape, and violence. Maybe we need more LGBTQI parents in the world to teach others how to love and raise children? At a time when our country only recently debated Marriage Equality, it surprises me how anyone could have voted No. But when law sets a precedent, behaviour change always follows.

Grandad and his Death

Vilhelm Larsen, My Grandfather.

Grandad and his death was a wakeup call. At 14 Mum brought Grandad up to Mount Isa to live with us for a year as he got diagnosed with Oesophageal Cancer. This brief period in my teenage years was a happy time as it was the only time my father didn't hit Mum. Why was this so? Possibly because on one occasion, when Dad attempted to; I remember my Grandad just picked him up with one hand and held him against the wall. The symbolism associated with this is so powerful. It represented a heroic Viking towering over this abusive, weakling figure of a man that was my father. But this time of bliss was short-lived, Grandad soon got sick and died at Mount Isa Base hospital.

On the day of his funeral, I so clearly remember my father coming up to Mum with a threatening tone in his voice and saying, "you haven't got your father here to protect you anymore". All I thought was what a cowardly and frightened man you are, that you need to resort to such an act. An alpha male, asserting such dominance over a woman at a time where she was most vulnerable. It's so sad that any man could lower himself to such a sadistic, evil act. It's only in embracing that moment; I realised compassion is the greatest forgiver, for maybe he did not know any better. In the absence of any male role models, I know I've grown up to be more courageous and honourable than most men I meet. It's time that men in this country start to Man Up to their responsibility to be men and get in touch with their feminine energy (the part of you that is receptive, soft, cares, cries, hugs, touches and caresses with tenderness); as we are all a balance of both.

Soon after this time, I was struggling to come to terms with my sexuality. I didn't have any role models in the 1970's (at least know anyone who was gay), and the only concept of being gay to me was that of being a paedophile. I didn't know anything else and deep down inside, I would think about killing myself. One saving grace about Christianity was my escapism into the fundamentalism of young Christian students. I called this my "happy clappy years", seeking solace in the church as a way of repentance and salvation. At 15, I found some liberation going to the state high school to complete my years 11 and 12. In many respects, the state high school was the counter-revolution to what seemed to be the revolutionary years of my Catholic education.

Standing Up to my Father

Standing up to my father was one of the most courageous acts. Mum heroically left my father when I was 16. She rented an apartment for Natalie and me to live in, temporarily our new home. For mum it must have been incredibly lonely and terrible, not knowing what to expect next and with no support services to help her. One night in a drunken rage, my father came to the apartment threatening mum with a knife. While she was "pleeing" for him to stop, somehow I felt this would escalate into something not so nice and possibly horrific.

David and Astrid, Christmas 2012 (Mum is my most trusted role model and one of most valued friends).

My father told Natalie and me to go to our bedroom, as he always did when he was abusive. As the verbal abuse continued, my father ended up dragging mum out of the house by her hair with the knife held firmly to her throat. However, in my heart, I knew I could not let this happen. All I remember in my dazed state is that I ran into the kitchen and got a knife out of the cupboard. I went up to Michael and without any fear said, "If you lay one hand on her you fucken bastard I'll kill you". With my perilous threat, my father dropped the knife, and the incident became lost for a moment in time. What was symbolic here, is that it represented the first time I stood up to my father and became the protector of Mum.

To Boston with Love

To Boston with love what an adventure. In the following year 1980, I graduated from school and then worked three jobs to save up enough money to leave Mount Isa in September 1981. I travelled to the United States of America (USA) to stay with my American family in Boston for three months. My Uncle Robin (my father's older brother) whom I felt connected to, was a product of the 'brain drain' of Australia during the 1950s – educated Australians seeking education, fortune and a new life abroad. During this time, I experienced one of the highlights of my life. Uncle Robin sent me on a train trip to Washington DC to have a personalised tour of the Capital Building, with a politician he knew called Congressman Bennett.

Congressman Bennett was a Republican and one of the longest-serving Congressman in US history. Soon after I arrived, I got to meet Congressman Bennett in his office, which appeared so massive and extravagant, like nothing I had seen before. My first impression was seeing this very distinguished grey-haired man in a suit with a pained gait and walking stick. After a cordial conversation, we then took the lift way down to some sub-basement level, which to my amazement led to an underground trolley car system, deep under Washington. This system must have been used to transport politicians to the Capitol Building and possibly other public offices. Congressman Bennett took me into the Senate while it was in session and surprisingly on to the floor of Congress. He pointed out the chair where the President of the United States would typically be seated and slyly asked me if I wanted to sit in the chair. With so much excitement, of course, I said yes. How surreal, here I was sitting in the President's chair in Congress. The most amazing thing about this moment was; I knew for the first time, I could do anything in life!

Living with the Brady Bunch

Living with the Brady Bunch felt normal. As I only had a three-month visa to stay in the US, regrettably I returned to Australia but not to Mount Isa. I settled in Brisbane but just for a short time and was lucky to stay with my best friend Brian and his family. Brian's family who I knew from my Mount Isa days, moved to Brisbane a few years earlier. His father always viewed him as a bit "different". This was another symbolic time in my life perhaps it was the first time; I felt like I belonged to a family. I shared a bedroom with my friend Brian, managed to get a job working at the AMP Society (insurance company) in Brisbane and would travel to work with Brian's father who also worked in the city.

I had this strange sense of being normal and for six months enjoyed the feeling it offered, kind of like a "Brady Bunch" family. But it was also a very awkward time, as I felt very much like an imposter. Brian's father would say things like, "Brian why can't you be more like David, stop mucking around and get a job". He was the rebellious one and resisted any normality that his family could provide. Brian truly drummed to his own beat and danced to it. Some nights Brian would climb out of our bedroom window and disappear into the darkness of the night. I was none the wiser but years later discovered that Brian was also gay and he was heading out to the gay bars of Fortitude Valley.

The greatest irony of this is; here we are as two young gay boys, living much like brothers and best friends. Brian was "the rebellious one", being true to himself and me being "the conservative, employed one", living a life in denial and fear.

Going Home to Adelaide

Going home to Adelaide was like completing a full circle. My restlessness was becoming a way of life, and at 19, I decided to move home to Adelaide. I stayed with family and managed to get re-employed at the AMP Society in their calculations department. Looking back, much has changed; the hours it would take to do the complicated mathematical calculations (on insurance policies); today computers could do in seconds. I only lasted six months doing this kind of work for it was so mind-numbing and deep down, I wanted to do something more meaningful with my life.

Nursing Group 7/83 Queen Elizabeth Hospital II, Adelaide, South Australia.

Around this time, I had a friend who was Nursing, and I thought I'd apply and give it a go. I had the good fortune of being accepted and started studying nursing from 1983-1986 at the Queen Elizabeth Hospital. During those days, becoming a Registered Nurse was in a hospital-based program – you received a Certificate in Nursing plus as a bonus, you got paid! God knows why I did Nursing because I found it so old fashioned and militaristic i.e., especially the culture and how hierarchical it was. I wanted to resign about a dozen times but somehow stuck with it, because nursing challenged something deep within me - the notion of overcoming my fear around caring or nurturing others. Maybe it was the wounded healer reaching out for answers knowing that by caring or healing others, I would also start to heal myself.

Another realisation, which was unbeknown to me when I first started nursing, was being surrounded by such an inspiring group of people. Little did I know 30 years later, most of these women (and one of the guys) would still be in my life today. In the lead up to our 30th reunion in 2016, I felt like I'd forget so many of the girl's faces and names. I wasn't sure what to expect, and with a little fear and trepidation, the reunion ended up being one of the most joyful events of my life. Of course, I remembered everyone's names, how could I forget such a remarkable group of people from such an extraordinary time in my life? I was so honoured to be around all these amazing and beautiful women I started nursing with; it felt like time hadn't stopped. No one looked older, and we were all just the same. As I reflect back on those years past, they were so fundamentally important. They set in train a series of events that ended up defining four critical aspects of my life:

- Accepting my sexuality i.e., being true to myself.
- Setting up my eventual move to Sydney i.e., symbolic of a new home and life.
- A new rewarding career, working in the HIV sector.
- A new journey in exploring a deeper connection with my spirituality.

At this time, what also assisted in turning my life around was reading my first book on eastern philosophy, a book about Buddhism. I call this my "lighting the candle moment" or the beginning of "Awakening", to being on the spiritual path. This moment set forth my quest and thirst for spiritual knowledge and study. It also activated a deep and innate understanding for me around the concept of reincarnation. Reincarnation seemed to resonate with the deepest core of my being. In 1985 I also came "out of the closet", so to speak and this was a very liberating moment for me being gay. However, this period was also set against a dark time; when HIV had only recently become a global issue surrounded by fear and discrimination.

Myself and the girls at our 30th year Nursing Group 7/83 reunion in 2016.

Coupled with this was the isolation of being gay in Adelaide, having a limited understanding of what this lifestyle meant. People rarely judged me, but I always remember being the first gay person that most of my friends and associates had met. If you think about it, no one had written a book on how to be gay or what it meant having a gay relationship. Even today, this remains an evolving part of the LGBTQI culture, as more and more people are telling their stories. Storytelling is so compelling, as it allows people to see our lives in various ways, often different from those conferred on them by others. Ultimately this casts a much broader foundation of acceptance and discovery by a whole range of people in our society. Nowadays it's quite funny when I meet younger gay men who seem entirely ignorant of history; I often say, "I did so much bloody trailblazing for you lot; everything that you accept as a right or way of life has had to be fought for". Our activism and protests have not been in vain and also without their struggles. It has always been with the intention of fighting for acceptance, equality, and respect. Fundamental human rights for everybody.

In the same year, I nursed my first HIV/AIDS patient Robert who was ostracised by the hospital staff. I still remember Rob with such clarity; he was an older man and quite frail. His skin was so dry and flaky that it caused cracks in his lower legs, like fissures and bled at times. I used to bath him whenever I could, as it appeared few of the hospital staff would touch him, and this experience left me with a deep sadness. How could health staff of all people be so inhumane? It's no wonder that this moment stirred up a deep injustice in me and I felt something needed to be done to change this most repulsive form of discrimination.

Upon graduating from nursing in 1986, I received the best theoretical and practical award for my Nursing Group 7/83, and with such pleasure; I appreciated my first academic achievement since leaving school. Starting work as a Registered Nurse was so exciting and such an accomplishment; setting forth my career as an experienced health practitioner, manager, healer and nurturer for

Me in my second year of Nursing, at the age of 21.

others. In saying this, I was always attracted to the "touchy-feely" type nursing, either fascinated with death and dying or working with those in traumatic situations. I only worked for six months as a nurse (in Haematology and Burns) before a successful entry into the first Diploma of Tourism offered in South Australia in 1987 – a class of approx. 30 students among 400 applicants. However, this did not last long, only a few months.

Around this time, my best friend and fellow nurse Kevin, who I met the year before - incidentally over a cardiac arrest - had just returned from Sydney with his partner John. While on their holiday in Sydney, Kevin cut out a newspaper advert, advertising for nurses to work in the new expanding HIV Unit at St Vincent's Hospital. When he showed me the ad, I had what I believe was my first epiphany in life. Within two weeks, I was in Sydney and how my spiritual journey unfolds is interweaved in the following chapters and themes in this book.

Beautiful Sydney, you've looked after me well for 30 years, thank you!

2

DEFINING SPIRITUALITY

- THE DIFFERENCE BETWEEN EGO AND SPIRIT

> *The problem is that ego can convert anything to its own use, even spirituality.*

— CHOGYAM TRUNGPA

Defining Spirituality

DEFINING **spirituality** can be framed or viewed in many different ways. Some people describe it as seeking a deeper meaning to life, and others define it as transpersonal growth, metaphysics, subconscious mind, understanding one's inner dimension, or being at bliss with life. Spirituality is different to religion; every person has a life experience that is meaningful, and it's like comparing two very different things i.e., something man-made (patriarchal) versus something innately Cosmic or Universal. My interpretation is the following:

> **What is it that makes YOU understand the deeper meaning of YOUR life and YOUR existence, no one else's, but just YOURS**
>
> — DAVID SHAUN LARSEN

Since the dawning of time, we have been predominantly ruled by man-made, patriarchal systems. These systems have operated purely from very traditional, command and control structures, hierarchal in form. Periodically, a third party, whether a saviour or leader has appeared (or some may say created) to provide a set of beliefs, commandments, and rules for humankind. Often this can evolve and take the form of what we call religion. Without integrity, religion can provide the foundation for ultimate control to indoctrinate people. It, therefore, can provide a dangerous weapon to dumb down the masses and force people to be closed to other ideas or beliefs. History has also revealed that these patriarchal systems have invariably used various methods to control people but just in different ways.

In essence, all religions have been created by men. Over time the method of control has varied from waging war; enslaving people; using drowning, hanging, torture and burning at the stake (such as witches) and using public displays of mutilation (cutting off various body parts, whether heads, hands, etc.). In more recent times, since the emergence of modern science and separation of Church and State; religion has tried to uphold its moral and social grip on everything. The consequences of this have been tragic and devastating for many people: -

- Influencing and infiltrating Corporate and Government decision making, via various representation and lobbyists.
- Blatant stigma, discrimination, and prejudice against LGBTQI people.

- Seemingly endless cases of physical and sexual child abuse.
- Use of various brainwashing ideology and techniques.
- Also, the emergence of modern day cult enclaves of fundamentalism has had the potential to cause destruction.

The positive reframe is that many religions are becoming more open-minded, transparent and accountable. However, those religious beliefs and faiths who lack integrity and are less transparent; are slowing losing their grip and stance in society. As more and more people see through the watered down truths (the same analogy can apply to Government), they evolve spiritually with the realisation that they don't need to rely on religion as a crux. For others, they are just plain happy to be atheists or live their lives under an alternative structure i.e., Corporate and Government control as an outlet for their lack of religion.

We are always alone but never lonely, just be one with the Universe.

Of course, there are people of Christian, Muslim or other faiths who are living evolved lifetimes, but it's possible at some point they will question their faith and Awaken to new possibilities. There have been many beautiful Christian people who have inspired me throughout life. One significant transformational moment that describes this the best is a Catholic Nun whom I worked with in the late 1980's - she provided pastoral care predominantly for gay men dying of HIV/AIDS.

At one of the first ever HIV Conferences in Sydney, in front of a mixed group of medical and scientific staff and fellow nuns, she gave a very heartfelt speech. She said she'd always thought she understood the true meaning of Jesus's love. But she went on to explain that it wasn't until after she started providing pastoral care for men dying of AIDS, that she realised they were the ones; who taught her what the true meaning of Jesus' love actually meant.

Religion can't Monopolise your Spirituality

Religion can't monopolise your spirituality. Spirituality comes from a much deeper sphere of awareness and consciousness, that is innately personal for you. Once you realise this, you don't need a religious framework to guide you. Presenting clear concepts around the difference between religion and spirituality is crucial. Although all religions have some common underpinnings regarding their values; they are also vastly different in their teachings and how people interpret them e.g., literal, fundamentalist and pluralistic views. There is no doubt the predominance of religion in many societies has started to fade i.e., the number of followers is waning.

I am by no means placing any value judgements on those people who follow religion. It's only disconcerting when people who say they are religious; use hate, fear, and judgement as weapons to disempower other people's cultural, social and spiritual values and lifestyles.

Historically, it's not been uncommon for people to use a biblical view, with patronising passages from scripture to justify and confirm all kinds of bias. Both slavery and apartheid were used in this way to argue cases for and against such actions. Also, gender was often, but wrongly used, to claim that God intended for men and women to play fundamentally different roles i.e., women being in caring and nurturing functions but not in positions of power or leadership.

Studying both Tibetan Buddhism and Triratna Buddhism, we can learn a lot about their purity as religions, especially if one use's an intelligence lens i.e., it's ability to reason and how it can evolve with our changing society. Tibetan Buddhism is a religion in exile, forced from its homeland when the Chinese conquered Tibet. The best-known face of Tibetan Buddhism is the Dalai Lama. Tibetan Buddhism combines the essential teachings of Mahayana Buddhism with Tantric and Shamanic, and material from an ancient Tibetan religion called Bon.[1]

The Triratna Buddhist Community describes itself as,

> an international network dedicated to communicating Buddhist truths in ways appropriate to the modern world.

Norbulingka Palace and surrounding park in Lhasa, Tibet, China, built from 1755.

It along with Tibetan Buddhism can intellectualise or explain some of the most relevant answers to our questions we ask because it uses logic. Although the Triratna Buddhist Community keeps with Buddhist traditions, it also pays attention to contemporary ideas, mainly drawn from the modern world of Western philosophy, psychotherapy, and art.[2]

Although I don't define myself as a Buddhist, I have incorporated aspects of Buddhist concepts, principles, and philosophy in my life. Spirituality is an evolving process of continuous Awakening to higher levels of awareness and understanding. The more I evolve, I realise how little I know about anything. Quite often, I have found life and its experiences to be humbling. I have only gratitude for the blessed journey it has afforded me, in particular, to be of service to others and share what I know.

Don't assume it's a good fit

Don't assume it's a good fit, even religion. If you are raised as a child to believe in religion or go searching for it later in your adult life, it doesn't mean it will always be right for you! We all have the ability to find out what is meaningful for ourselves. For many, religion leaves them feeling abused, brainwashed, disempowered or misguided and for others, it's a gateway to something else (even the belief in nothing). My experience of growing up with a Catholic education and teaching is sometimes similar to experiencing one of those moments in life that you'd rather forget.

On one particular occasion when I was a student nurse working in Theatre. I was ably waiting for the Registered Nurse to pass me an excised tumour that the Surgeon was delicately cutting out of a middle-aged woman who had an ovarian cyst. It was about the size of a bloodstained basketball, and I had to more or less collect it, as the nurse placed it in the bucket I was holding.

A photograph of me squashed into a narrower than normal seat, on a KLM flight to Amsterdam (14 hours).

As it turned out, I wasn't holding the bucket so firmly, and the cyst just hit the ground and exploded like a balloon full of water. It was one of those moments I'd rather forget, let's just say the aftermath wasn't stunning! Was it my error or was the cyst just too big to fit into the bucket? Hmm, we may never know. All I knew at that moment, was Theatre Nursing wasn't for me. As a consequence, it propelled me to find out which speciality was right for me. I just knew it had something to do with helping people who were suffering in some way.

The Buddhist beliefs about suffering; Universal compassion (or loving kindness) and the impermanence of life, speak to the illusory nature of life. Once we truly understand on a spiritual level that all life is an illusion - nothing stays the same, we repeat cycles of birth and death, over and over and eventually, our physical bodies will decline; then and only then can we transcend.

Western Astrology - Our Universal Harmonic Resonance

Western Astrology - Our Universal Harmonic Resonance is based on interpreting mathematical correlations between celestial positions and earthbound life. Astrology originates as far back to Egyptian, Babylonian, Greek and Roman culture and later Arabic and Western civilisations. Often described as a pseudoscience, by scientists, Astrology has always been a part of our early religion and culture and interweaved with Greek philosophy. Therefore, it's always been a part of what I call our, 'Original Science'. My Astrology teacher is an incredible woman named Kerrie Redgate. She came into my life at a very tumultuous time, soon after my first partner Michael died of HIV/AIDS when I was 28. It was a time of intense, personal grief and loss and in the darkest of moments; I sometimes wondered how I would summon the strength to get through it. For those who have never experienced such a thing in their life, it was a time where there was so much stigma and discrimination, not only towards gay and lesbian people but also immense fear towards people living with HIV.

Kerrie Redgate, my teacher, and inspiration.

I first met Kerrie in 1993 and was initiated into Astrology. She did a natal (or birth) chart for me interpreting it from a present and past life perspective, incorporating Buddhist philosophy. It was one of those, "Oh My God" (OMG) moments! It was not only a life-changing experience but set me forth on a new path of deeper, spiritual understanding in life - basically, it was an indescribable but enlightening experience. I then studied with Kerrie for one year in 1994. The class was a very well structured, 4-semester intensive program. Studying Astrology enabled me the opportunity to start learning my craft. I mostly did this by doing other people's natal charts such as friends and acquaintances I'd met. Throughout my life, this has always been my outright unconditional gift for others.

Few astrologers claim to know how Astrology differs from a scientific understanding of life. However, Kerrie is leading the field in a lifetime quest to ensure that Astrology is once again understood. I believe it is an experimental (and one day will be seen, as a scientific) tool that people can use to understand the screenshot of the Universal Harmonic Resonance at the moment of their birth.

All I know is that it works. This "screenshot" of your universal energy at the moment of your birth, represents a spiritual roadmap or astrological blueprint of your life. I have studied my craft for well over 23 years and during this time, have done hundreds of validated readings for people. I describe Astrology, as understanding the twelve Universal energies that surround us, and how the associated movement and harmonic resonance of the planets impact on us, not only as individuals but also as a planet (more on that later).

> Personal Astrology uses a 'screenshot' of the **Solar System** and the **Earth's Field** at the moment of your birth. (Western 'Tropical' Astrology does *not* use the distant galaxies and fixed star patterns as its Zodiac; though ancient Indian Vedic Astrology does.)
>
> This screenshot is actually a representation of *frequency patterns*, defined using the ancient astrological language (some of which is still used by NASA today), which reveals a unique pattern of *sympathetic harmonic resonance* with your higher spiritual consciousness at birth, and which consequently 'hard-wired' your brain in that moment.
>
> As all thoughts—all phenomena of 'mind' (as energy) at all levels—emit particular frequencies, this screenshot of *sympathetic harmonic resonance* (being your birth-chart) contains the **imprints** of a **significant past** and your **aspirations** for this current life.
>
> Only the Astrologer can *interpret* this 'screenshot'.
>
> — KERRIE REDGATE - ASTROLOGER, AUTHOR,
> CONSULTANT, RESEARCHER, TEACHER
> HTTPS://EXCEPTIONALPURPOSE.COM

Science and its irrefutable quest for scientific evidence or proof cannot explain everything, and unfortunately, it seems to cast aside any unproven concept or belief with sheer scepticism i.e., unless it is proven, it remains untested. Of course, Science has dramatically improved the quality of our lives and enhanced our understanding of evolution and nature. However, many of the things that truly matter to people are not scientific, such as a person's belief systems and innate spirituality.

Traditional Chinese Medicine

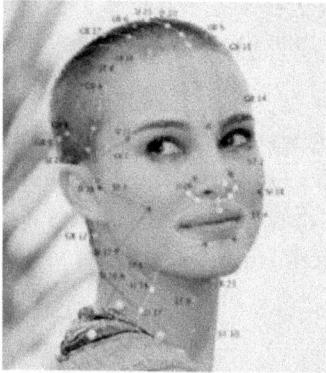

There are about 400 acupuncture points. The meridian system is a concept in traditional Chinese medicine (TCM) about a path through which the life-energy known as "qi" flows.

Traditional Chinese Medicine has been my primary form of medicine to support health, for over twenty years. When I first started using Acupuncture and Chinese Herbs in 1995, it was then described as an alternative medicine by science; as it was not proven e.g., how could 12 invisible Meridian Lines move energy throughout the body, which also has hundreds of acupuncture points? Qi (Chi) energy flows through this meridian or energy highway, accessing all parts of the body.

Meridians have been studied and mapped throughout the body. They flow within the body and not on the surface, meridians exist in corresponding pairs, and each meridian has many acupuncture points along its path.[3] Fast forward to 2017; you can now study TCM at several Universities (even consider a PhD in TCM) and claim acupuncture treatment as a rebate on every health fund in Australia. One-day I believe science will be able to explain the unexplainable.

Everything associated with spirituality is not that difficult to understand, remember no one person can monopolise your understanding of spirituality. Quite often the answers to our questions are right there before our eyes. We just need to be more open and start to seek the deeper meaning to things and the interconnectedness between them. It follows logic and no surprise to me, that there are 12 Universal or Astrological energies and 12 meridian lines.

In Hinduism, Jainism and Buddhism there are also seven chakras or energy centres that move our prana or life force. A chakra is thought to be an energy point or node in the subtle body. Chakras are believed to be part of the subtle body, not the physical body, and as such, are the meeting points of the subtle channels called Nadi. Nadi is believed to be channelled in the subtle body through which the life force (prana) or vital energy (non-physical) moves.[4]

The Crown Chakra is the seventh chakra and sits at the top of the "chakra ladder" and connects us with the Universe and the Divine source of creation. It makes sense that we draw down the Universal or divine energy through our chakras and meridian lines that co-exist as two different energy systems.

The Seven Chakras or Energy Centres

The seven chakras or energy centres a brief overview: -

Base chakra (the energy vortex at the base of the spine) relates to our primaeval or base energy often where we can "get stuck". It represents our deepest beliefs, feelings, and fears about security, survival and love. Holding on to these beliefs, and feelings can eat away at you, you can easily "become the victim" and as always, be destined to repeat it over and over.

The Seven Chakras or Energy Centres.

THE SECOND CHAKRA (the energy vortex in the middle of the abdomen) - when we operate at this energy centre, experiences are more often associated with our sexuality, sex, emotions and relational issues e.g., pain, suffering, poor self-esteem, and shame.

The third chakra (just below the navel in the abdomen) - when we operate from this energy centre we start growing up (evolving) and able to challenge our false beliefs. We're also freer to experience life with our eyes wide open, explore self-esteem issues, and seek knowledge and establish friendship circles much like a teenager does. However, our moral choices aren't always that well guided.

The fourth chakra (our heart chakra) - when we operate from this energy centre we are much better equipped to drop our moral prejudices, but this often comes with much pain and suffering. We also start to understand the broader world; critically examine our self-esteem issues and concepts of conditional love i.e., I do this for you, and you do this for me. This is the stage of personal transformation.

The fifth chakra (the vortex of energy at the throat) - when we operate from this energy we bring a higher voice to our work, can speak out against injustice and bring more vitality and meaning to our lives. Vigour provides us with the ability to take responsibility and respond to the world with courage, clarity and strong intention. We take action and speak our beliefs.

The sixth chakra (the vortex of energy on our temple or often called third eye) - when we operate from this energy centre, we have greater intuition and wisdom; a much more profound vision and start seeing things that others do not understand or care to see. Therefore, this provides us with much more inner guidance. Here, our relationships fundamentally become connected with our deeper Self (Soul), and we live life with a higher purpose or mission.

The crown chakra (the vortex of energy on the top of our head) - when we operate from this energy centre we have greater consciousness; become selfless, working from our highest compassionate nature and experience life as bliss and with abundance. For others, it might be "Micro Moments of sheer Happiness" and experiences of blessings, kindness and humility and the interconnectedness between everything.

THE INTERCONNECTEDNESS between everything extends as far as we can see, permeating everything and into the outer realms of the Universe. The interdependence of energy is in harmony with the Universe and leads us to discover that there are Universal Laws that guide everything.

> This our ancestors did, according to the reckoning of our culture, from the Creation, according to the common law from 'time immemorial', and according to science more than 60,000 years ago.

— THE ULURU STATEMENT FROM THE HEART 2016

Our Indigenous people were privy to these realms. When you think about it, Australia has the oldest, continuous spiritual civilisation on earth that is approximately 60,000 years old and we must look to them, for they have the answers.

I write about this in **Chapter 8: *Australian Indigenous Culture - The Oldest Spiritual Culture on Earth.*** However, the Australian Indigenous people and their culture are essential for our healing and survival as a nation. It's their untold connection to the Dreamtime and innate understanding of the true essence of our nation's spirituality. It's essential for our country's spiritual Awakening. I predict that Australia will become a Republic in 2023. This time is critical for our nation, especially around the transformation of our identity. Restoration of our Indigenous people out of the victim role we have created will thus give them the respect they deserve. Their culture then becomes ingrained, rightfully so, in the heart of our new constitution.

So however you define your spirituality and the awe-inspiring interconnectedness between things, it is up to you; but I'd like to think there are some **INNER Values**:

> **Intention itself is everything**, as long as it is with the right intention!
>
> **Nourish the mind, body, and soul**, with gratitude; it's simple!
>
> **Name injustice in the world for what it is**, without fear!
>
> **Empower others with love, compassion, and kindness!**
>
> **Raise the consciousness of those around us,** by becoming the Spiritual Warrior!
>
> — DAVID SHAUN LARSEN

The spiritual warrior is someone who is awakened to their spirituality and is truly on their spiritual path. While they still need to live on the earth plane; they seek a deeper meaning to life, its existence and global issues.

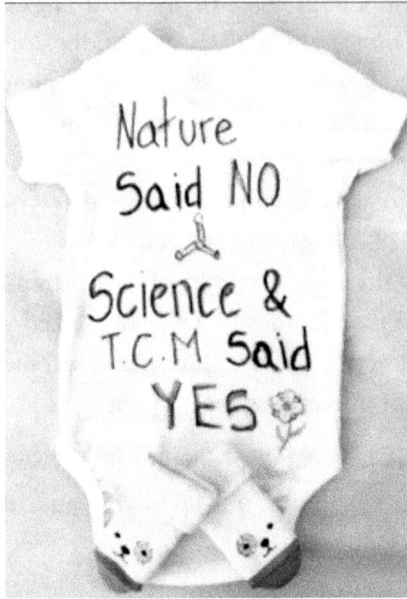

Science has its limitations but with a little help from TCM
anything is possible, even the birth of a newborn.

You may decide on creating your own set of INNER values (even with a different acronym) that is unique to your spirituality. Whatever your INNER values are, remember it is your individual and unique gift and no one else's.

3

OUR SOUL EVOLUTION

- THE EVOLUTION OF THE SOUL OVER MANY LIFETIMES

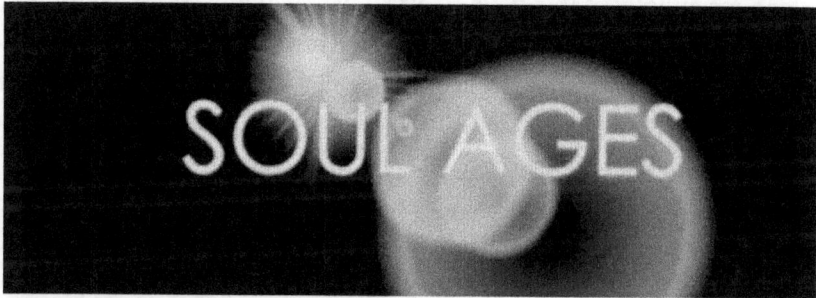
SOUL AGES

> In my next life, I want to live my life backwards. You start out dead and get that out of the way. Then you wake up in an old people's home feeling better every day. You get kicked out for being too healthy, go collect your pension, and then when you start work, you get a gold watch and a party on your first day. You work for 40 years until you're young enough to enjoy your retirement.
>
> You party, drink alcohol, and are generally promiscuous, then you are ready for high school. You then go to

primary school, you become a kid, you play. You have no responsibilities; you become a baby until you are born. And then you spend your last 9 months floating in luxurious spa-like conditions with central heating and room service on tap, larger quarters every day and then Voila!

You finish off as an orgasm!

— WOODY ALLEN

In Your Next Life

IN YOUR NEXT LIFE, imagine the joy of finishing off your life as an orgasm! So what do you want in your next life? All I know is that sometimes, I feel I am not of this world. I know I am here to do something meaningful at this time in our human evolution. This opportunity might possibly be in politics or guiding Humanity in some way, especially in the new world or global crisis that I write about in **Chapter 18: *Humanity and 2023/2024*.** I use the word evolution, because just as humankind has evolved, so does the soul. Once again logic prevails, why wouldn't our soul evolve? Unless you believe in one life, which doesn't seem logical or you don't believe in anything at all, then we just live and die. That's pretty depressing, but hey I won't ever know until I die, but one thing I know with certainty (as a person with a lot of experience around death and dying) is that something continues. It's the unexplainable feeling that it is so. Ah, a different day, a new roadmap and a whole lot of new amazing lessons to learn.

In my early nursing career, I sat at the bedside of many people who died, especially back in the early days of HIV/AIDS in the late 1980s/early 1990s and working in palliative care in the mid-1990s. This time taught me three invaluable lessons about the meaning to life. I can guarantee you that on your deathbed you will be thinking or reflecting on only one or all three of these things to varying degrees: -

- The value or meaningfulness of your relationships i.e., partners, family, and friends;
- Questioning whether you have made a difference in life however you define that and
- Questioning the need to leave a legacy or something behind, so that the memory of who you are continues.

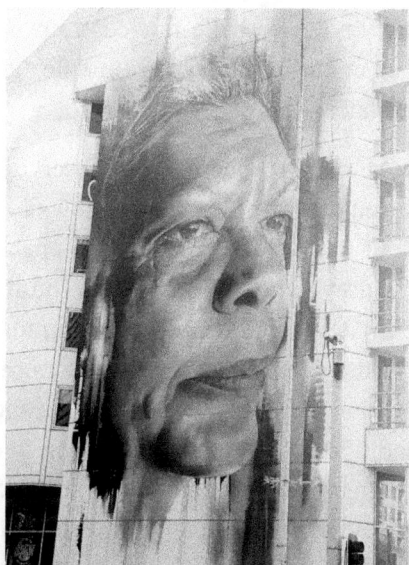

A mural of an Aboriginal woman painted on a high rise building in Sydney. For me, it embodies our soul evolution away from attachment. It's like the image transcends the material plane.

Some people may never reflect on these things but for those who are truly evolving, they always have "Lightbulb" moments, and it is sad to see people reflect, quite often with regret. But in saying this, if you have any doubt that your soul doesn't evolve, you won't find value out of this book. I'm not attempting to convert the unconverted but just present an example of life giving you the answer to something right before your eyes.

Our Soul Evolution

Our Soul Evolution is not dissimilar to the stages of the Human Life-cycle. In our modern world, the Human Lifecycle can be mapped through a number of distinct stages, which are shared by all humans e.g., birth, childhood, adulthood and old age. However, along this journey, we also experience milestone events and clearly marked times in our lives where we know we have moved from one stage of life to another e.g., such as in our teenage years, middle age and as we generally get older in our later years.

Let's examine these distinct phases and observe how they are no different to The Seven Stages of Soul Evolution - regarding the behaviours and actions - which you'd expect to see in people at certain ages. The spectrum of soul evolution represents the birth of our ego nature (or pure attachment) at one end of the spectrum, to eternal spirituality (non-attachment) at the other end. It's really about the polarity of life that exists in everything that we see. Whether it's about our expression of love (being conditional or unconditional); the transition from night to day or feeling extremes of temperature both hot or cold, it's all the same. Polarity is everywhere and in all things. Therefore, I call Polarity one of the Laws of the Universe. Given that it exists; thus, it is what it is. No one can doubt the existence of polarity in all things as "fake" news, more on that later.

Seven Stages of Soul Evolution

Seven Stages of Soul Evolution are classified in a way to enable the reader to understand the complicated process that occurs but in a simplified form. Our soul evolution is a simple concept and given that it uses the Universal Law of Polarity, it acknowledges that there is infinite duality in everything. This polarity can also be viewed as our attachment with ego, money and material things but as we evolve, the emergent qualities of spiritfulness (service, love and selflessness) become more prominent i.e., the benchmarks for the path of the spiritual warrior. Spiritfulness is my way of coining a new word, which refers to "living and being with spirit".

Human Life stages / Soul Evolution stages

1. Birth/Infancy – Characterised by birth the first year of life, the infant is completely dependent upon its parents or custodian for its survival. **Baby Soul -** first few incarnations where we experience no responsibility, it's just about food, shelter, emotions and survival.

2. Childhood. Toddler at first, then socialisation takes place from 1-12 years, and the child is susceptible to many learned behaviours and habits. **Younger Soul -** Start to learn about the consequences of our actions but are still overly attached to their ego nature (extreme narcissism, emotion, greed, status, money, power and fundamentalist religion).

3. Adolescence. Characterised by the ages 12-18, a critical period which includes puberty and when the child becomes a teenager. **Young Soul -** Less evolved beings living within their own spectrum of evolution. They start to learn about responsibility and the impact of their actions but are often still attached to their ego nature and follow the pack mentality (narcissism, judgment, greed, status, money, power and religion).

4. Adulthood. A time of building the things that you want to achieve in life, often with a sense of responsibility and accumulating things/wealth. **Adult Soul -** Evolving beings that are living in their own spectrum of evolution. Start to learn about responsibility and the impact of their actions but often still attached to their ego nature (greed, status, money, power and religion).

5. Midlife. Characterised by the ages 37 – 52 a time of contemplation and mid-life changes which can bring on a complete change of course or life path. **Awakening Soul** - Newly evolved beings starting to Awaken (light their flame of consciousness) and see glimpses of the spiritual path, discovering the meaningfulness of life. However, they often get drawn back to their ego nature (this can take years). Note: the process for the Awakening soul can occur at any age, the earlier, the better.

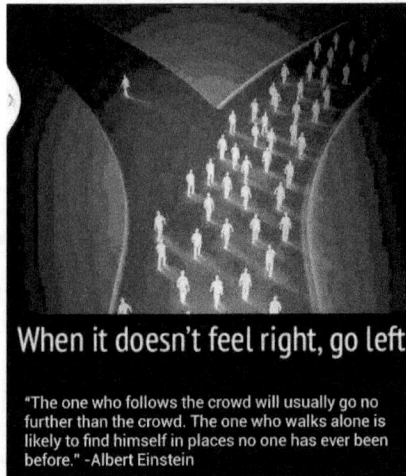

When it doesn't feel right, go left

"The one who follows the crowd will usually go no further than the crowd. The one who walks alone is likely to find himself in places no one has ever been before." -Albert Einstein

A photograph showing two paths diverging. "The one who follows the crowd will go no further than the crowd. The one who walks alone is likely to find himself in places no one has ever been before" Albert Einstein.

6. Older age. Characterised by the age 52 onwards. Gaining wisdom, respect and authority and being seen as someone who can guide others. **Older Soul** - Evolved beings living within their own spectrum of evolution and often have lifetimes where the Universe is testing them to grow, learn about hardship, stand against the pack mentality, often feel outcast and very drawn to things more meaningful in life. They are here to lead the way.

7. Old Age. Characterised by the age 80 onwards (or equivalent in developing societies). The age where people start living beyond their normal life expectancy and are seen in many cultures as an Elder. **Old Soul -** beings living within a very evolved spectrum of evolution and often have lifetimes where they come to the earth plane to raise the consciousness of Humanity at various levels. They have themes of imprisonment; sacrifice and live the spiritual path like no other.

How do we explain it?

The concept of Soul Evolution is in synergy (or synergistically connected) with the period of pregnancy; the time when a baby is being formed in the mother's body. During pregnancy, the spirit (in some ways) is studying the connection to its chosen family and circumstances surrounding its early childhood situation; in which it will be born. When a newborn baby enters our world in human form, conscious birth takes place. This moment is when a baby takes its first breath, and it also represents your Astrological blueprint or roadmap of your life. Much like our DNA determines the colour of our hair, eyes and predisposition to genetic diseases; an Astrology chart is no different, and it represents your astrological DNA. It's like a soul is waiting for the right time or window to be born; so that it can resonate with a specific Universal Harmonic Resonance or energy pattern. Thus this pattern becomes a freeze frame of the Universal energy at the moment you take your first breath.

Studying where people sit in their soul evolution can sometimes be complicated. This is very much relative to the person's current situation, circumstances and experiences in life and I call this their manifested Soul age. But in reality, their true Soul age may be different and depends on a variety of factors such as: -

- Age and characteristics of the person;

- Invariably, this is linked to how the person lives their life, whether driven purely by narcissism and ego or the will of selflessness - without the, "what am I going to get out of it" nature;
- Making a substantial effort to realise what they are truly here to do in life;
- Possessing the ability of insight to understand the consequences of their actions towards others;
- Having the conscious ability to understand that right intention is everything;
- Time left to achieve their Soul purpose, which is also dependent on the above variables.

As an example, a person's true Soul age may be that of an Older soul; however, they manifest a lower form of their soul evolution to fit in like a chameleon because the actual purpose of their life is yet to come. In essence, it cannot be fulfilled until there is a change in the environment, the world, or circumstances in their life i.e., an experience of illness or events yet to occur at an older age in life.

In reverse, it is highly unlikely that a Younger soul can manifest a higher energetic form unless they are receptive to change e.g., they're prepared to undertake an accelerated growth lifetime (for whatever reason) or what is called a "spiritual growth lifetime". The latter is where the Universe is initiating you to grow,

> Ok you think you can do it this way, but let's see how you can do it; if I throw these set of circumstances at you.

This type of life is difficult with lots of hard knocks and life seems harder than most other people's lives. However, on a more positive note, the Universe is asking and expecting you to grow, in reality; it's a blessed lifetime! Older souls will always come back and choose lifetimes where they initiate themselves to grow through experiencing more extreme situations; with the purpose to accelerate their growth without the Universe forcing it.

Baby Souls & Younger Souls

- *Our Soul Evolution away from Attachment*

Baby Souls & Younger Souls are predominantly earthbound souls of the lowest order and most associated with survival instinct; out of control emotions; extreme narcissism; greed and status; position and wealth. Their defining features also includes judgment; emotional insecurity and fear of anything that they do not have a formed understanding of. Hence why they relate most to fundamentalist religions, framed with extreme religious views i.e., Isis, fundamentalist Christians, Islam, etc. We must have compassion for them, for, in essence, they do not know what they do not know. Fear and judgment force them to act out their primaeval view of the world, often by force and hate. However, the time has come for the Universe to reverse things in its tracks and this can only be achieved by dramatically shifting humanities' path of destruction and that of our planet.

In terms of Younger Souls, they often have this unwarranted connection to following the pack, as a concept, I call this the "teenager pack mentality". This behaviour can be very dramatic, unpredictable and emotions run high. There is often severe greed, selfishness, lack of self-esteem and a need for love and belonging. Trump's behaviour for

A beautiful butterfly set for flight.

that matter represents the ultimate Younger Soul i.e., he has the soul evolution of an 8 to 15-year-old, as it varies at times. God forbid how terrifying someone like this is as leader of the most powerful country in the world, very frightening indeed!!! The two scenarios of Younger Souls who embody and embrace the misuse of power (think

of Hitler) and their potential for manifesting this on the world plain are: -

- Those Younger Souls who have developed extreme narcissistic and sociopathic qualities (totally devoted to their ego nature) or
- Older Souls who have the fallen "Lucifer concept" i.e., fallen angels who haven't been able to restore themselves to the highest order but choose to dwell and inflame the misery of Humanity.

Both types of souls, use Younger Souls to promote fundamentalist approaches around coercion, abuse of power, division, hatred and often violence. Ultimately Younger Souls want to mature and become adults and start learning about responsibility and the impact of their actions on others. However, they often remain attached to their ego nature. When Younger Souls become adults, they begin feeling things that they haven't felt before, and the Universe starts to awaken them to emotions like sympathy and experiences of grief and loss, and forgiveness. They often have a deeper focus on aesthetic and cognitive (intellect and thinking) needs, masking it in the form of intellectual elitism.

Awakening

- Our Soul Evolution Midpoint

The midpoint of the Soul Evolution spectrum is purely about "Awakening the Spirit" – these are the blessed Young Souls who are evolving or Awakening i.e., lighting their candle's spiritual flame of consciousness. It is a highly emotional and intense time yet at this point of discovery they see glimpses of their true spiritual path i.e., yearning to experience the deeper meaning to life. However, in saying this, they often get drawn back to their ego nature (time and time again) therefore this process can take many years. In seeking this deeper meaning to life, they experience a deep tension between the polarity opposites of our "Soul Evolution" spectrum. But by focussing less and less on the tangible or material things in life, they start to get a better view of the other end of the spectrum, much like coming out of a clearing fog. At this point, they finally go on the path of the spiritual warrior and find it easier to serve something much greater than oneself. Key to their Awakening are the **Older/Old Souls who are here to lead the way**.

Older Souls are evolved beings who live within their own spectrum of soul evolution, they are: -

- Often not of this world (literally speaking);
- Very sensitive and have lifetimes where the Universe is testing them to grow, often with a sense of purpose;
- Are born as natural healers and learn about hardship;
- Stand up against the pack mentality;
- Speak out against injustice in the world;
- Often they feel outcast or don't fit in and
- Very drawn to things more meaningful in life.

They are all here along with the Old Souls to lead the way.

Old Souls & Kindred Spirits

- *Our Soul Evolution towards Enlightenment and Meeting of Souls from Other Worlds*

Old Souls are beings of the highest order that are living within a very evolved spectrum of evolution and are not of this world with a primary focus on self-actualisation and transcendence. Old Souls live life with "pure intent" to shine light into a world that is mostly in darkness, but somehow they find a way to shine through the darkest of clouds. Their lifetimes are about guiding others, opening people's hearts and often come to the earth plane to raise the consciousness of Humanity at various levels i.e., nations and mankind. They have themes of imprisonment; sacrifice and live the spiritual path like no other but often need to immerse themselves among everyday people to experience and understand the human condition. The symbolism of their lives and deaths for that matter are very significant for Humanity and our survival. Their life and death teach us invaluable lessons however we often don't truly value their lessons (and sometimes distort their teachings) until well after they have left the earth plane.

I was so privileged to meet Princess Diana in 1996 when she visited patients at Sacred Heart Hospice - a rehabilitation/palliative facility, St Vincent's Hospital Sydney. It is, without doubt, one of the most touching experiences I've always remembered in life. I've never been in the presence of such an Old Soul, and when she walked into the room; I felt something so enlightening about her aura or energy field (like being touched by an angel but words cannot describe it). I also remember preparing an Astrology Chart to give to her as a gift, but on the day I shrunk into my fear; as I didn't think it was kosher (plus she was only carrying a small purse, it would barely fit). It was common knowledge that she believed in and used Astrology in her daily life.

I am an Ancient soul, caged in a young body.

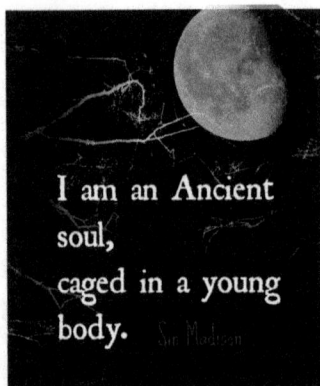

Old Souls find their way to shine in the World.

The patients were gathered into the day room (a room where patients would attend activities/social events) in a great circle (wheelchairs and beds), with hospital staff behind them. Of course, the crazy mass of media was banned but sitting impatiently outside like vultures. Princess Diana chatted to many patients on the day, devoting her attention to those most in need. We were privy to many of their conversations, exalting her skills which were endearing, full of empathy and humour. However, I remember there was one patient who stole her heart; she intuitively knew that he looked so lost. He was a frail, young man dying of AIDS with a sad, vacant look on his face (he hadn't smiled since he came in). He couldn't see anything (as he was visually impaired) and didn't know what to expect sitting there comfortably in his Jason recliner chair. Princess Diana's advisor was informed of his condition, and she immediately asked for a chair to be put right next to him. Princess Diana sat down and lovingly embraced him with all her heart; placing one hand on his knee (rubbing it gently) while the other arm was wrapped around his other shoulder, holding it ever so firmly. She then lent over and started whispering in his ear; only they were privy to what was spoken, but in an instant, he would've felt the warmth of her breath.

At that moment his face beamed with the most amazing smile I have ever seen, it was a pure act of loving-kindness and compassion. These qualities are the inherent features of Old Souls. The number of Old Souls in the world may be few but they role model the essence of the evolved human spirit; have true presence of being and an innate understanding of Humanity i.e., Princess Diana, Nelson Mandela, Martin Luther King, Krishnamurti, some may say Aung San Suu Kyi to beings such as Buddha and Jesus Christ (the embodiment of the highest order).

But please read on, for it is my view that we have a significant number of Old Souls living on the earth plane right now who are destined to be here for the next Global shift, which is necessary for **Humanity and will occur in 2023/2024**. This period will be one of the most significant times in our human existence. There will be a massive global event which forces Humanity to transition; thereby, raising our global consciousness. This time will be purely governed and underpinned by our acceptance of Universal Laws around balance and harmony; compassion; being of service and always using the right intention.

If Humanity can't evolve at this pivotal time, it makes sense that the Universe will force it upon us. Many of us get the feeling that something terrible or unforeseen is about to happen and it's just around the corner. For those that get it, you are truly kindred spirits! The kindred spirits I tend to meet are evolved souls from other worlds and they understand that there is a diverse group of spiritual families living among us.

Me with Princess Diana (Madame Tussauds Wax Museum, London).

Often you have this innate feeling of not belonging; life has taught you many life lessons or initiations and that many people just don't get you or you just don't get them for that matter. There are themes of searching for a place to call home, and not feeling like you can achieve what it is you're here to do with your life. If you could, the world or our current environment must change for you to do so. For those earth-bound souls or other souls (for that matter) who get it and are "Awakening" very quickly; come on the journey for you will now be able to evolve to other worlds. It's not an elite club and is open to all those who seek the deeper meaning to life, its existence and the global issues of our time! In essence, it's about the transcendence of Humanity to something much greater, limited only by what our current understanding can comprehend.

The Dawn of Aquarius: A New People, A New Consciousness,
A New Era ... Humans Are Free

4

CHALLENGES FOR HUMANITY

- DEEPER INSIGHTS INTO THE ISSUES THAT MATTER

We are just an advanced breed of monkeys on a minor planet of a very average star. But we can understand the Universe. That makes us something very special

> *I did my best to notice when the call came down the line. Up to the platform of surrender, I was brought, but I was kind. And sometimes I get nervous when I see an open door. Close your eyes, clear your heart, cut the cord.*
>
> *Wave goodbye, wish me well, you've gotta let me go. My sign is vital, my hands are cold, and I'm on my knees looking for the answer. Are we human or are we, dancer?*

— HUMAN LYRICS, THE KILLERS 2009

The Meaning Lies in Us

THE MEANING LIES IN US, and Stephen Hawking knows the science of Cosmology like no other scientist or physicist. He states, "We can understand the Universe. That makes us something very special". But we are at a crucial time in our history, for most of us will experience and witness some of the most significant challenges for our Humanity. In essence, our planet is being forced to evolve. The question in the lyrics asks, are we human or are we, dancer? As Humanity evolves our umbilical cord is finally going to be cut. When this time comes, Humanity will be a dancer set forth on to the Universal stage, however our next performance will be focussed outward rather than inward.

Many of us are already have a feeling that our world is changing dramatically; possibly in a way that we have never seen before. We have grave concerns about our environment, and it's quickening destruction; there remains inequity between men and women, and we have wars that are displacing millions of people but do we care? Where is our humanitarian spirit? We still don't have true equality, with an extreme divide between those that have and those that have nothing. We are preaching about racism and division like no other time, and our political systems are corrupt and divided. They strive to keep people "stupid", and out of desperation people are forced to bury their heads in the sand.

> Meaning doesn't lie in things. Meaning lies in us. When we attach value to things that aren't love – the money, the car, the house, the prestige – we are loving things that can't love us back. We are searching for meaning in the meaningless. Money, of itself, means nothing. Material things, of themselves, mean nothing. It's not that they're bad. It's that they're nothing
>
> — MARIANNE WILLIAMSON

I feel, on the whole; most people would rather not know what is coming and are relieved by their ignorance through the pursuit of greed, security, position, and comfort to dissolve their apathy. But this is nothing to be proud of, a temporary delusion and path of what I call the selfish warrior. Ultimately it's your choice, as there are alternative options. If your awareness is closed, then it's inevitable that you will become vulnerable to the manipulation of others. As our senses become shut down, we end up cowering to others who can control us, and they say everything you want them to say. As a consequence, this then purely feeds your ego nature.

The Challenges for Humanity

The Challenges for Humanity we face are only proportional to our inaction or inability to fight for change. Does that sound depressing? Yes of course it is, but if we all bury our heads in the sand, there will be no one to fight the Challenges for Humanity. There is no time like any other in our human history where world events are escalating to something that is going to result in the possible death and destruction of our planet, but we can intervene! There is a need and urgency for greater activism and community participation in the things that matter. I believe we need some early or possibly radical intervention for our survival, the survival of our planet and Humanity. It just involves getting off our backside, making a pledge and doing something right now!

I believe one of the most significant shifts in our global consciousness is about to take place in the next five to six years. Why this timeframe, I have observed that there are transformational global shifts that always occur approximately every fourteen to fifteen years. Usually, following the initial global event or impact; subtle undercurrents of great trans-formational change continue through each period.

The next global shift will be revolutionary and powerful in nature; its energy operating from the space of addressing the global inequality that pervades our world. If our actions are mostly focussed towards the "me, me, me" culture without concern for the bigger picture; than the global consequences of the energy shift will be proportional to what is required for us to evolve as a planet. Therefore, the more self-obsessed and selfish we are as individuals (devoid of any meaning) then the more severe the consequences of the next global shift. At the moment, I'm not feeling very confident. In many respects, I believe it's the Universe's way of showing Humanity how we need to change, evolve and transform our consciousness over time. It's so pure and simple.

THE WORLD'S WEALTH INEQUALITY

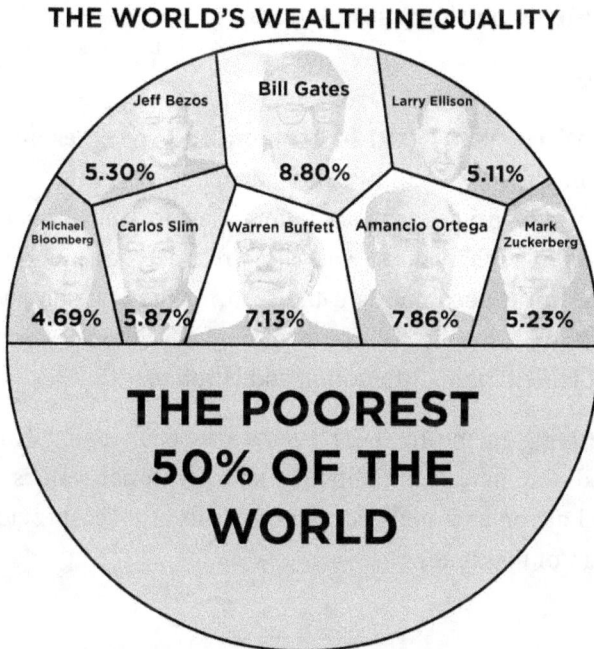

Sources:
https://www.oxfam.org/
https://howmuch.net/articles/the-worlds-wealth-inequality

howMuch .net

Wealth Inequality it's pretty depressing! Also, notice there is not one woman among the wealthiest men on earth. As civil-rights activist Dorothy Cotton said, "we are ordinary people, living our lives, and trying…to 'fix what ain't right' in our society".

Global shifts in our consciousness always involve significant transformational change and power. Humanity must come to realise that the impact of these shifts not only exert a generational influence on individuals but also influences and transcends humankind on a social, political and spiritual level.

Everything we do is about the sum of the interactions of all of us; not only for our planet but also for that of the Universe. As above, as below.

— DAVID SHAUN LARSEN

Global Shifts over the past 100 years

1914 – 1939

Globally World War I (1914-1919) and Interwar Period. This time was also marked by the Influenza Pandemic of 1918, the spread of psychology and psychoanalysis (attempting to transform our understanding of inherent values) and the Great Depression. The shift in energy also influenced and laid the seed for the Russian and Chinese Civil Wars and a timeline of events throughout the Interwar period and the rise of Hitler, Stalin, Mussolini, and Hirohito.

The underlying theme of these events was challenging Humanity to understand the inherent traditional and territorial values of home, family and nation and our need to protect this at all cost (evident in our nationalism of that time).

1939 – 1956

Globally World War II and culminating in the Korean War - A turbulent time on a massive scale and marked the emergence of the Cold War and ended with major wars such as the Vietnam War. Beginning of the baby boomers (this generation have an intense will, dramatic self-expression, power, and pride) and there was massive immigration during and post World War II.

Over 60 million people were killed, which was about 3% of the 1940 world population, estimated 2.3 billion.[5] Supposedly the war to end all wars. The underlying theme of these events was challenging Humanity to learn about the limitations of conditional love. The ultimate way to experience and develop the maturity of the heart is through grief and loss e.g., death, displacement, war and destruction.

1956 – 1971

Globally this was marked by the time of the Vietnam War, the Civil Rights Movement, and the emerging Counter Culture revolution - This was the time, where our definition of civil rights was revolutionised, dissolved, and transformed. Marked by the height of the cold war, moon landing (connection to Cosmos); the assassination of President JFK and Martin Luther King. It also marked the signing of The Civil Rights Act (1964) and Equal Employment Opportunity. The use of LSD, Cannabis, and worship of the mother goddess emerged.

It was the time of the Counter Culture revolution an anti-establishment phenomenon i.e., the Peace and Flower Power movement (attuning into the higher vibration of service to Humanity). It also saw a massive sea change in our relationship to health and well-being; with a revolutionary emphasis on natural foods, lifestyles, and holistic and naturopathic health practices. Ultimately, this time was attempting to awaken Humanity to our connection with the Cosmos e.g., the significance of the moon landing and realising the damaging effects of war. The Peace movement was the counter-revolution to war and many returned veterans received mixed public support and inadequate long-term health care for conditions such as post traumatic stress, etc.

1971 – 1983

Globally this time was marked by the emergence of two powerful movements for change. The Women's Rights (Liberation) and Gay Rights Movements and the rise of Neoliberalism - these global movements gained momentum. This period was the start of the electronics and digital revolution, height of the sexual revolution, 70s fashion, and disco. Also marked the Iranian Revolution, Pol Pot and his famous killing fields.

The struggle for equality was the predominant theme throughout this decade with many protest marches, and demonstrations and our younger generation were redefining what was rightfully just. This period ended with the emergence of HIV and the publication of "A Neoliberal's Manifesto" in 1983.

1983 – 1995

Globally this time was marked by the fear and discrimination associated with the Impact of HIV and embracement of Neoliberalism - Emergence of the global impact of HIV/AIDS and widespread embracement of neoliberalism. This period ended with the discovery of combination therapy for HIV/AIDS in 1996 which lead to HIV being a long-term chronic illness, as opposed to a death sentence. Since the beginning of the epidemic, more than 70 million people had been infected with HIV and approximately half that number 35 million have died.6

This is more than 1.5 times the number of military war deaths from World War II. Also, this period ended with the genocide in Rwanda which left the world in disbelief (where over 800,000 people were killed in less than 100 days) and the rise of the Taliban as a militia (1994-1996).[7]

1995 – 2008

<u>Globally</u> this time was marked by the Global Quest for Knowledge and Rise of the Internet - This was also the time of many brutalities in the name of religion i.e., the rise of the Taliban as a Government (1994-2007), Sept 11 attacks 2001 and the War on Terror. However, we also saw a substantial economic boom across the world and in essence, this was the start of globalisation i.e., easy borrowing, economic expansion, and technology. Around this time we had much easier travel; access to money and education, that was expanding our horizons and convincing us that anything was possible. *Medicines Sans Frontières* was awarded The Nobel Peace Prize 10th December 1999.

The emergence of the world-wide-web gave us access to information of an unprecedented scale. The Web had broken down previous barriers in many unthinkable ways. In reality, it made our lives unrecognisable by 2008 and when we looked back at this time; we couldn't have imagined in 1995 such change was possible.

2008 – 2023/2024

<u>Globally</u> this time was marked by the Global Financial Crisis (GFC) and major Global Power-Shifts - The time which heralded the world financial crisis, thus began a process of global power-shifts and major structural and socio-economic changes. It is a time where Government and especially Corporations rule; the rise of the "nanny state"; loss of rights and civil liberties (including charities) and ongoing major power shifts (some yet unknown).

This has been characterised by the emergence if ISIS; Russia flexing its weight; Brexit (UK leaving the EU) and the election of Donald Trump in 2016 (Corporate CEO). Also, it represents the lifting of nuclear-related sanctions on Iran in 2016; North Korea and its nuclear threats and China positioning itself as the number 1 global economy in

2014. **Australia will become a Republic on 26th January 2023, most likely before 2024.**

———

2023/24 – 2039

Globally this time will be represented by the hopeful Evolution as opposed to Revolution of our planet. It is often symbolised by a sudden shock event (without warning); with the purpose of bringing the transformational change our planet needs. The chain of events set forth our next Global Shift in Human Consciousness. **See Chapter 10:** *Humanity and 2023/2024 - Our Opportunity to Embrace the next Global Shift in our Consciousness.*

———

The Next Series of Chapters

The next series of chapters relate to my spiritual insights around major societal and global issues that are either impacting our way of living today and the planet. Understanding the deep threads between these issues is crucial and integral to how we can harness these insights and teachings, for the betterment of individuals and our planet. It's not intended to be an exhaustive list or read, for that matter, but I hope you will get something out of it. Briefly, I will cover: -

- **Gender Equality** - *The Answer to our Evolution*
- **Politics -** *A New Political Movement for the 21st Century*
- **The Environment -** *The Urgency to Protect our Planet*
- **Australian Indigenous Culture** - *The Oldest Continuous Spiritual Culture on Earth*
- **HIV and its Global Impact -** *A Global Disease to Challenge Humanities' Fear*
- **Humanitarianism** - *Our Global Responsibility for Humanity*

- **Diversity in Life -** *Acceptance of Universal Sexuality and Cultural Diversity*
- **Mental Health and Substance Use -** *Resilience, The Use of Drugs and Alcohol and the Search for Recovery*
- **Dis-Ability -** *People with Ability who are born to challenge our perceptions about life*
- **Happiness and Wellbeing -** *Our Measure of Social Progress*
- **Living, Loving, Ageing, and Dying -** *The True Essence of Life*

The Dawn of the Aquarian Age | The Wise Magazine

5

POLITICS FOR OUR AGE

- A NEW POLITICAL MOVEMENT FOR THE 21ST CENTURY

> *The great question...is whether the time has not now arisen for the creation of this Australian continent of an Australian Government and an Australian Parliament. I believe the time has come.*

> — SIR HENRY PARKES, TENTERFIELD ORATION,
> 1889

Has Politics Lost its Way?

HAS POLITICS LOST ITS WAY? Politics as a movement and system has lost its way, and real meaning for the average Australian or American for that matter and this profoundly resonates in the hearts of most of us. Both countries are portrayed prominently in this chapter, as our people are crying out for change but be careful about what you ask or how you vote.

For a nation that parodies disinterest in politics; Australia uncannily divests an enormous amount of our energy, conversation and time complaining about it! In many ways, the apathy and disregard for politics among the electorate is very disturbing and not surprisingly feeds directly into the hands of the power moguls i.e., the corrupt corporations, lobbyists, and an array of disenchanted groups that rally to the cause. Also, the economic pessimism that permeates our societies today and the fear of impending change - not dissimilar to a readjustment that we might need to make - if we experience a sudden life event, illness or even ageing itself. Adjusting to change is something that can occur over a short period or with rapid onset.

Malcolm Turnbull was posing for a selfie on Twitter for APEC 2017 - later it was revealed that there was one more person who had posed for the selfie, only to be cropped out (Vietnamese President Tran Dai Quang). Vietnam was the host of APEC.

The readjustment that our society needs to undertake as we make a transition from one economic period to another will be a painful and challenging experience for most people. I fear that we are about to enter a period of significant economic readjustment. The election of Malcolm Turnbull as Prime Minister in Australia and Donald Trump as President of the United States has been anything but disappointing for both countries. However disappointing it may be; the significance of these men coming into power is also a positive for the world, as it feeds the movement for critical change that is desperately needed.

> **Malcolm Turnbull** @TurnbullMalcolm - Catching up with @realDonaldTrump & President Xi at #APEC2017; working together to secure our region's safety & prosperity

These type of men only operate with selfish intent, putting self-interest above everything else. So what is selfish intent and what does it look like? Recently there was an infamous selfie taken by Malcolm Turnbull at APEC in November 2017. There is nothing wrong with an odd selfie now and again. However this selfie was deplorable, later it was revealed that the Vietnamese president Tran Dai Quang had also posed for the selfie (he got cropped out). Some may argue that this is insignificant, but it's not when Vietnam was also the host nation for APEC.

Somehow I don't think this is working together to secure our region's safety & prosperity, especially when the host nation is viewed as lesser significant.

Let's Go Onward Together

Onward Together slogan

Let's go Onward Together. The election of Donald Trump is not the beginning of a new era; it's the beginning of the end. It's more the end of an old era, with the death throes of right-wing conservatism in the world e.g., it becomes the vehicle that will finally take down right-wing conservative politics in the next generation. Whenever we try to release any old pattern of thinking or ways of working; the situation seems to get tenser for awhile, until we settle into the new situation. Our response in times of change is to react naturally! When we embrace change with positivity and move forward, we're developing something counter to the old ways of thinking. Therefore, what the world needs is a new Counter-Revolution, to change this sad state of affairs. Hillary Clinton officially announced in May 2017 the formation of a new political organisation aimed at funding "resistance groups" standing up to President Donald Trump.

The idea for a Clinton political group started after Hilary Clinton met with a group of young activists. She, therefore, launched "Onward Together" as a way to encourage people to get involved, to organise, and even run for office.[19] "Onward Together" was in essence, a way for the Democrats to boost their electoral hopes while subtly questioning Trump's authenticity. Clinton certainly doesn't want to be silent in the coming years, and she wrote,

> Onward Together is dedicated to advancing the vision that earned nearly 66 million votes in the last election. By encouraging people to organise, get involved, and run for office, Onward Together will advance progressive values and work to build a brighter future for generations to come...
>
> From the Women's March to airports where communities are welcoming immigrants and refugees to town hall meetings in every community, Americans are speaking up and speaking out like never before.
>
> The challenges we face as a country are real. But there's no telling what we can achieve if we approach the fights ahead with the passion and determination we feel today, and bring that energy into 2017, 2018, 2020, and beyond.
>
> — HILLARY RODHAM CLINTON, ONWARD TOGETHER

Where are Our Leaders?

Where are our leaders? Politicians have lost the ability to lead. There seems to be a need to motivate and spur up activism among young people. In Australia with compulsory voting, there are believed to be close to 800,000 young people under 30 who have not registered to vote and if they did; they could change the outcome of the next election. Cuts this year to the Australian Electoral Commission, framed as a restructure to the Northern Territory based office also means that the Commission doesn't have the staffing to track people who haven't registered to vote. Therefore, what a perfect way to influence the outcome of the next election. I guess if you assume most people under 30 are slightly more left-leaning than it makes sense for a right-leaning party in power to try and do everything possible to stay in power.

Bernie Sanders who at 75 was the longest-serving independent in U.S. congressional history and ran for office as the Democratic Nominee up against Hilary Clinton

All around the world, people are rising to define a new vision for our collective future. What Australia needs is its own Bernie Saunders, who at 75 was the longest-serving independent in U.S. congressional history running for President of the United States.

Why does there seem to be such a lacklustre pool of Australian political leaders? Have they been mostly constrained by towing the party line or possibly unable to lead, because of the ineffective political system itself? Also, the influences of news and media; the reliability and factualness of information and where people source their information from, is potentially dumbing us down. Lack of knowledge ends up satisfying our craving thirst as a people that are viewed by many politicians as "stupid". For all intended purposes, we then only have ourselves to blame, as we get the culture and political system that we deserve. The charity sector in Australia, one of the last cornerstones of our civil society and democracy, is now under attack. The Liberal Government in Australia is targeting community organisations who engage in advocacy on public policy issues. How low can a government go, it's fundamentally repulsive?

Yes there are a lot of "stupid" people in Australia and the US for that matter, and forgive me, but I mean "stupid" in the nicest possible way.

I have been one of those stupid people in the past, not concerned about the bigger picture, our democracy or trying to make sense out of the fake pledges made by our politicians.

Therefore by "stupid"; I'm referring to the decent, common-sense people (that part of society), that care more for the distractions of life that feed our ego rather than our minds and spirit. Politicians will always tell you what you want to hear but look behind the meaning; does it come from a space of compassion and unity or does it come from a space of judgement, division, and hate. You are a greater fool if you rally to the cause of the latter.

The Charity Sector is one of the cornerstones of our democracy. The Liberal Government is now targeting community organisations who engage in advocacy on public policy issues.

"Intention" in life is everything; the "right intention" is the part and sum of us that cares very deeply about our culture, our way of life and inherent values. I fear countries like the US are closer to a situation of a civil war. Trump's vision for America can't exist alongside the progressive vision created by Obama. One or the other has to prevail in the next few years. And this is what precisely happened in the lead up to the US Civil War 1861-1865. After a long-standing controversy over slavery, state's rights, protectionism and American nationalism, war broke out in April 1861. Let's hope the past does not repeat itself.

Statue of Sir Henry Parkes, Centennial Park, Sydney

Sir Henry Parkes my Great, Great, Great Grandfather

Sir Henry Parkes my Great, Great, Great Grandfather, was an incredible man with a vision. Politics runs deep in my blood. Sir Henry Parkes was an inspiring leader and the father of our Federation (my Uncle who lives in the US used to refer to him, as the George Washington of Australia). Sir Henry Parkes was the longest serving Premier of any state or former colony in Australia and was Premier of New South Wales on five separate occasions. Parkes also had many other talents, one of which was as a writer, which is extraordinary for someone who lacked any formal education. Maybe politics and writing is my calling too!

Sir Henry Parkes contribution to Australian politics and way of life was extraordinary. Parkes was dedicated to the idea of keeping Australian society racially homogeneous and sincere in his chosen role as guardian of the constitutional convention.[20] The Centennial Park Trust in Sydney has listed seven reasons why he was such a prominent figure in Australian politics.[21]

Here are the seven reasons:

- **Rags to Riches Tale**– born into poverty, Parkes had very little formal education, suffered early setbacks with business failure in England and came to Australia as a penniless immigrant in 1839.
- **Determined and Hard Working** – despite an early life of hardship and supporting a young family, Parkes worked odd jobs as a labourer, factory worker, shopkeeper, and journalist.
- **Held Ideas and Ideals**– he started a newspaper *The Empire* in the 1850s which were destined to be the chief organ of mid-century liberalism. He also helped set up the Australian League to educate people about the rights and duties of citizens in a democracy. He fought for jobs and fair wages by opposing the free labour, sourced through convict transportation. He argued for universal suffrage.
- **Stood for Public Office often without Personal Gain** – he sought out and was elected to the NSW Parliament in 1854 and represented his constituents for long periods without pay. He left public office on some occasions to stave off personal bankruptcy and financial problems.
- **Worked His Way to the Top**– he chaired a committee to investigate the condition of the working classes (especially his concern for children). He brought the first nursing sisters who trained under Florence Nightingale out to Australia. Parkes also was instrumental in educational reform, as he believed teachers should be remunerated for their work.
- **Great Speech Making Ability**– despite a lack of education, Parkes developed great oratory skills to inspire, unite and impel his audiences to action. Many of his speeches linger long in Australian history, and his *Tenterfield Oration* in 1889 was possibly the most influential speech that eventually led to the uniting of the colonies and the Federation of the nation of Australia.

- **Creation of Centennial Park**– the famous Centennial Park in Sydney (along with other public spaces) was one of his crowning achievements. The Park was established to commemorate the 100th anniversary of European settlement in the colony. At its opening in 1888, Parkes stated,

> This grand park is emphatically the People's Park, and you must always take as much interest in it as if by your own hands you had planted the flowers, the park will be one of the grandest adornments to this beautiful country.[22]

— SIR HENRY PARKES

Statue of Sir Henry Parkes, Centennial Park Trust, Sydney

My Poppa and Coming Out as a Gay Man

My poppa and coming out as gay at 21 years of age has nothing really to do with politics. However, my Poppa (George Murray) deserves a special mention; he was my father's father. Poppa was also the Grandson of Mary Parkes, one of Sir Henry Parkes daughters. Mary Parkes (3 March 1848 – 15 December 1919) married a gentleman called George Murray, and I believe they had several children.[23] George eventually set up a business as a printer and lithographer. George died in 1898 and Mary in December 1919.[24] One of their sons was my Poppa's father. I remember Poppa very well. One very fond memory I have before he died, was when I came out to my father about being gay. My Poppa had remarried a lady called Ali and lived a happy life in Adelaide for the remainder of his years.

Me standing in front of a statue of Sir Henry Parkes in Centennial Park, Sydney.

On the night I came out to my father, I was at my Poppa's apartment, and my father came over to visit but was drunk, what a surprise! When I told him I was gay, he threatened to hit me, but my Poppa was very accepting of my homosexuality. He said to my Dad "Michael just grow up, accept David for who he is, basically get over it". My father in his grief and anger, wanted me to sleep with one of his lady friends (sex worker friends) who ran a brothel in Adelaide, and as quickly as he could, he phoned her. As a means to appease him, I started chatting with her on the phone, and I remember her saying, "oh dear is your father drunk? You know, and I know, there's nothing wrong with you being gay, and of course, your father is just a bloody idiot", and I said "God yes". We just chatted and laughed, and I guess my father had no choice but to leave wounded and disappeared into the night, like a stray dog.

But the saddest thing is that my father never used this event nor any other experience in his life to bring about some personal transformational change, especially for someone who was gifted with opportunity in life and lots of it when he was young but squandered it away.

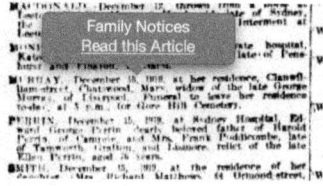

Obituary Notice, Sydney Morning Herald 1917.

There is Nothing to Fear about the Future

There is nothing to fear about the future if you just scratch the surface and look for the connections. I believe the personal transformation the planet needs is taking place in Australia, Asia, Europe and the US. There are hints, all around us, of what will occur or is needed to happen in the world. The Brexit vote in England; the election of Donald Trump; The North Korean nuclear threat; the rise of Russia and the more significant economic alliance between China and Europe are just the beginning of the end of this era. These events are going to bring some of the most expected and unexpected convulsions, that world has ever seen. These events will also produce some of the most significant changes in the world and although we shouldn't be fearful of the consequences, those who have "Awakened" will welcome them with great opportunity. There is nothing to fear about the future. Once we emerge out of this time, we will observe some of the most accelerated changes we will ever witness on our planet in our lifetime.

> We are suffering just now from a bad attack of economic pessimism. It is common to hear people say that the epoch of enormous economic progress which characterised the 19th century is over; that the rapid improvement in the standard of life is now going to slow down —at any rate in Great Britain; that a decline in prosperity is more likely than an improvement in the decade which lies ahead of us.

I believe that this is a wildly mistaken interpretation of what is happening to us. We are suffering, not from the rheumatics of old age, but from the growing-pains of over-rapid changes, from the painfulness of readjustment between one economic period and another...

— JOHN MAYNARD KEYNES, ECONOMIC POSSIBILITIES FOR OUR GRANDCHILDREN (1930)

This decade is very reminiscent of the 1930's, during this era we saw the emergence of right-wing politics that gripped much of the world with fascism (the rise of Hitler, Stalin, Mussolini and Hirohito). Peter Leyden wrote in his informative article, *Why Trump's Inauguration is Not the Beginning of an Era—but the End* that, "it's easy for politicians to whip up public fears against these changes and rally people to go back to the old ways, to make America great again".[25]

The Positive Reframe: Trump does the World a great Service

The Positive Reframe: Trump does the world a great service, Leyden states that California is the future and although in many ways Trump is heading down the path of fascism it won't last long. He believes that Trump is ultimately going to do America and the world a service by becoming the vehicle for change that will finally take down right-wing conservative politics for generations. His insights are convincing for the following reasons: -

- Trump has managed to get the entire Republican conservative establishment to buy into his regime.
- By doing so, Trump is creating an administration that is all about rule; some may say dictatorship.
- Therefore Trump represents the ultimate in Corporate government control. He is blatantly selling out to the wealthy, the industries bleeding our oil and carbon and celebrating an elite style of capitalism, like an episode on a reality TV show.

- Trump will therefore completely alienate the growing political constituencies of the 21st century: the Millennial Generation, professional people, people of colour, people who value education and our wiser sex, namely women (especially those who embrace their innate power).
- Trump will eventually repulse a significant number of more moderate Republicans. And finally, the white working class people who got him elected, however they will never admit that they voted for him.
- The analogy is going to be closer to what happened to the conservative Republicans coming out of the 1930s — they were out of power for the next 50 years.

Some may counter-argue that California is not the forerunner of the future, questioning:

- Who is this process intended to be for?
- Will it feed into more inequality in the world?
- Is the issue of globalisation and capitalism driving such changes?
- Is the left being counter-intuitive to the changes it wants to create?
- Is turning to the past, not a bad thing it may not be progressive but is it regressive?

Even if these ring true, one could say; isn't it better to model some positive progress for the future that will hopefully raise humankind out of the vulnerable state of affairs our world finds itself today? All progress must start somewhere, but we need to continually ensure that it is equitable and inclusive for all, reaching all classes and the entire population of our planet.

US States Renamed for Countries with Similar GDPs, 2015

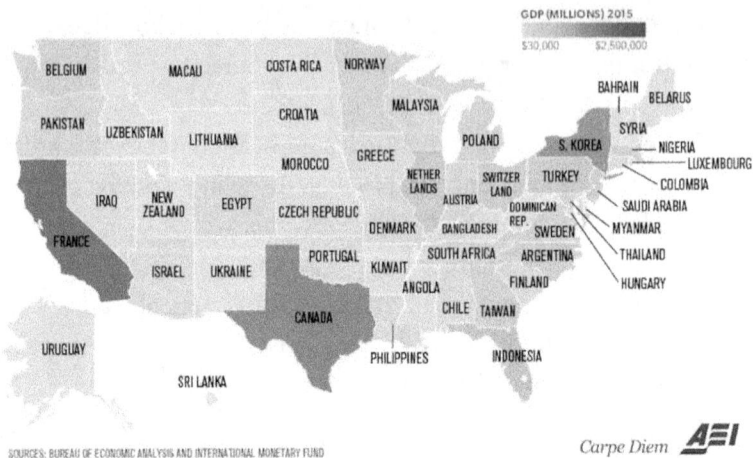

GDP (MILLIONS) 2015

$30,000 $2,500,000

BELGIUM   MACAU   COSTA RICA   NORWAY

BAHRAIN   BELARUS

CROATIA   MALAYSIA

PAKISTAN   UZBEKISTAN   LITHUANIA   POLAND   SYRIA   NIGERIA

S. KOREA   LUXEMBOURG

MOROCCO   GREECE   COLOMBIA

NETHER   SWITZER   TURKEY
LANDS   LAND

IRAQ   NEW   EGYPT   CZECH REPUBLIC   AUSTRIA   DOMINICAN   SAUDI ARABIA
ZEALAND   REP.   MYANMAR

DENMARK   BANGLADESH   SWEDEN

FRANCE

PORTUGAL   SOUTH AFRICA   ARGENTINA   THAILAND

ISRAEL   UKRAINE   KUWAIT   FINLAND   HUNGARY

ANGOLA

CANADA   CHILE   TAIWAN

URUGUAY   PHILIPPINES   INDONESIA

SRI LANKA

SOURCES: BUREAU OF ECONOMIC ANALYSIS AND INTERNATIONAL MONETARY FUND

Carpe Diem   AEI

Leyden believes the backlash or counter-revolution will be fast and furious. And it won't just be Trump that goes down — it will be Prime Minister Turnbull and large swaths of conservative politicians everywhere, hopefully before it is too late for the World. I believe like Leyden that the next 3 to 7 years are going to see a severe revolutionary change in politics — to the left, not the right. It's possible that Hillary Clinton wouldn't have brought about the kind of transformation that the world currently needs. She is more likely to help the convulsion to the left by driving the "Onward Together" movement, as a grassroots activist organisation, that will rely on the further public donation if it's to be successful.

The days of conservative ideology will be long gone, the out-dated modes of working and ideas will perish and be noted only as a scholarly learning in our history books. The world needs to move on. The events leading up to Humanity and 2024 is going to bring a new leadership the world needs to enable it to make the next global shift. I believe this shift will bring 15 years of overarching Aquarian energy, where we will make the full transition to digital technologies; unimaginable scientific discoveries; acceptance of diversity in sexuality and culture; reshaping capitalism to rebalance massive inequalities; human-itarianism, and making a significant progression with climate change.

Let's Go Together

Let's Go Together as one and a movement for political change in the 21st century. It's necessary to go together and embrace positive change for the greater good of Humanity; progressive Governments and tech-nological innovation. The most progressive societies on earth such as the Northern European Nations (Netherlands, Scandinavian Countries, and Germany), Canada, New Zealand, California and New York State in the US are embodying the next economic and technological period of growth. They wholeheartedly resist any political movement towards the right. Also, I believe there will be enormous political shifts occur-ring in Taiwan, Korea, Hong Kong, Japan, Singapore and China, although in China with increasing civil unrest. How this impacts on the world and plays out is uncertain?

Conservative ideology and politics will be a thing of the past. Australia is emerging out of this period, and places like California represent a microcosm of this, for I believe it is an "energetic centre". California has traditionally been a place that spurns a culture of innovation, new ideas, movements for change and sets trends. If you think about it, the early settlers had a sense of "Go West, young man" but those early pioneers were possibly already ahead of their time. Although framed around fertile farmlands and the need for westerly expansion, I feel California has always been something much greater, even outside of the US .

The future economy of the world is already working in California, and it has surpassed France as the world's 6th largest economy in 2016.[26] Also, for the vast majority of its citizens, Trump lost to Hillary in Cali-fornia by 4.3 million votes.[27]

Resist, insist, persist, enlist

— HILLARY RODHAM CLINTON

Now the time has come to bring about real change; all we need is a critical mass of people who care enough to create a COUNTER-REVOLUTION. Surely those people who cause so much pain in the world by preaching about division, war, and hate; WE the real people can bring about through love and understanding. We can't be silent anymore; we need to drive the change, we need to speak out and stand shoulder-to-shoulder and add our voices to fight for justice FOR ALL. If we are to create the Politics for Our Age, we need to start with a new political movement for the 21st century. *People just like you and me.*

> **If you want to go quickly, go alone. If you want to go far, go together**

— PROVERB

Play Your Part in Creating Change for Australia

6

GENDER EQUALITY

- THE ANSWER TO OUR EVOLUTION

> We've begun to raise daughters more like sons... but few have the courage to raise our sons more like our daughters.

— GLORIA STEINMAN

> The beauty of standing up for your rights is others see you standing and stand up as well.

— CASSANDRA DUFFY

The Search for True Equality

THE SEARCH **for true equality** is pivotal at this time in our history, as we still haven't actualised equality for all; especially with a growing divide between those that have and those that have nothing. Therefore, working towards Gender Equality is an absolute necessity and is more than equal representation. It is strongly tied to women's rights and often requires policy changes to achieve the goal of gender equality.[16] According to UNICEF [17] it means,

> *That women and men, and girls and boys, enjoy the same rights, resources, opportunities and protections. It does not require that girls and boys, or women and men, be the same, or that they be treated exactly alike*

On a global scale, achieving gender equality also requires that we work to empower women and work against harmful practices such:

- Female mutilation and sex trafficking.
- Femicide (the intentional killing of females whether women or girls because they are females).
- Dry sex (the act of drying a vagina with herbs, a cultural practice perceived by men as increasing their sexual pleasure).
- Sexual violence.

Women are far less likely to be politically active than men and are far more likely to be poor, uneducated and victims of domestic violence. They have less access to property ownership, training opportunities, accessing credit and gainful employment – many of the things that determine how we socially advance and progress as people and nations.

In many respects, we live in an unjust world, and the forces of change are now opposing it.

Gender Equality is about Balance

" When we live in a world that is very unjust, you have to
be a dissident

— NAWAL EL SAADAWI, EGYPTIAN FEMINIST,
WRITER, AND PSYCHIATRIST

Lastly, the reduction in the number of deaths associated with HIV since
2010; has been more significant among adult women compared with
adult men. Men are more likely to delay starting treatment, less adher-
ent, blunt the preventive effects of treatment, and lead to men
accounting for 58% of adult AIDS-related deaths (UNAIDS, 2016).[18]
Whether HIV or another disease **men often have poorer health
outcomes** in most western societies due to them less likely to seek out
healthcare. Therefore, men's health is being addressed with more attention and focussed support.

Striving for Equality is our Evolutionary Intention

Striving for equality is the evolutionary intention that Humanity needs to establish balance and harmony in the world.

The Evolutionary Intention

However, to achieve this, we must first Awaken to our connection with the Cosmos. The Global Shift that occurred in the early 1970s (and energy preceding it) was a significant time for Humanity. Understanding the energy resonance and the counter-revolution (anti-establishment phenomenon) of the 1960's is an important concept. This time was attempting to reconcile and evolve the prevalent belief of devotion to service of others. Given that war was an expression of this energy, the energy shift at that time was trying to connect Humanity to our Mother Earth nature and that of healing.

Ultimately this process was attempting to awaken Humanity to our connection with something much higher; our understanding of the Cosmos, e.g., the significance of the lunar landing for Humanity and realising the damaging effects of war. Many returned veterans suffered major trauma and stress that impacted on their lives for the long haul. They received little public reaction and support when they returned home and access to the long-term health care they needed (such as post-traumatic stress and other conditions). In many respects, this reaction resulted in a distortion within the embodiment of our human spirit, i.e., limited awareness and a lack of empathy and understanding from the public. One can only imagine the profound imbalance and disconnection people experienced caused by patriarchal rule.

The over-arching effect of our Masculinised culture has been counterbalanced throughout time by women effectively, becoming detached in response (often by no choice of their own). In effect, women become drained and trapped by their thinking, appearing to analyse and criticise men. The more over

> On average 1 woman a week is killed by a partner or former partner in Australia.
>
> Lisa McAdams

masculinised our culture, then the more extreme the response, such as domestic violence and abuse; whether played out by men or women. In Australia and the USA, the effects of this are possibly our nations' most significant threats. It has helped create some of the highest rates of domestic violence, objectification of women, underlying racism; and alcohol and drug misuse in the western world. In its purity, this is a very straightforward concept to understand without judgment towards men or women.

Suicide is the number one cause of death for men aged 15-44 in Australia, and same-sex attracted Australians have up to 14 times higher rates of attempted suicide than their heterosexual peers.[19] Both Australia and the USA have a poor track record in politics, Australian's (both men and women for that matter) publicly vilified our first female Prime Minister Ms Julia Gillard, and the USA, did the same thing very much to Hilary Clinton who ran for President last year. Although defeated she won the popular vote, go figure!!!

These statistics are not "fake news", and the wounds run deep in our psyche. History always has a way of rewriting events and one day I can only hope we reflect and look back with utter disgust. We have even demoralised our Indigenous community to the brink of despair resulting in suicide rates for Aboriginal and Torres Strait Islander men, doubling that of Non-Indigenous men. I am hopeful that things will change because if it doesn't, it ultimately limits our ability to evolve and mature as a country and rightfully so, become the nation we are meant to become.

We can change this, especially if we start to raise our sons more like daughters and evolve into a Nation with a humble but grand vision for the future. I see this changing with a new form of grassroots political activism that celebrates: -

- Its love of diversity, fairness, and equality;
- Protecting our ecosystems and environment;
- Our amazing humanitarian spirit;
- Our new scientific and technological endeavours;
- Our ability to be innovative, progressive and ahead of its time;
- An efficient and non-discriminatory social safety net, free education and universal healthcare;

- The egalitarian spirit and way of life and being fair and outward looking;
- And reveres all our Elders and has our Indigenous people at the heart of our constitution.

Norwegian Navy.

To change this, it's easy, but there is much work ahead of us, and we need the foresight and commitment of people to stand up to adversity. If we look to the Scandinavian societies, they embody true gender equality in the world. History will show that women in the Viking era (circa 800 to 1100 AD) were very much respected as equals, and although the Vikings were brutal, they encountered and influenced many cultures from Afghanistan to Canada. Their ability to be innovative, their curiosity to discover new worlds and travel the high seas, gave them advantage. It wasn't just about rape and pillage (who wasn't brutal at that time) but also a race of people who sought to be heard, to settle, to farm new lands and experiment. Over time they integrated themselves into new cultures and religions. The fusion between pagans and christians.

Women actively participated in all forms of public life whether as leaders, warriors, medicine/healers, teachers, sacred goddesses and in traditional roles, highly regarded as mothers. Little do most people know, the Viking conquests (which also included women) across Europe and elsewhere wouldn't have been possible without the robust industry of cloth weaving, to weave sails for the Viking ships. The textile industry was a female-led industry and women even as housewives, were seen as business managers, especially in all aspects of the trade.

The Global Gender Gap Report

The Global Gender Gap Report is the evidence base for demonstrating the extremes in Gender Inequality in the world. Gender Inequality is one issue that we can change within a relatively brief period. Being more mindful of Gender Inequality is an important starting point and actively challenging others who perpetrate it no matter what their sex, speaks to our universal compassion and understanding. **<u>Gender equality is the goal</u>**, but it is our practice of being mindful around promoting neutral and equitable ways of thinking that help in achieving the goal. The Global Gender Gap Report[20] measures gender parity or similarity between countries regarding gender gaps in Equality – based on a wide range of indicators such economic participation (income and wage equality); equality in politics, educational attainment; and attainment of health and survival.

However, the human experience is what most counts. As a man who is a pro-feminist, I feel qualified enough to speak about this:

- Being a victim of childhood domestic violence;
- Someone with deep spiritual insight and is proud of their Norwegian heritage (which celebrates gender equality).
- Observations from experiencing cultures across the world, whether my time when working, travelling and living in Africa and the Middle East and elsewhere.

My experience of doing humanitarian work from ages 38 to 42, was a time full of adventure and escapism but it also consolidated many things in my life i.e., being fulfilled with a new sense of liberation and purpose. The events and things I witnessed in life have been challenging on all levels yet so powerful and life-changing. I also knew I was changing as a person, in ways so subtle, regarding my beliefs, cultural perceptions, thinking, optimism and how I saw the world.

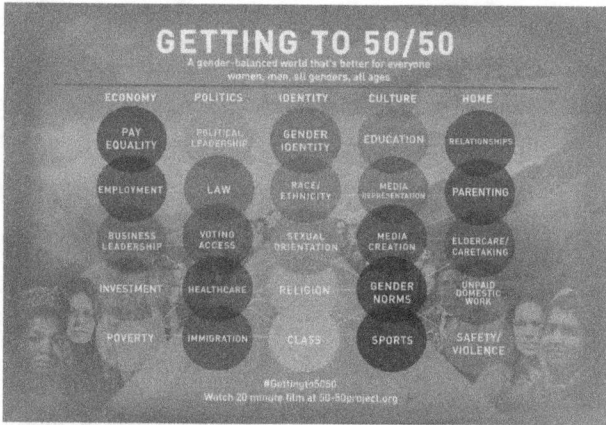

Courtesy of Getting to 50 /50 Let's Create a Fair World for
Women and Girls

One of the most significant lessons this experience taught me, was the
stark reality that life is vastly different for women depending on where
you live. It became bleating evident to me, that those countries which
are the most progressive and wealthy, such as the Scandinavian and
Northern European countries are near parity regarding gender equality.
Whereas those countries who experience some of the most extreme
poverty, tribal conflict and inequality in the world such as many
African and Middle Eastern countries, women are disempowered. I am
quite convinced that there is a correlation between how progressive,
happy and evolved your society is with changes in gender equality.

What does the 2016 Global Report reveal?

What does the 2016 Global Report reveal? If we examine the top 10
countries compared to the bottom 10 countries; the top ten are (in #
order) #1 Iceland; #2 Finland; #3 Norway; #4 Sweden; #5 Rwanda; #6
Ireland; #7 Philippines; #9 New Zealand and #10 Nicaragua. These
countries are far more progressive regarding their political empowerment; attaining educational equality; health and survival between men
and women and greater economic participation than Australia and the
USA (which sit depressingly low in ranking at 46 and 45 respectively).

Also, Switzerland, Germany, South Africa, The Netherlands, France, Latvia, Denmark and the United Kingdom are all in the top #20. The Scandinavian countries and The Netherlands are also happier than Australia and the USA on the World Happiness Report.[21]

The bottom ten countries are #136 Cote d'Ivoire; #137 Morocco; #138; Mali; #139 Iran; #140 Chad; #141 Saudi Arabia; #142 Syria; #143 Pakistan and #144 Yemen. Most of the countries that sit in the bottom 20 countries are mostly from the Middle East and northern Africa.

My theory is that deductions can be made from this data. The higher up you sit in the Global Report, generally the more liberal and progressive the country. It achieves higher rates of gender parity (similarity); educational attainment; higher wealth if nations close their gender gaps; decreased rates of domestic violence, drug and alcohol misuse, and are more environmentally friendly. It's a basic no-brainer, things really need to change in Australia and the USA for that matter because of our poor global ratings in terms of gender equality i.e., compared to other Western societies.

How does this ranking present itself, I call it for what it is, "the Ugly side of Australia".

In comparison to other western countries,

- Australia is ranked 10th in the world as one of the most drunkest counties (Vouchercloud compilation of World Health Organisation data 2010-2015);
- Australia has some of the highest rates of domestic violence and related death of women;
- Australia and the USA have ingrained racism at the core of our societies;
- Australians are the world's biggest users of ecstasy, especially among youth (United Nation's 2014 World Drug Report);
- Australia has the highest use of methamphetamine in the English-speaking world or indeed almost any other country (TIME, 2017);

- Male suicide is the number one cause of death in people aged 15-44 (three out of every four suicides in Australia in 2015 were men, and this rate rose to 4 times that of women in the USA).[19]
- There is also clear inequality between same-sex and heterosexual peers in our rates of suicide, acceptance of relationships and drug and alcohol use;
- Australia's "king hit" culture is apathetic.[22]

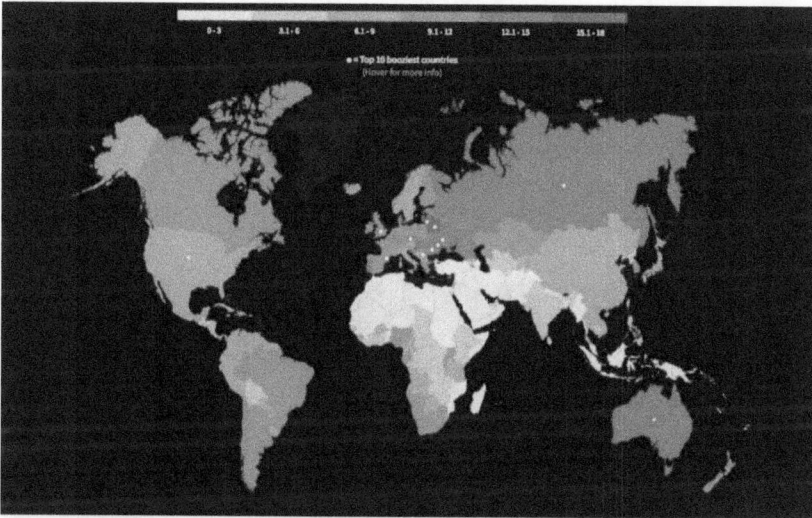

These are the world's drunkest countries - Australia is ranked 10th in the world.

These statistics are not surprising, especially when Australia rates so poorly in regards to Gender Equality. However, the devastating effects of these statistics are frightful and need to be corrected and corrected urgently; otherwise, our Great Southern land will slip into the depths of despair as a nation that has no heart. Conservative politics and politicians have strangled our country for far too long, with little appetite for change or the willingness to experiment or do anything radical. Data from the Australian Census in 2016 has revealed that the average Australian politician is a white middle-class man, aged 51 with a wife and two children and two or more investment properties.[23]

Our apathy as a nation seems to be counter-intuitive to any desire for change or reform to fix things; therefore, we only have ourselves to blame. As civil-rights activist Dorothy Cotton said,

> *We are ordinary people, living our lives, and trying...to 'fix what ain't right' in our society.*

Hold Heart, the Forces of Change are Occurring

Hold heart, the forces of change are occurring right across our nation. We need to let it happen, as its a form of expression without resistance. The resistance to swinging to the right in our more progressive societies speaks of hope. The resurgence of Women's marches across Australia and the world, are taking on greater significance as a movement for change.

Two adorable girlfriends Fran Bowron and Steph Sands - both women are making an incredible difference in this World.

The resurgence of Women's marches across Australia and the world, are taking on greater significance as a movement for change. Australia is finally attempting to address its high rates of ingrained domestic violence through resourcing community-based organisations and health service projects (we are saying enough is enough). The tireless work of Australian Marriage Equality and other movements to create change for Marriage Equality have finally achieved their goals.[24] The revolutionary Man Up movement is also one bloke's mission to save Aussie men and the creation of Man Sheds that have sprung up across the country.[19,25]

The success of the Hillsong[26] movement as a revolution for change has been a positive thing for Australia and the world because as a movement they embody some of the most anecdotal evidence for achieving gender equality. The success of Hillsong is often ascribed to its ability to bring women on the journey of spiritual development and enlightenment. Maybe this feeds into the reality of our age and what Australia is meant to become a Republic; a nation that truly speaks to equality between men and women at its heart. We need to give credit where it is due, for all these movements for change are genuinely tapping into something that is innate and deep in our spiritual psyche as a nation. Let's Wake up Australia! Far more needs to be done, we need to ensure that:

- Funding to address domestic violence and access to crisis accommodation for women is improved;
- Legal protection for women is drastically improved to give hope for women who have left their partners because of domestic violence;
- The high rates of suicide among men are addressed and support further funding for men's health;
- Our media portrays positive images around the cultural and sexual diversity of our nation and our television stops serving mind numbing reality shows that are dumbing us down. Look

to Australian film as the answer. Why is it more innovative and unique?

- There is a quota for women in politics given the lack of diversity in Australian politics - it's obvious that men in suits haven't done a better job, given the apathy for our current political system.

Stopping the cycles of Inequality will require a radical change in our thinking and in our political representation. Without this change we will be stuck in the quagmire, of violence, aggression, and guilt; and therefore, we become the perpetrators of such cycles. Is this the legacy we want to leave to our next generation? On the other hand, we can achieve harmonious relationships, if we commit to the principles of truth, justice, and tolerance. The spiritual warriors are those people who aren't afraid to look within, change the way they think, open and heal their hearts and become the wounded healer for others. This kind of healing transformation is what our planet needs right now.

We need to build a critical mass of people who demand change and work towards the creation of a new **Political Movement for the 21st Century** and partner as equals to bring a silent revolution for change. I can sense it; I hope you can?

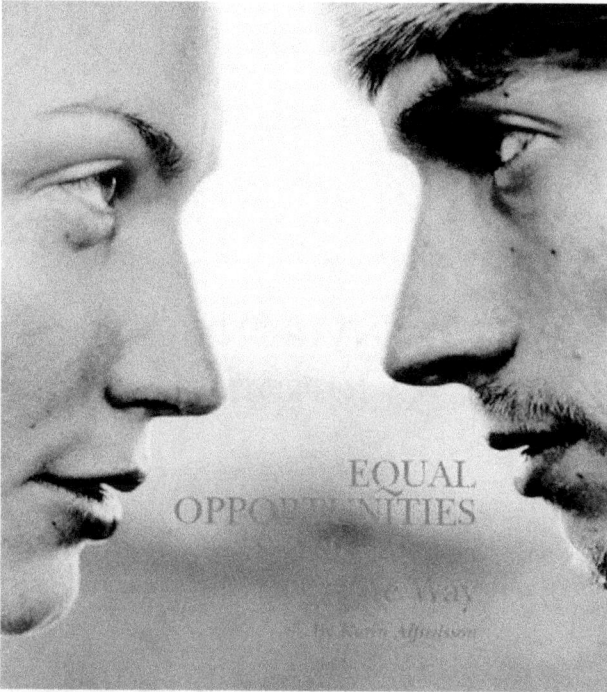

EQUAL
OPPORTUNITIES
the Way
by Kevin Allanson

7

THE ENVIRONMENT

- THE URGENCY TO PROTECT OUR PLANET

" *Look deep into nature, and then you will understand everything better*

— ALBERT EINSTEIN

" *Why do we need to fight our government to protect the environment? The urgency to protect our planet over-rides any value of government and corporations. Our most vital legacy is to ensure that our children inherit a world they can live in.*

— DAVID SHAUN LARSEN

Every Living Thing is Vulnerable

NEARLY ALL SPECIES **that ever lived are extinct**; it's a reminder that every living thing is vulnerable to the fragility of our planet. We might think that we sit at the top of the pecking order but in the Universal scheme of things we are just a blip on the radar. The stark reality is that our time on this planet is precious and how we live and who controls how we live, dictates how we evolve. Therefore, it makes sense if Humanity is to evolve further as a species, any limitation to this; is only bound by the cause and effect of our actions, decisions and that of our collective wisdom today.

Kimberley Ranges, Western Australia.

The virtual control of Government and Corporations is something that I believe demands greater account-ability and transparency. They are failing to meet our civil and enduring right to live on this planet. Our society needs to take more civil action around the things that matter, such as under-standing the bigger picture to protect the environment. We need to dream big; for our moral protests are barely being heard.

Imagine if there is a global catastrophe or an unimaginable climatic event; the emergency related to this crisis will give us no other choice but to act. In such a scenario, we would need to rise as one and go out into the world, like shooting stars to ensure the survival of Humanity and whatever remaining life we manage to save. We may scoff at such an idea but how do we know it's not impossible? If it eventuates, it is likely to be sudden and happen without notice; in a heartbeat. At that moment, we may wonder why didn't we seize the power of now. The future of our planet is far too important to be left just to our Leaders, Government and Corporations.

Climate Change

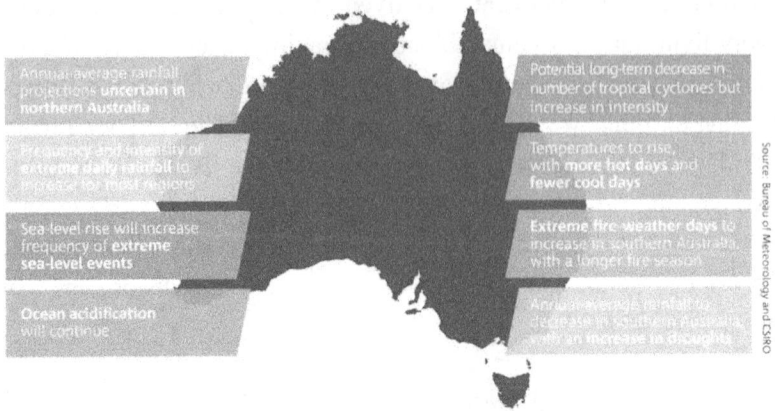

Annual average rainfall
projections **uncertain in
northern Australia**

**Frequency and intensity of
extreme daily rainfall** to
increase for most regions

Sea-level rise will increase
frequency of **extreme
sea-level events**

Ocean acidification
will continue

Potential long-term decrease in
number of tropical cyclones but
increase in intensity

Temperatures to rise,
with **more hot days** and
fewer cool days

Extreme fire-weather days to
increase in southern Australia,
with a longer fire season

Annual average rainfall to
decrease in southern Australia,
with an increase in droughts

Source: Bureau of Meteorology and CSIRO

Climate Change is real, and the current state of play is that our planet
is teetering on the edge. It is a delicate, self-regulating ecosystem that
is gradually becoming destroyed. Climate change is not "fake news",
and our handling of the environment will be OUR most important
legacy our children will inherit. Humanity has made a profound impact
on this delicate ecosystem and our ability to sustain life and our civilisation into the future, as we know it, is untenable i.e., our selfish greed
and willingness to conspire to a world of inequity is deplorable. Our
footprint is what matters the most, and the most significant travesty
facing our planet is our population growth. The select few, who accumulate most of the world's wealth and power, have this needless desire
to exhibit their reckless extravagance and greed. They are mostly
Young Souls who have no conscious nature or willingness to evolve.
However, there are some Old Souls among them who through their
philanthropy are changing the lives of others, making a difference in
the world and guiding the way.

The issue of climate change has become a paralysing issue for Humanity. The majority of Young Souls want us to believe it doesn't exist and
will do anything to dispel scientific evidence, keep us in denial and
create an environment, to excuse the pun of utter despair. Therefore,

most people have become complacent forcing a silent kind of impotence around our ability to act. For those who are starting to wrestle with the big questions and looking for a deeper meaning to life know in their hearts the answers but inadvertently prefer to bury their heads in the sand. They often revert to what they know best i.e., comfort, security and denial. Only those Awakening or have Awakened will be able to rise to the challenge of protecting our Environment and become the true spiritual warriors fighting for the survival of our planet. If our world's destroyed, we won't be able to rewrite history for there won't be any history to rewrite.

An old water tank at a friend's (Cliff and Andrew) property in Walligan, Hervey Bay.

The Power of Now and Protecting the Environment

The power of now and protecting the environment is imperative! If we are to become dancers and choreograph our next amazing journey through the tiniest eye of the Universe, it can only start and end with the power of now and protecting the environment. It's such a remote possibility, but if we embrace the opportunity to evolve and divert all our energy from war into creating technology to enhance and to protect our environment; we may well become honoured as we obtain a seat at the Universal Council of the most evolved civilisations. Films like Star Wars and Star Trek may well be science fiction, but I'd rather think they speak to something far more significant, the potentiality of Humanity, new frontiers, civilisations and worlds we have never encountered before.

Can we deliver such a dream or is it possibly out of our reach? It's not impossible, but it must start today and without question, provide a sustainable world of opportunity for our children. Our Indigenous people knew it; their Dreamtime enabled them to look deep into nature and respect the privilege it afforded for their existence and survival. They lived deep in harmony with nature. Our nations are made up of a smorgasbord of cultures, economies, societies, and people. On the whole, our world isn't very forward thinking, and in many ways, we think with very tunnelled vision; rarely learning from past mistakes and live in a reactionary world often with our issues siloed from one another.

In essence, the superiority of our economic thinking and lack of insightfulness drives our complacency and inability to connect the dots and respond to the issues that matter, such as addressing: -

- Social Justice and Inequality;
- Cultural Divides;
- Humanitarianism and,
- Environmentalism.

We desperately measure the world by values, benefits, and costs; GDP being the centrepiece of our economies and we place barriers around border control and migration with such condemnation. How do we even tolerate ourselves as a Humanity, especially around our negligence towards lessening the suffering of others? Often by no choice of their own; are born or driven into poverty, marginalised by society and are made vulnerable; including our Indigenous people.

Wattle flowers, Kimberley
Ranges, Western Australia.

Humankind urgently needs to wake up and develop systems of thinking, operating and viewing the world from an "interconnectedness" between all things. We need to become wiser, creating global systems and visionary ways of doing and seeing things for the greater good of Humanity. It's a no-brainer, and I feel the only way to achieve this is for some global event or situation to raise our consciousness out of the mire that we are faced. The powers to be aren't going to take responsibility and act. Power equals knowledge, and we have "THE POWER and KNOWLEDGE" to change things; for protecting our planet, and the environment underpins everything. Our economies are just "embedded" within our societies, which are "embedded" within our nations and that of the planet. All these systems are interconnected, much like our environment is connected to the sacred essence of life and our spirituality. Therefore, our environment is also conducive to the development and enrichment of our spirituality. Everything by nature is spiritual.

If we are to emerge into the 21st century as the true spiritual warriors of our planet; Tom Hatfield, a British author, states that thinkers such as Raworth, believe measuring environmental performance, will play a much more extensive part compared to the mere financial success of our societies.[27]

> Our carbon, land, nitrogen and water footprints will be part of our own ways of monitoring our personal and national lifestyles, alongside our health and sense of wellbeing
>
> — KATE RAWORTH, ECONOMIST AT OXFORD UNIVERSITY'S ENVIRONMENTAL CHANGE INSTITUTE

Whether from the impact of mining, pollution to climate change, it's no surprise that our societies still place so much value on economic cost benefits versus the intrinsic value of our environmental wealth. We can't pretend anymore that the environment doesn't count, especially if we don't care to count it.

Humanity and 2023/2024 is possibly the next global shift and essentially the crux time for nations, Corporations, and Government. It will be both the end of an era and the beginning of new era. A counter-revolution will emerge in the years preceding this time, as an antidote to the apathy, narcissism, and greed of our current world. A new global emphasis of empathy and compassion will emerge out of the possible chaos and revolution that will unfold. If we are to restore a new world arrangement like no other time in our human history, then there is no time like the present to act. Our current actions if they go unheeded offers a foreboding warning of the world to come.

The Community Conversation

The community conversation in Australia is that we do care about the environment, although we are not always well informed about the detail - people access information, through various media and other news sources. Whenever we hear about environmental issues and proposed solutions for the way forward, many of us seem helpless to know how to act or create the change that is needed. The bleating obvious is that we resonate with it because we truly care about our environment.

Most of us want to leave it up to someone else i.e., other people whom we think are better placed to fix it or have the political power to advocate or work the system. Let's face it; it's easier to have "our heads in the sand" or "sweep it under the carpet". It's the easiest default option. Why would you bother walking the path least travelled, it's a hard slog and bloody hard work? It's easier for us to doubt, think we are not capable or just can't be bothered! This is a lazy response! If you take the time to go within to seek the answers, then in your heart you'll genuinely know or realise that there's an environmental emergency going on. An emergency not dissimilar to our planet having major convulsions and god forbid a massive heart attack. If we don't fix it or defibrillate it right now, we are truly destined to go down the path of no return. This environmental emergency is simply about the death of our planet and life as we know it. Let's not gloss over it anymore; for you have the power to change this right now, nothing more nothing less.

A Naked Beach, Kimberley's Western Australia.

I love to reminisce. In the early days of the HIV/AIDS epidemic in the 1980s; the so-called AIDS victims and community were forced into an impasse. Solutions required drastic force. Hence the formation of Act Up.28 ActUp is an international direct-action advocacy group working to bring about the end of the loss of lives for people living with HIV through legislative change, medical research and treatment and policies. As painful as this may seem our innate destiny and universal rights to dignity, freedom, and justice include our right to live against the forces of evil at whatever time in our human history.

Study history and you will find that there have been many people who have inherently gone against the grain and fought for our human rights. They have all worked to advance the true qualities of our society as we know of it today. Ronald Reagan wasn't perfect as a President and presided over one of the most disastrous administrations in US history. Government inaction led to a battle line drawn between the people versus the government. This inaction was a time where people had to fight for their civil liberties. They also had to challenge some of the most hatred fear and discrimination our planet has possibly ever seen through the global impact of HIV/AIDS – read more about this in **Chapter 9:** ***HIV and it's Global Impact*** - *A Global Disease to Challenge Humanities' Fear.*

I have enormous respect for all those people & souls who have fought for injustice in the world and have the utmost respect for their human dignity, at a time of extreme adversity.

The Solution

The solution involves understanding that everything is interconnected, even the conversation about HIV/AIDS and our environment. In some ways, Environmental activism is no different to that of HIV activism. Although both are global issues, there is not the same urgency yet to protect

Australian Wattle, Kimberley Ranges Western Australia.

our planet. We either can't see its impact, choose not to or refute the evidence. The protection of our environment deserves a much better, critical response and what we are witnessing is just the tip of the iceberg. If we are going to be complacent, then we deserve nothing but the consequences for our collective actions e.g., if we are to create any significant change, then we need to address our environmental issues right now. It's the most significant issue for our planets' survival, and the only way we can do this is to form a grassroots activist movement to effect change right up to the top, not only for Governments but also Corporations.

Governments essentially are ruled by Corporations and their various sponsors, such as the media and lobbyists. We may choose to gloss over the facts but just look to the most potent example of this in the world i.e., the United States of America (some may say the Divided States of America) and Donald Trump. Trump is just a corporate CEO who is now the President of the most influential country on earth. I'm not sure if this is liberating or brings terror to your soul? Only you can decide. Maybe ask your children or those you can confide in, who will always provide you with the most authentic or truthful answer to your questions.

How Do We Effect Change?

How do we effect change? People power is the only way to affect change, and we need everyone. Join an activist organisation such as Australian Conservation Foundation or GetUp29, speak out and protest against your elected members of parliament, these are all ways of effecting change. Why GetUp? GetUp is a well-respected grassroots organisation which has a lot of older members and not affiliated with any political party.

> We need to think big for we have no other option than to do this at such an immense scale. We need to think huge billboards, demonstrations, radio ads, and thousands and thousands of phone calls
>
> — GETUP

Let's be at Peace with our Environment.

The most current pressing issue in Australia is the Adani coal mine - the world's biggest coal mine and environmental emergency since the Franklin Dam. If approval goes ahead, the new proposed coal mine and the terminal will ship its coal out through the Great Barrier Reef. The Reef is one of the seven natural wonders of the world and how can we be its custodians if we allow such an envelopment (an enclosing or bad development).

Citizen engagement and people power can have the ability to change this and campaigns such as #StopAdani Challenge[30] can bring that much-needed change. This movement is made up of a diverse group of people, from suburban grassroots activists to traditional owners, farmers and locals directly affected by the mine. The envelopment of Adani has evolved into a situation of blatant corruption, including a billion dollar government handout to flooding of sensitive wetlands with toxic, black coal sludge.[31] Australians have nothing to be proud of if they agree with such an envelopment. It represents nothing but a terrible stain on our great nation - another one of those classic stories of corruption, destruction and criminal history. The company's environmental record overseas is tarnished and with this incident, how can we trust that such an envelopment?

We continue to argue about the effects of Climate Change in a world where we are seeing rises in global temperatures, like no other time in human history. The Great Barrier Reef is experiencing mass coral bleaching, a phenomenon caused by global rises to sea surface temperatures. Scientists certainly don't want to think that our Great Barrier Reef could be in its 'terminal stage'. New aerial surveys have found that two-thirds of our Great Barrier Reef has been hit by severe coral bleaching for the second year in a row.[32] Guess what, we know how to fix it; we just need to stop pollution caused by agriculture, tourism and mining and burning fossil fuels, like coal. We now have a real chance to turn this story around not only for our survival but that of the environment and our planet. It's about the Urgency to Protect our Planet.

BREAKING NEWS

An election has been announced to be held sometime in our future. Hopefully an election for our next President. But like every election how you cast your vote makes a real difference. Citizen or people engagement at every level is critical. We are standing on the precipice for change, and how we remedy this is entirely up to us.

Which side of history do you want to stand on? If you are looking for direction? We only have two choices. Vote for responsible leaders who want to protect our Environment or Vote for those leaders who want to Destroy it.

Many of us feel disillusioned with Australia's two-party-preferred voting system. We must be vigilant like no other time before. Apathy is our worst enemy. Vote for a party that has a vision and wants to renew our economy from the declining industries of the past to one with a vision for our future.

> Citizen engagement at every level is central to a strong and vibrant democracy...we've seen what's possible when people come together to resist bullying, hate, falsehoods, and divisiveness, and stand up for a fairer, more inclusive America.
>
> — HILLARY CLINTON, ONWARD TOGETHER

If we look to the forest for inspiration, there is indeed something much more unknown and majestic than us.

8

AUSTRALIAN INDIGENOUS CULTURE
- THE OLDEST CONTINUOUS SPIRITUAL CULTURE ON EARTH

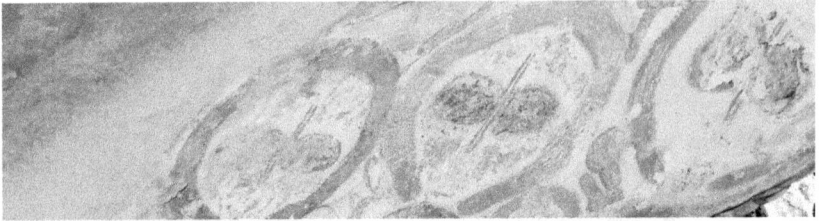

Proportionally, we are the most incarcerated people on the planet... Our children are alienated from their families at unprecedented rates... And our youth languish in detention in obscene numbers. They should be our hope for the future. These dimensions of our crisis tell plainly the structural nature of our problem... In 1967 we were counted, in 2017 we seek to be heard. We leave base camp and start our trek across this vast country. We invite you to walk with us in a movement of the Australian people for a better future.

— THE ULURU STATEMENT FROM THE HEART

I RESPECTIVELY ADVISE **Aboriginal and Torres Strait Islander people that this chapter may contain images of deceased indigenous people and ask that you read this with caution.**

The Failing of our Education System

The failing of our education system is exemplified by how little young people know about history. I attended school in Mount Isa, and I learned surprisingly little; if anything that I can remember about our Aboriginal and Torres Strait Islander people, culture or history. Mount Isa and the surrounding region was home to the **Kalkadoon** (properly **Kalkatungu**) who ruled what is called the emu foot province and were living on these lands for over 40 thousand years. Their forefather tribe have been called 'the elite of the Aboriginal warriors of Queensland'.[1]

> The Kalkadoon's acknowledged a leader, and they always knew precisely where he was located. Once or twice a year delegates from the wandering bands of Kalkadoon people would assemble at the leader's camp and be instructed on raids or attacks on neighbours and at times two or more of these wandering bands would join forces.
>
> — CHERN'EE SUTTON CONTEMPORARY
> ABORIGINAL ARTIST

They would rarely leave their country, they protected their land ferociously and were known to surrounding tribes as fearsome warriors.[2]

The Kalkadoon people were fiercely independent and would mark the boundaries of their territory with an emu or cranes foot that was either painted on to rocks or trees or carved on to the sold granite rock as a warning to other intruding clans. Interestingly, they would rotate their campsites for a few weeks at a time and live off the land until their resources became scarce and not return for 2 or 3 years, so the wildlife and vegetation could replenish and survive.[2]

This story inherently speaks to our Indigenous people's respect for the land and ability to live alongside nature, honouring the delicate equilibrium that existed with our ecosystem. Such incredible people! The older I get, I always have my eyes very wide open. I am eager to learn and have an intense thirst for understanding and knowing more about our Indigenous people, their culture, traditions and maybe even one day their languages. I have learned more since leaving school, yet I am still amazed at how little I don't know.

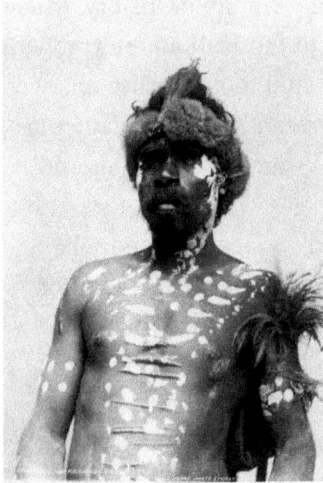

Image of a Warrior of the Kalkadoon People - Kerry Photo Sydney. Charles Henry 1857-1928

I'm in awe of the 250 or more nations that once crossed our continent (and still do to varying degrees today); the diversity of its people and languages; their storytelling; enormous respect for their Elders and aboriginal art, music, spirituality and even weaponry, mining, farming, and sport. On the darker side, I have also learned about our ingrained racism as a nation. This dark side includes their untold genocide; dispossession and incarceration as people; the endless lists of deaths in custody; extinction of the Tasmanian aboriginals; the stolen generation; their fight to be counted as people and our nation's struggle to Close the Gap on our Aboriginal and Torres Strait Islander people's health and life expectancy.

As I write this book and start talking about this chapter with people I meet; I'm still so surprised and amazed at people's ignorance. To be honest, I'm so sick and tired of Australia's ignorance and people who continue to perpetuate this myth of a "hand out mentality" that our Indigenous people supposedly have. Often their defence is not grounded in any reality and is always based on some experience from their childhood or hearing about abuse, violence or what has happened to a third party person, friend or relative. There is also this perception of favouritism, that they deserve something more than me and questioning, "Why do I always have to identify on official forms whether I am either Aboriginal and Torres Strait Islander or not?".

A photograph of my nephew Linkyn (aged 11) playing the digeridoo. He is very proud of his Indigenous culture and history.

It's so demoralising and mortifying to me; it's no wonder I am writing this chapter in the hope that it's not too late to progress the healing and reconciliation process. In all these situations, I just wish I could say, "I'm Indigenous" like my 11- year-old nephew Linkyn does, who proudly wears his Indigenous status on his sleeve. It melts away any form of racism when he smiles and says these words; it makes people think and challenges the stereotypical views. Most people still can't seem to apprehend that Aboriginal and Torres Strait Islander Australians can be of any colour whether black, brown, white or any shade of grey.

I hope one day, someone like our great film director Bruce Beresford (who recently remade the famous "Roots" miniseries of the 1970s) or an up and coming Indigenous film director, can tell our own story not too dissimilar to "Roots" i.e., tell the story of our the intergenerational trauma our Indigenous people experienced from settlement right up until the Referendum of 1967 or even better to when we become a Republic. It's all about the symbolism, nothing more, nothing less; once people realise it, we can all move on together!

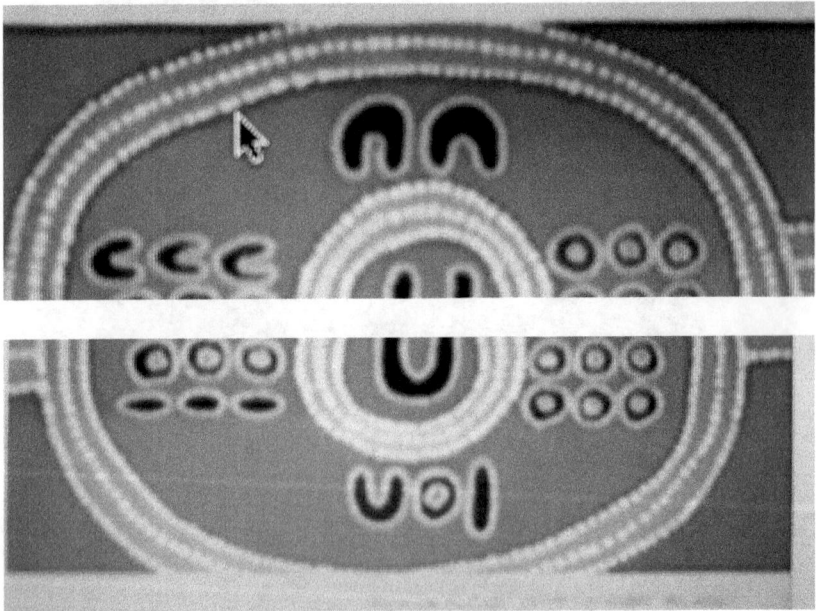

Two halves of an Indigenous Art painting deliberately shown as broken; to represent how far we have not come regarding Constitutional Reform in Australia.

The Uluru Statement

Hundreds of Aboriginal community leaders met at Uluru in late May 2017 to find common ground on a way forward. This capped off a dozen regional meetings around the country.

Our Aboriginal and Torres Strait Islander tribes were the first sovereign Nations of the great Australian continent and its adjacent islands, and possessed it under our own laws and customs. This our ancestors did, according to the reckoning of our culture, from the Creation, according to the common law from 'time immemorial', and according to science more than 60,000 years ago.

This sovereignty is *a spiritual notion: the ancestral tie between the land, or 'mother nature', and the Aboriginal and Torres Strait Islander peoples who were born therefrom, remain attached thereto, and must one day return thither to be united with our ancestors. This link is the basis of the ownership of the soil, or better, of sovereignty.* It has never been ceded or extinguished, and co-exists with the sovereignty of the Crown.

How could it be otherwise? That peoples possessed a land for sixty millennia and this sacred link disappears from world history in merely the last two hundred years?

With substantive constitutional change and structural reform, we believe this ancient sovereignty can shine through as a fuller expression of Australia's nationhood.

Proportionally, we are the most incarcerated people on the planet. We are not an innately criminal people. Our children are alienated from their families at unprecedented rates. This cannot be because we have no love for

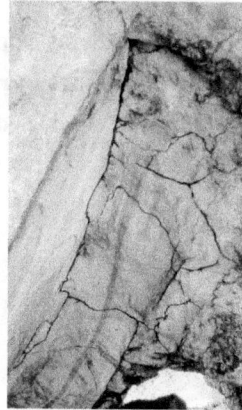

Indigenous rock art The Kimberley, Western Australia

them. And our youth languish in detention in obscene numbers. They should be our hope for the future.

These dimensions of our crisis tell plainly the structural nature of our problem. This is *the torment of our powerlessness.*

We seek constitutional reforms to empower our people and take *a rightful place* in our own country. When we have power over our destiny our children will flourish. They will walk in two worlds and their culture will be a gift to their country.

We call for the establishment of a **First Nations Voice enshrined in the Constitution.**

Makarrata is the culmination of our agenda: *the coming together after a struggle.* It captures our aspirations for a fair and truthful relationship with the people of Australia and a better future for our children based on justice and self-determination.

We seek a Makarrata Commission to supervise a process of agreement-making between governments and First Nations and truth-telling about our history.

In 1967 we were counted, in 2017 we seek to be heard. **We leave base camp and start our trek across this vast country. We invite you to walk with us in a movement of the Australian people for a better future.**

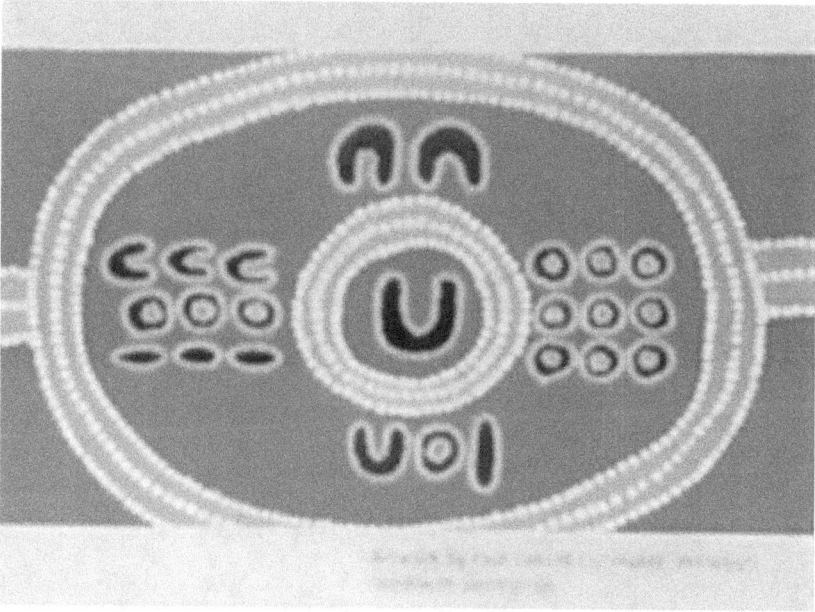

The same Indigenous Art painting brought together to represent the Unity of Constitutional Reform in Australia.

Welcome to Our Past

Welcome to our past, let's suspend disbelief but imagine that you (including the cultural heritage that you may identify with) belong to the oldest, continuous spiritual culture on earth. Imagine that one day, your land was invaded and you were brutally forced to change the way you live, and behave and become disconnected from the spiritual essence and heart of who you were as a person. Welcome to the past...

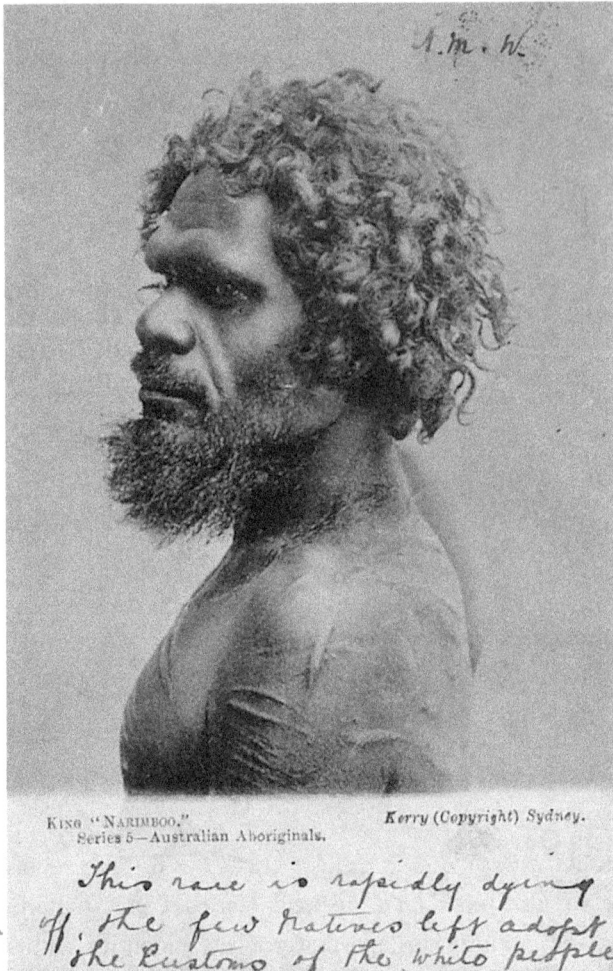

King "Narimboo" Aboriginal Man, Fine Art America.

"This race is rapidly dying off; the few natives left to adopt the customs of the white people" - *an example of the sheer racism that existed.*

As a result of this you were literally forced into a state of despair and victimisation, which included: -

- **Death from new diseases;**

- **Forcibly displaced off your traditional land** (your home and that of generations before you);
- **Suffered genocide** (some estimates of over 500,000 people or even more, we may never know); **65,180 is the number of Aboriginal Australians, historians estimate were killed in Queensland alone from the 1820s until the early 1900s** [3]. You work out the maths…
- **Treated as a basic barbarian** (the lowest of low life);
- **Deliberately not allowed by law to education** and
- **Not even worthy of being counted as a person**, in what we so-called, a civilised nation.

Lastly, to top it off, in today's Australia, you then embody the most extreme statistics of drug and alcohol misuse, male suicide, domestic violence, HIV infection and living with chronic diseases. But sorry to finally put a nail in the coffin; you also become the most incarcerated people on our earth and die much earlier than most people around you.

Intergenerational trauma is something inescapable that all Australians need to finally understand and the effects that it has had on our Indigenous people. We must also stop questioning why Indigenous Australians can't just "get over it" and "move on". The impact of colonisation (our invasion) and the horrifying abuse and dreadful atrocities that were committed in the past, continue to this day to contribute to some of the most significant health and social inequalities than in any other western nation. For example, poor health outcomes compared to non-Aboriginal Australians, including an average life expectancy for males that is 21 years less and for females almost 20 years less than the total population.[4]

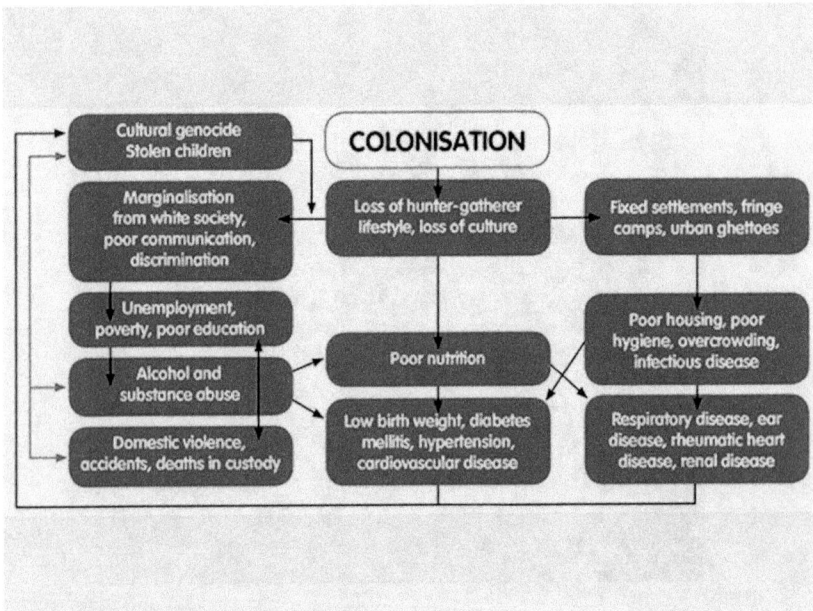

The effects of Intergenerational trauma - a visual guide that explains why we need to man up as a nation.

> " The trauma and suffering that Indigenous people have experienced over generations have contributed to the burden of disease, substance misuse, and incarceration

— AUSTRALIANSTOGETHER.ORG.AU

Pause for a moment, because this is disturbing and even writing about it creates such a pain in my heart; for I am not proud to be an Australian, not in a country that controls our civil liberties and dictates our rights. What is even more troubling is how we allow our politicians that we elect to create, legislate and tell our story. That's the greatest irony, and we are only perpetuating it.

If this doesn't create a shiver, trauma, and pain, at the deepest level and heart of your psyche, how can we honestly truly be responsible as Australians for our destiny? We need to finally name it for what it is, speak with truth and compassion and search deep in our souls. This is not about an apology, empowerment, rights or reconciliation but it's about something that is far greater and much more powerful. It's speaking to the soul of our nation which is crying for hope and restoration. This is our moment for transformation so that we can become attuned to the spirituality of our great land. It's the land of our Indigenous people, it always has and always will.

Through the Uluru statement, our Indigenous people sought to become heard. They have the compassion to embrace us, for they see the future and know we can become one and walk together on our journey. Hence why it is a *Statement from The Heart*. They know the soul and spirit of our great nation is broken, and we need to finally man and woman up; because if you genuinely want to make a difference in this world, it starts right here, right now and in this nation.

We can no longer gloss over the past, for this past is one of the greatest travesties in our human history. The only decent, mature and right thing we can do is pay our respects to all our Elders past and present and raise our Indigenous people out of this dark history of abuse, hate, bigotry, and discrimination and allow them the dignity to reclaim their heart. As Sir Henry Parkes (our Father of Federation) said about the great nation he imagined, and we created in a former time, for a former people,

> Surely what the Americans did by war, Australians can bring about in peace
>
> — SIR HENRY PARKES, FATHER OF FEDERATION,
> TENTERFIELD ORATION, 1889

The Australian constitution was created for a nation that was built for a former time. My triple great, grandfather Sir Henry Parkes had a vision for Australia as a union of a disparate group of colonies, without respect for our Indigenous culture. What we need to do today is to tell the new story of what our great nation could become. What would that story be? Well, the story I want to tell is of the Republic of Australia, which embraces our Indigenous people at the heart of our new constitution. It is a story that tells the truth about settlement and the powerlessness of the struggle of our Indigenous people; yet tells a story of our spirituality, the love for our children and hope for the future.

Indigenous Rock Art The Kimberley, Western Australia (W.A.) - is a sparsely settled northern region of W.A. It's known for large areas of wilderness; defined by rugged mountains, dramatic gorges, semi-savanna and isolated coastline.

Therefore, surely what we can now do as a nation is bring about constitutional change, nothing more, nothing less. We can only do this if we start telling a new story, and not just imagine it but make it happen. We need to stop contributing to the myths that we cannot create change, for if you speak up and demand change, you can create the new story for our nation and that of our Indigenous people.

There is no greater agony than bearing the untold story of what our great nation could've become. It's time that the former great Indigenous nations of Australia are recognised and embodied at the heart of our new constitution. We need to walk with our Indigenous people in a new movement. This movement is the emergence of a new 21st century nation, the great Republic of Australia.

Let's Start Dispelling the Myths

Let's start dispelling the myths as there are many things about Indigenous history that you probably didn't learn about in school. Indigenous rights campaigner Julian Cleary outlines some of these below. Cleary says they are some of the most interesting, humbling, and inspiring facts that have been whitewashed from our history lessons.[5]

Martumili Ngurra canvass National Museum of Australia - A bearded Aboriginal man, walking among long grass with a smoking stick.

- **You learnt about the First Fleet. You didn't learn about Indigenous settlements.** Early explorers described Indigenous, irrigation systems, agriculture and grain harvest right across Australia. 30,000-year-old grindstones have been found near Walgett, NSW, and ancient stone fish traps at Brewarrina, NSW; may be the oldest human-made structures on earth. And today at Budj Bim, Victoria, you can visit the remains of stone houses and an aquaculture system that pre-date Egypt's pyramids by at least 4,000 years.

- **You learnt about Matthew Flinders. You didn't learn about Aboriginal international trade connections.** Well before British invasion, Yolngu and other Aboriginal groups exchanged goods, ideas and culture with Macassan sailors from what is now Sulawesi, Indonesia. The Macassans arrived in search of sea cucumber (trepang) to trade in China. In 1803 when Matthew Flinders was circumnavigating the country, he met a Macassan fisherman who told Flinders he had been harvesting trepang on the northern shores of Australia for 20 years. This story lives on in the ceremony and language of the Yolngu.

- **You learnt how to play Aussie Rules Football. You didn't learn about Marngrook.** Marngrook is a game played by Aboriginal groups across southern Australia. This almost certainly influenced Australian rules football, although the Australian Football League still disputes this. The 'Protector of Aborigines' and author William Thomas wrote about an Aboriginal football match played at Pound Bend, Victoria, in 1852. Thomas wrote that the players kicked the possum-skin ball high with the instep of the foot and "leap as high as five feet or more from the ground to catch the ball". Tom Wills, credited as one of the founders of Aussie rules, lived in the Grampians (Gariwerd) as a young man. He reportedly grew up surrounded by Djab wurrung children, learnt their language fluently and played Marngrook with them.

- **You learnt about cowboys and Indians. You didn't learn about Aboriginal resistance leaders.** In the late 19th century, Jandamarra and the Bunuba People resisted the violent encroachment of squatters onto their country in the Kimberley. Jandamarra had been a talented police tracker, but his people were being shot and poisoned, and the survivors were being enslaved around him. "Jandamarra died on his own soil defending his country. A true Australian hero." Paul Kelly, Singer/Songwriter.

- **You learnt about the suffragette and civil rights movement. You didn't learn about the Aboriginal and Torres Strait Islander civil rights movement.** It wasn't until the federal election in 1963 that all Aboriginal and Torres Strait Islander adults were able to vote – more than 50 years after Australian women got that right. This was the year Martin Luther King gave his "I have a dream" speech. At the same time in Australia, there was a growing movement of Indigenous activists and supporters demanding civil rights.

Dreamtime Sisters by Colleen Wallace Nungari.

There are so many other historical moments in our Aboriginal and Torres Strait Islander people's history and struggle for human rights. These moments cannot be adequately covered in this chapter. It's our inherent responsibility as Australians to learn, know and understand about our Indigenous Australian history. The sheer importance of this is something that we cannot ignore for it will enrich us all as people, and I throw down the gauntlet for you to find out more.

Constitutional change is possible

Constitutional change is possible and is something that is imperative for our Nation, following The Referendum 1957-1967. In 1967, after ten years of campaigning, a referendum was held to change the Australian Constitution. Two negative references to Aboriginal Australians were removed, giving the Commonwealth the power to legislate for them as a group. This change was seen by many as a recognition of Aboriginal people as full Australian citizens. The refer-

endum campaign effectively focused public attention on the fact that
Aboriginal and Torres Strait Islander Australians were second-class
citizens with all sorts of limitations - legislative and social - on their
lives.[6]

> The Dreaming means our identity as people, the cultural
> teaching and everything that's part of our lives here, you
> know?...it's the understanding of what we have
> around us

— MERV PENRITH (WALLAGA LAKE, 1996)

Australians are well known for our relaxed and easy-going nature. Where do you think we get this from as a nation? We have lived side by side our Indigenous People for 200 years or more, and I'd like to think that THEIR easy going natures have rubbed off on us somewhat. Our Indigenous people have always had a chilled and relaxed way of being and in many ways the expression, "She'll be right mate" is symbolic of this. Fellow Aussies will know that it can either refer to an outlook of optimism or apathy i.e., whatever is wrong will right itself with time. Professor Sussex [7] said in the Sydney Morning Herald before colonisation there were about 250 Aboriginal languages in Australia.

It's time that our Indigenous people are recognised, and we walk with them in a new movement for change.

There are more than 200 languages spoken every day in Australia - about 70 of these are Aboriginal, and approximately 130 are European and Asian.

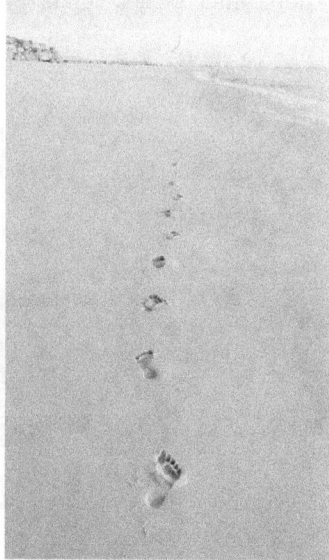

We are also known for our love of dolphins, dugongs and whales; it's like it's ingrained in our DNA and we will fiercely do anything to protect them. I'd like to think that we get this from our Indigenous cultures, as they have lived side by side with our whales, dolphins, and dugongs for thousands of years. Think of Hervey Bay in Queensland which is the gateway to K'gari (Fraser Island) - the national park that spans pretty much most of Fraser Island has been renamed "K'gari". This has been a partial victory for the Butchulla people (traditional owners) who are campaigning to rename the whole island. Hervey Bay is also home to the annual whale migration from Antartica. Anywhere where mother whales go (and feel safe enough for 4 months of the year) to have their baby calves, nurture them, then begin the migration south; must be a special, spiritual "energetic centre".

Lake Mackenzie, K'Gari (Fraser Island). K'Gari is home to the Butchulla people.

The Butchulla people have always known this and have revered the whales. Many streets and landmarks in Hervey Bay also have Aboriginal names. Hervey Bay even has a "Paddle Out for Whales" which is an annual event held in the whale watching capital of the world, as part of IFAW's National Whale Day celebrations. The event is held to help raise awareness of the many issues whales face today. The number and diversity of events all over the country on the day illustrates how valuable whales are to Australians in our unity and commitment to protecting them.[8]

A lot has been covered in this chapter, and I hope the readers are left with some valuable insights into the rich culture, history, and resilience of our Indigenous people. Our Aboriginal and Torres Strait Islander people are the fastest growing population group in Australia, and I think it's time that the Great Nations of our Indigenous people are recognised and embodied at the heart of our New Constitution. Let's walk with our Indigenous people in a New Movement for change. Let's make what seems to be Impossible, Possible.

Our Dreamtime - let's leave base camp together and start our trek across this vast country. We are all interconnected and once you understand the oneness we have with this great land our spiritual journey will continue like it always has.

9

HIV AND ITS GLOBAL IMPACT

- A GLOBAL DISEASE TO CHALLENGE HUMANITIES' FEAR

> *Frolance Besa, you came into my life for a sheer moment, however short our journey was, you embodied love. Your presence of being, your humbleness and simile were something to lament, your acceptance and selflessness were from up above.*
>
> *Bless you darling and may your memory live again, your story is not forgotten and deserves to be told. You didn't come into my life out of vain, your spirit, courage, and beauty were truly so bold.*
>
> — DAVID SHAUN LARSEN

HIV the First Epiphany in my Life

THIS CHAPTER IS DEDICATED to Frolance Besa who embodies the untold story of every person who has died from HIV in the Third World and the former staff and patients of 17 South (HIV/AIDS Unit), St Vincent's Hospital, Sydney

I started my 30-year journey working in HIV at St Vincent's Hospital in April 1987 at the age of 23. I was a very innocent, young gay man who started work within days of arriving, fresh off the plane from Adelaide. I initially lived in the old nurse's quarters on the 5th floor which was the boy's floor for nurses who lived onsite. The building is no longer there; it's now a part of the Garvan Research Institute. I remember it was a blessed time working on Ward 17 South (the first HIV/AIDS Unit in Australia).

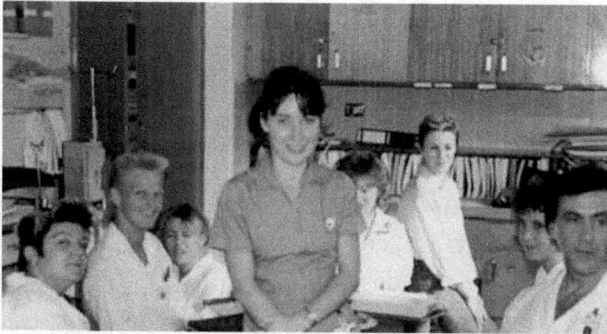

That's me on the left (yes with the mullet). Working as an RN - at the handover in the Nurses station, Ward 17 South (HIV/AIDS Unit) St Vincent's Hospital Sydney circa 1997.

I had the pleasure of working with such a collective group of dedicated and professional staff. But more so, I was blessed to be in the presence of so many beautiful people who died from AIDS-related illnesses. I've given up counting how many people, nearly all men, with whom I sat with at the time of their death. Some were artists, creative types, flight attendants, lawyers, doctors, business owners, activists, sex workers and others. I remember there were three categories of men that I observed which often determined how long people would live and also die of HIV. There were those that lived in denial and often carried deep pain and sadness. Then there were the professional patients, those that lived and breathed their illness to the very end, as it seemed to define them as people. Lastly, there were those who embraced it and got on with their lives. The last group were to some extent the survivors, but everyone had aspects of the spiritual warrior, just some more than others.

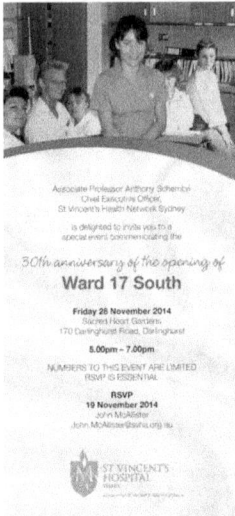

Associate Professor Anthony Schembri
Chief Executive Officer,
St Vincent's Health Network Sydney

is delighted to invite you to a
special event commemorating the

30th anniversary of the opening of
Ward 17 South

Friday 28 November 2014
Sacred Heart Gardens,
170 Darlinghurst Road, Darlinghurst

5.00pm - 7.00pm

NUMBERS TO THIS EVENT ARE LIMITED
RSVP IS ESSENTIAL

RSVP
19 November 2014
John McAllister
John.McAllister@svha.org.au

ST VINCENT'S
HOSPITAL

The 30th Anniversary Invitation to celebrate the opening of Ward 17 South, St Vincent's Hospital in Sydney.

The scale and scope of the HIV/AIDS epidemic in those early days were insurmountable. Imagine the agony of a community witnessing illness and the pain of death, day after day and year after year. Imagine attending funerals for colleagues, friends, and family every week. I relate my experience of working in HIV, being not dissimilar to working in a war zone. The nurses used to write the names of those who died on a whiteboard, and in December 1987 we had 16 names on that board.

Humbly I felt honoured to help and comfort so many people on their journey to the other side, especially at a time where there was so much widespread community fear, stigma, and discrimination. I can only vaguely remember the faces of the men I looked after during this time and uncannily; time itself has a way of giving you selected memory loss. Why some memories leave deep imprints on your brain and others don't, I don't know. It might be the Universe's way of protecting us, as we get older. Maybe the storage vault of memories starts to get too full, and you seek to cherish the memories that most matter to you.

In the late 1980's and early 1990s, I did five years of HIV nursing and given that I was caring for predominantly gay men at the time; it didn't surprise me that one day I would fall in love and that I did. Michael

Wayne Garnam was like no other patient I'd met, and I used to describe him as one of my favourites (my code for "like him a lot" but I needed to stay professional). During Michael's stay on the ward a lot was happening, and on successive admissions he was getting sicker with PCP pneumonia, needing occasional CPAP machine for breathing and intravenous medication. Around this time, I also resigned, as I was planning to go on my big trip to Europe and possibly stay away for one year if I could.

I remember one weekend after coming back from days off; I noticed when I walked past Michael's bed it was empty and I immediately got this pain in my gut, like a terrible dread that he must have died. When I arrived in the office, one of the nurses gave me a handwritten letter, and it was from Michael. He apparently discharged himself and thought if he got sicker he'd rather die at home then on the Ward. Michael also mentioned that if he got better; as a way of

Michael Wayne Garnam 1961-1992.

saying thanks, he wanted to take me out somewhere. Michael was very sick when he left for home, what an amazing Arian spirit he had.

What followed was a series of dates where we got to know each other better, a trip to the Blue Mountains, a few visits to his mum's place and I even stayed at Michael's home a few nights before I left for Europe. Sadly, it had to end! Michael took me to the to the airport, and saying goodbye at the time felt like one of the hardest things I ever had to do, the tears were flowing, but in my heart, I knew I was in love for the first time in my life. What happens next? I write about it in **Chapter 15. *Living, Loving, Ageing, and Dying*** - *The True Essence of Life*. It was a fantastic journey; no words can describe the experience and little did I know I would be working in Africa approximately 15 years later.

For all the staff who worked on 17 South, we couldn't have done all the things we did, without our hearts on our sleeves. Times were tough.

> There truly were angels among us and knowing this, enabled us to draw deep from that well of compassion.
>
> We rose to meet the challenge, and we did so with such dignity; as it seemed to be our duty to alleviate the suffering of others. It took us above the fear and discrimination of that time and what we had experienced was purely in itself love.

— DAVID SHAUN LARSEN

The Bridge To Africa

In 1997 I had the opportunity to set up 'The Bridge' Australia's first residential care facility for people with HIV related Cognitive Impairment/Dementia, mental illness and associated conditions. This facility was part of a statewide service administered by Royal Prince Alfred Hospital in Sydney. 'The Bridge' provided long-term residential, rehabilitation and respite care services however the facility relocated to Concord.

I managed the service for five years, and the staff and residents became a part of my family. I have so many fond memories of that time and working there was crucial to my decision to go and do humanitarian work in Africa. It's something that I had always dreamed of doing in life. However, it was my struggle with the ego that deterred me from making a firm decision in my head. That inner voice kept saying things like, "You'll never meet a partner there"; "You'll be away from your family and friends" and "What about your comforts of life, you won't have those in Africa".

It's not that my work in Sydney wasn't meaningful, it just became clear that access to affordable health care was a luxury compared to people living elsewhere. When you compare life here versus somewhere like

Africa, you can't close your eyes to the extremes that people face with poverty. It makes you question more and more, what's life all about. Where is the equity in the world? It became innately clear to me that just by our birthright, we have so much opportunity while many others have nothing. I needed at some point to prove to myself that I cared and wanted to do something to change the situation in the world in terms inequity and showing compassion.

The beautiful Victoria Falls in Africa.

In late 2002, the opportunity presented itself to go and work for Médecins Sans Frontières (Doctors Without Borders). MSF is the world's leading independent organisation for medical humanitarian aid and was awarded the Nobel peace prize in 1999. Every day more than 30,000 MSF staff assist people caught in crises around the world.[40] After five glorious years of managing 'The Bridge' I was about to go on the biggest adventure of my life. Africa, here I come...

Out in Africa

All I knew by MSF standards that I was going to what they called "the Hilton project" as they had a speed boat and satellite television which was highly unusual for an MSF project. The project's base was in a town called Kashikishi, Nchelnge District on Lake Mweru; a vast inland freshwater lake 100km in length that separated Zambia on one side from the Democratic Republic of the Congo on the other.[41] The reason for the speedboat became clear, Zambia had two islands that were on Lake Mweru, Kilwa and Chisenga islands, as they were responsible for providing HIV health care as part of the broader project remit.

A photograph of a pride of lions I took on my first safari in Africa.

Arriving at Lusaka airport I had no idea what to expect and what was to come, but my first impressions were so memorable; being greeted by a beautiful woman called Clare Nkwanga-Jolly. Clare was our Office Manager among the many other things that she did for the project and the staff, based in Lusaka the capital city of Zambia. She is still a dear friend to this day (limited to the occasional Facebook posts as we follow each other's journeys in life) and her smiling face and warm personality put me immediately at ease, so comforting for a first timer in Africa.

I had so much going on in my head, "I can't believe I'm here", "wow this is Africa", "where I am going to", "it's so hot", "not sure if I should be nervous or excited" so many thoughts. However, what I remembered the most, which stimulated every sense was the joy of just being here - the fresh air and its array of smells, the warmth of the people and the smiling children. It's what I call the rawness of life, and

I now know what people mean when they say Africa just gets under your skin. There's no place like it on earth.

There are currently more than 36.7 million people living with HIV with approximately 17 million on Anti-retroviral treatment. The scale-up of antiretroviral therapy is fast on track and has surpassed expectations. Global coverage of antiretroviral therapy reached 46% [43–50%] at the end of 2015. Gains were the most significant in the world's most affected region, eastern and southern Africa. Coverage increased from 24% [22–26%] in 2010 to 54% [50–58%] in 2015, reaching a regional total of 10.3 million people.[42]

South Africa alone had nearly 3.4 million people on treatment, more than any other country in the world. After South Africa, Kenya has the most extensive treatment programme in Africa, with nearly 900 000 people on treatment at the end of 2015. Botswana, Kenya, Malawi, Mozam-

Clare Nkwanga-Jolly.

bique, Rwanda, South Africa, Swaziland, Uganda, the United Republic of Tanzania, Zambia and Zimbabwe all increased treatment coverage by more than 25 % between 2010 and 2015.[42]

Stories From The Field Medicines Sans Frontieres, Nchelenge, Zambia (August 2003)

- **This is a letter from one of our field staff David Murray who is on his is first mission with Médecins Sans Frontières.** David is from Sydney and has been working as a nurse in Nchelenge, Zambia since January. He dedicated this letter to Florence Besa who died from HIV/AIDS in 2003.

MAP OF ZAMBIA
Kasama
Chingola
Kitwe
Ndola
Chipata
Kabwe
Mongu
Lusaka
Livingstone
0   miles   300
ZAMBIA

I have been lucky enough to work with some really nice people here. Neetie, one of my housemates, who was working on the Malaria project, left last week. It is always sad to see people leave. And although you are quite often very different people, the experience of living and working so closely together binds you for some moment in time. I have learned a lot from everyone who I have had the pleasure of living with. Rachel, the new ARV Doctor, arrived last week. Rachel and I will work very well together. She has lots of good ideas and is very enthusiastic. I am very pleased.

My next role within the project is to work on the ARV side of the program, developing a system and looking at requirements for compliance and counselling. The roll-out date seems to be getting longer and it might not be until November. There are plans for Rachel and I to go to Malawi to visit the Médecins Sans Frontières-France project there, maybe in late September. Next week I will be handing over one of my catchment areas, Kabuta, to Emmanuel, a new Médecins Sans Frontières Clinical officer who starts on Monday. It is a strange feeling to hand over some-thing that you have invested an enormous amount of time and energy in. But I am pleased that someone else will be able to take it that next step further.

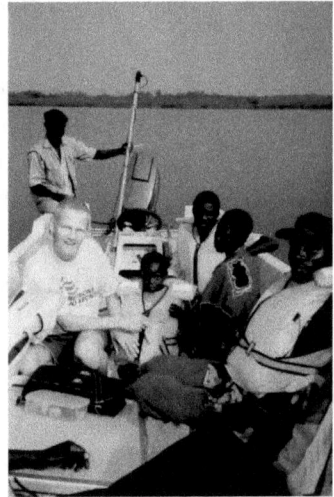

Transporting patients from Chisenga to the mainland. Stopped en route at a fishing village to pick up a few sick patients. Although we restrictions on the number of patients we could carry, on occasion we often overloaded the boat.

At the moment I am still going to Chisenga Island one day a week. That will be a hard one to hand over as it is like my "little baby". I have had some great breakthroughs. I did some ongoing counselling with the caregivers last week, and it was so rewarding to see the fruits of my labour coming into being. So the next step for our project is to start running support groups at the village level in each of the catchment areas.

However, a major obstacle is still the stigma people experience being HIV infected (people are fearful of publicly disclosing their status within the villages). We are trying to encourage our caregivers to know who their HIV patients are and get them to come to the Well Care Clinics (HIV Clinics) with them. The support groups will be a further development. Médecins Sans Frontières is currently running the Well Care Clinics, so another challenge is to get the Clinical Officers who are employed at the Rural Health Centre to take ownership of their clinics which can sometimes be very hard.

Chisenga Island caregivers 2003. I recruited approximately 18 caregivers (earlier in the year) and provided them with a 3-day training program on HIV which was run on the mainland.

The caregivers on Chisenga Island have informed me that they had five patients publicly disclose their status within the community, including one man in his local church. The reaction so far has not been too adverse, and it looks like they are ready to come to the support groups. I've been working with the caregivers; providing training around counselling and facilitating support groups, with the aim of providing these groups in every village on the island.

That way, when someone comes for HIV testing and tests positive, we can admit them straight away to our program and refer them to the local village support group. There's been such a wonderful feeling of seeing great change, and mobilising the community to be proactive. And it's not possible without the wonderful work that the voluntary caregivers do.

The speedboat MSF had to transport staff and patients between Chisenga Island and the mainland. We operated the Chisenga clinic one day per week. The boat was also used to go to another island that was in Lake Mweru.

I enjoy following the stories of my patients, as it gives some personal meaning to the human face of HIV. One of my patients, who is very special to me, is a 24-year-old girl who only recently tested HIV positive around the same time as having a miscarriage. She has such a beautiful energy, speaks English very well and is always very eager to know everything about her health. To my distress, she has been very sick with pneumonia for weeks. She had PCP (pneumonia) and TB

Pneumonitis, a combination of two quite debilitating illnesses. Fortunately, she seems to be picking up quite a bit.

It is nice to hear stories about individuals as opposed to lots of facts and figures. There are many other people whose stories are equally deserving like Charles and Mary (husband and wife couple) and Grace (widow of 5 children) in Kabuta. More on them later... Cheers for now....Lots of Love....David

MSF started the administration in Antiretrovirals (ARVs) in February 2005. Frolance didn't improve with TB treatment and was unable to get better from having pneumonia and sadly passed away in November 2003. Frolance was only 24 years old when she died but for me she was an Older soul who touched me with her presence. She embodies the story of untold millions of people who have died from HIV in the developing world.

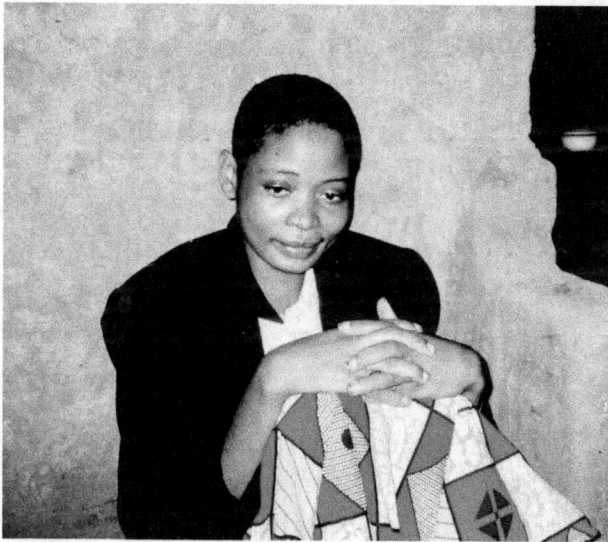

Frolance Besa 2003 Nchelenge District, Zambia.

The Integrated HIV/AIDS Project in the northern district of Nchelenge, included voluntary testing and counselling, home-based care, advocacy, and education. Médecins Sans Frontières had been in Zambia since 1999.

COUNTRY PROFILE (2004)

Zambia Population: 10,872,000; Life expectancy: 42 years and MSF expatriate staff: 16 MSF national staff: 183

Vale Adjunct Associate Professor Levinia Crooks, AM

28 November 1960 – 16 October 2017

Prior self-publishing my book, I learned that a dear colleague Levinia Crooks had passed away. I first met Levinia in 1997 when I was employed to set up, *The Bridge HIV Residential Care* facility. Levinia and another colleague, **Associate Professor Dr Roger Garcia, University of Sydney** were instrumental in getting *The Bridge* development approval through the local Glebe Council. Levinia deserves a special mention in this book as someone who has truly dedicated her life to the great work that is being done in the HIV field.

Dedication from the the Australasian Society for HIV, Viral Hepatitis and Sexual Health Medicine (ASHM). Posted by ASHM 17th October 2017.

Professor Levinia Crooks, AM.

It is with great sadness that the Board and staff of ASHM announces the passing of Adjunct Associate Professor Levinia Crooks, AM on 16th October 2017 after a long and courageously fought illness. Levinia was 56 and is survived by her mother, Judy.

Levinia's contribution to the work of ASHM has been untiring, far-reaching, extraordinary and exemplary. She was Chief Executive

Officer from November 1999 to September 2017 and has been a leading advocate in the field.

Levinia served for over 30 years as a champion for people's rights in the health sector. She began in the 1980s supporting her friends and colleagues impacted by HIV/AIDS, conducting social research to inform the development of counselling and support services for people living with HIV. She also served as President of the AIDS Council of NSW and Bobby Goldsmith Foundation, as well as on the Board of the Australian Federation of AIDS Organisations.

She applied her considerable experience and skills to push for dramatic changes in the viral hepatitis response and greater attention to sexual health needs. Her drive and focus on the needs of the workforce in HIV, viral hepatitis and sexual health pioneered ASHM as a provider of high quality resources and training. In this capacity, she has written a wide range of educational resources and provided robust advocacy for many initiatives that resulted in increased access to HIV and viral hepatitis treatments.

In 2008, she was made a Member of the Order of Australia for her contribution to HIV policy, her care for people with HIV and her contribution to health generally. In 2015 she was further honoured with the ACON President's Award in recognition of a lifetime dedicated to improving the health and well-being of people affected by HIV and AIDS.

Levinia leaves us all a major and extensive legacy to carry forward and build upon, with countless lives in our region positively impacted by her energetic, pragmatic, visionary, brave and can-do approach. Moreover, she will be remembered as a warm and generous friend to so many ready to roll her sleeves up, get on with the work at hand and bringing her formidable intelligence, wit, and problem solving abilities to the table.

Vale Levinia! You are sorely missed.

The Latest Science: What's New?

The International Council of AIDS Service Organisations (ICASO) has developed a brief to provide the HIV community and others, with the latest current information. This also includes an analysis of new and updated clinical data on the effectiveness of antiretroviral therapy (ART) in preventing HIV transmission to sexual partners of people living with HIV.

The Latest Science: What's New? Clinical study findings, released in 2016, have added to prior evidence demonstrating that HIV cannot be sexually transmitted if the person living with HIV has a fully suppressed viral load i.e., is taking HIV medication (ART) and the amount of virus in their blood (their viral load) is Undetectable.

An HIV undetectable status means HIV cannot be transmitted. **Undetectable = Untransmittable.**

> Scientists never like to use the word 'Never' of a possible risk. But I think in this case we can say that the risk of transmission from an HIV-positive person who takes treatment and has an undetectable viral load may be so low as to be unmeasurable, and that's equivalent to saying they are uninfectious.
>
> It's an unusual situation when the overwhelming evidence based science allows us to be confident that what we are saying is fact.
>
> — DR. ANTHONY FAUCI, DIRECTOR OF THE U.S. NATIONAL INSTITUTE FOR ALLERGIES AND INFECTIOUS DISEASES (JULY 2017).

Available At: Undetectable = Untransmittable Community Brief October 2017 ICASO

Living with HIV has been a Blessing in Disguise

Living with HIV has been a blessing in disguise because, after all the years of working in the HIV sector, I never thought I would get the virus. Not because I was scared or anything, I just didn't think it would be my process. I mean of anyone; I seemed to be the most affected person i.e., working in HIV, nursed so many people who died, lost friends and a partner. I remember my diagnosis well, the big awakening for me came on 27th December 2010, as I got quite sick and it was just before New Year.

I had just returned from spending Christmas with mum, Allister (my partner at the time) and his family in Corowa, near Albury New South Wales. I remember feeling very unwell on the drive home, the voice in my head said, "maybe I'm just getting a cold" and a cold it was. Little did I know I was having a severe seroconversion illness - a massive immune response that usually occurs 3-4 weeks after infection. I had very high fevers, a spotty rash from the waist up (which seemed far worse than my distant memory of getting measles as a kid) and noticeably swollen glands under my arms, neck, and groin; which seemed to come on quite suddenly. Given my insider knowledge and being a nurse, I just knew I had HIV. In some ways, I felt cheated around my diagnosis because it deprived me of any chance to experience the "big denial phase" that I used to witness in so many others.

I guess it's easier to bury your head in the sand for a few days or a few weeks or months for that matter; until you at least work it all out. But no, I moved through the shock of diagnosis and accelerated into acceptance around living with HIV very quickly. What is helpful for anyone at this time, is the love and support from family and friends. Allister was always very supportive and caring.

Now the lesson not what to do; especially if your doctor is about to tell someone that they might have HIV. The day after getting sick, Allister took me to a medical centre nearby because my GP practice at the time was closed. The doctor examined me, took some blood, then I went home and didn't think about it anymore; because I just wanted to enjoy my New Year. New Year was only days away and I could already sense that pre-New Year excitement that starts to happen, especially if you live in Sydney; with its spectacular summer, beaches, tourists and World renowned fireworks display.

I received a phone call from the Doctor (whom I initially saw) the day before New Year's Eve. He stated that my blood test for HIV, "was veering towards being positive". "Really?" I exclaimed but speechless for a minute. "So what is veering towards positive mean?" I asked. He just explained that the blood test was possibly positive, but hadn't been confirmed yet and left me hanging with no explanation. Moral of the story is; you just don't give results like this over the phone, it's highly unprofessional. Significant life-changing results like this always need to be delivered in person.

What a roller coaster ride my journey with HIV has been over the years, and you know what; I wouldn't change a thing about it. Although infected with HIV, I feel blessed for the journey living with HIV has taught me. It has shown be about acceptance and an invaluable lesson around stigma and discrimination and other people's judgement. You see people for who they indeed are. For me life's good; I am fit and healthy, do work that I enjoy and don't experience any side effects from my medication. For the most part, I am happy and content with life.

NO SHAME ABOUT BEING HIV+

WORLD AIDS DAY · 12/1
#RiseUpToHIV

This feature story on HIV activism appeared in the Mardi Gras Festival Guide 2016 with me are two amazing HIV activists Abby Landy and Theodore Timothy Tsipiras (photo courtesy of Ann-Marie Callihanna, Photographer for the Sydney Gay and Lesbian Mardi Gras).

All I can say is if life deals you a card that's not what you expected (such as a sudden illness, death or some other unpleasant experience) you only have three choices. You can embrace the experience for what it is; go into denial and play the avoidance game or kill yourself, which is somewhat extreme but I'd never judge anyone who took their own life. I'm very proud to be a gay man living with HIV today as many others have suffered extreme illness, loss, and death. Although I, along with so many others in the world, have contributed to the fight for acceptance and support, it gives me so much hope that we will prevail towards Ending HIV!

In saying this, there is also much more work to be done especially in the developing countries such as Africa and Asia Pacific region, that are still enduring a far more significant burden of HIV. I believe many life lessons can be learned from all the courageous people who have died from HIV. In essence, all I can say is cherish your social connections and those that you love; try and make a difference in the world in whatever capacity you can; challenge stigma and discrimination and think about what sort of legacy you want to leave behind. But above all else, remember to let the memories of those that we have all lost and loved, live again.

The amazing staff of the HIV Outreach Team. I've worked with most of the staff for many years and some for ten years when I was Program Manager.

10

HUMANITARIANISM
- OUR GLOBAL RESPONSIBILITY FOR HUMANITY

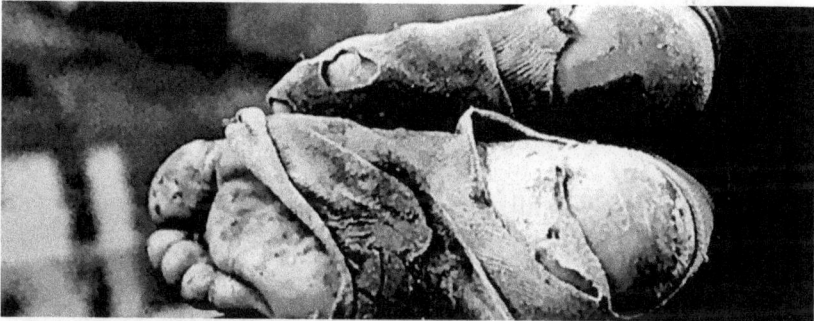

" *Our volunteers and staff live and work among people whose dignity is violated every day. These volunteers choose freely to use their liberty to make the world a more bearable place...One bandage at a time, one suture at a time, one vaccination at a time.*

— JAMES ORBINSKI, MSF INTERNATIONAL
PRESIDENT, THE NOBEL PEACE PRIZE SPEECH 10TH
DECEMBER 1999

Your Playing Small does not Serve the World

YOUR PLAYING **small does not serve the world** and nearly twenty years after this famous Laureate speech was made in Oslo, Norway; we still live in a world that hasn't changed significantly.

> Despite grand debates on world order, the act of humanitarianism comes down to one thing: individual human beings reaching out to their counterparts who find themselves in the most difficult circumstances...
>
> And, uniquely for Medicines Sans Frontières, working in around 80 countries, over 20 of which are in conflict, telling the world what they have seen. All this in the hope that the cycles of violence and destruction will not continue endlessly.
>
> — JAMES ORBINSKI, MSF INTERNATIONAL PRESIDENT

For the most part, we still create war and destruction on a scale unfathomable. The Government of the day just finds someone new to blame and to direct their futile need for power and control. Humanity more than ever, at any time in our history, needs to reach out to our fellow human beings who are in crisis. Those people who are experiencing hardship, suffering conflict, and enduring violence at the hands of militia or terrorists. What appears to be something so built into my genetic makeup is the quality of humanitarianism - that part of me that I thought was common to all human beings.

> Life's most persistent and urgent question is, 'What are you doing for others?'
>
> — MARTIN LUTHER KING JR. CIVIL RIGHTS ACTIVIST AND CLERGYMAN

Me thinking about the deeper meaning of life.

Unfortunately, the older I get; I realise that this isn't so! I feel that there is a humanitarian spectrum aligned with our identity as humans however it indeed mirrors our soul evolution, nothing more and nothing less. The older you are as a soul, the Universe expects that you would be like a "Bodhisattva" - an evolved being much like Jesus Christ who has come to the earth plane to alleviate the suffering of others. This is the belief that all human beings deserve respect and dignity and should be treated as such. Therefore, we are all ultimately working towards advancing the well-being and welfare of Humanity as a whole. It's innately in our genetic makeup as human beings; whether you think so or not. Compassion and kindness are critical, but without understanding the world at large, you end up playing small.

> Your playing small does not serve the world. There is nothing enlightened about shrinking so that other people will not feel insecure around you.
>
> — MARIANNE WILLIAMSON

Few Australians realise that Australia along with New Zealand are some of the most humanitarian nations on earth; in terms of volunteers who freely choose to,

> Use their liberty to make the world a more bearable place.

In other words, proportionately we punch above our weight in terms of humanitarian endeavours, if not by the actions of our Government (not abiding international law) but the individual liberty of its citizens. The latter is the story we should be telling our children. It's just that our Government is not as liberated and our society on the whole still chooses to celebrate the endeavours of our actors, media personalities and sports stars than our humanitarians and scientists and other great people advancing the welfare of Humanity.

The UN Human Rights Committee stated in November 2017 that Australia should bring Manus and Nauru refugees to immediate safety. Our mandatory detention policy is inhumane and unlawful and Australia cannot "pick and choose" which international laws it follows[43].

> Australia should end the practice of "offshore process-ing", immediately close Nauru and Manus Island, and "take all measures necessary to protect the rights of refugees and asylum seekers affected ... ensure their transfer to Australia or their relocation to other appro-priate safe countries.
>
> — UN HUMAN RIGHTS COMMITTEE 2017

There is nothing enlightened about Australia shrinking on the world stage in terms of its Humanitarian responsibilities.

The Stories That We Should Be Telling

Information courtesy of Conversations with Richard Fidler.

Picture of Creswell Eastman (ABC RN).

The stories that we should be telling are about people like, Creswell Eastman, who has saved a million brains. Professor Creswell (Cres) Eastman[44] has led projects to abolish Iodine Deficiency Disorders (IDD) throughout the developing world. Children born to mothers deficient in iodine can suffer a range of defects including mental retardation, deafness, speech and physical impairments.

He is an international leader in projects to abolish IDD over the past decades. Cres and his teams have been effective in Malaysia, Laos, Thailand, Vietnam, Indonesia, China, and Tibet. His transformative work with populations in remote areas of China led him to be dubbed, "the man who saved a million brains".

During his first visits to Tibet, Cres discovered that 13 per cent of the population was born with cretinism as the result of iodine deficiency. In the course of his field work in Asia, Cres almost lost his life to altitude sickness. Cres' current focus is on the recurring problem of IDD in Australian and Thai populations. He is concerned that IDD may be affecting the ability of Australian children, and in particular, Indigenous Australian children, to perform at school.

> My association with Tibet began in the mid 1980s with visits out to the Tibetan Plateau in Qinghai. But on my first visit there, I had never seen as many people in villages with cretinism anywhere else in the world. So it

145

was a massive problem, in fact it was absolutely over-whelming... It's such a big problem in China because over two-thirds of the population live in rural areas, many of them having to just sustain themselves through what they grow.

In other words, they are born, live and die within a few kilometres... most of the fields, most of the earth and the water are iodine deficient. And it doesn't get in from imported foods or processed foods... So the higher the altitude, the more remote you are, the worse the problem is... If the average IQ of Tibetan children is only 85, and that's what it was before this program started, and people with IQs of 85 can't be educated, they don't really get beyond primary school.

— EASTMAN CRESWELL (CRES)

Cres argues that to ignore this problem means turning one's back on the basic human rights of these people and "the most important human right you've got is to realise the intelligence you've inherited from your parents."

Further information:

Cres is a Clinical Professor of Medicine at the University of Sydney Medical School, and Principal of the Sydney Thyroid Clinic at the Westmead Specialist Centre.

To subscribe to the *Conversations* podcast, paste

http://www.abc.net.au/local/podcasts/conversationspodcast.xml into your podcasting application.

Never Lonely but Alone

Never lonely but alone, is a state of feeling so integral to my time doing humanitarian work. Humanitarians aren't some sort of heroes with superhuman gifts. We are just like anyone else, but with a passion and caring to provide a decent standard of living for all mankind and with the realisation, that our destiny is dependent on it.

Me with a group of volunteers that I trained and worked with, in Nchelenge District, 2004.

I have always found this feeling of being alone in the world but never lonely - a classic feature of Older souls. This was intensified for me when I did my Humanitarian work because none of my friends and family could ever really understand what I had experienced or observed. In addition, when you are placed in situations out of your comfort zone, it kind of forces you to grow and to rise to the challenges that it presents or succumb to the fear or inability to go on.

When I worked in the role as a Project Coordinator, it was even more isolating. Imagine not only being the manager but having to live with the people you manage. There was always this time period after work, which I called the debriefing period. This is where I'd be listening to staff offloading their daily woes, usually over an alcoholic beverage. It was like a ritual, by the time we ended up having dinner, I finally felt like one of the team; just like any other expatriate staff. However, there were many days when the going got tough; some nights I'd find myself sobbing or crying to sleep. It was like therapy, as I reflected on the day with no one to talk to. I just had to force myself to sleep and find the strength and resilience to do it all over again. I admire anyone who does these roles for any length of time, for it's not always that easy.

A community group being facilitated by Renato an MSF Doctor who ran the mental health program.

The urge to be a Humanitarian is something quite indescribable. The only analogy I can use actually relates to the intense feeling of depression but exalted in reverse form i.e., the feeling of experiencing immense personal satisfaction and pleasure beyond anything imaginable. I always had a feeling that I needed to do something to alleviate the suffering of others in the world and always will. It's just that the feeling became more intense and stronger as I got older. It's interesting (as an observation), the opportunity to do humanitarian work presented itself soon after I recovered from depression in my mid to late 30s.

I never thought in my wildest dreams (working in the HIV field for most of my life), that it would lead me down a path of being a humanitarian. As scary as it seemed at the time, the opportunity to eventually work for MSF was like jumping into the void. This new and unknown endeavour would force me out of my comfort zone. Little did I know, I was totally unprepared for the immense freedom, challenges and personal joy this work would offer me in return.

Stories From The Field Medicines Sans Frontieres, Nchelenge, Zambia (April 2004)

- **This is a Story from the Field by David Murray** who is an HIV nurse from Bellevue Hill who has just returned to work on an HIV project in Nchelenge Zambia. Last year David went on his first mission with Médecins Sans Frontiers and he found it so rewarding he chose to return to the same project
- **This time around David is working as the Project Coordinator for our field project.**

HI EVERYONE,

This is my first email to let you know what has been happening since I have been back - mostly project news. I had a really nice time back in Australia and appreciated all the kind support. I have many fond memories to keep me grounded for the next six months.

A group photograph that was taken with my MSF housemates, 2004.

Life here hasn't changed at all and I have managed to slip back into some normality with ease. I spent my Sunday today decorating my room, as I haven't had any time this week to do anything except work. One of my dear friends/housemate and work colleagues Sue is leaving tomorrow. Sue has just spent six months doing lots of fabulous work coordinating the psychosocial side of our program. She has expanded the program from a core group of 5 VCT (Voluntary, Counselling, and Testing) counsellors to 11.

Me in a photograph with a Sub Chief and his delegates in
Nchelenge Zambia 2003.

She has also spent a lot of time getting the counsellors up to speed to
cope with other complex counselling issues such as ongoing counselling, support groups, prevention of mother to child, adherence to
antiretroviral treatment and dealing with the increasing impact of
having more children in our program. Hence our team is putting on a
barbecue (or brie) to send her off. So our house is a little busy at the
moment with all of us preparing the food (marinated goat) and organ-
ising the logistics of keeping the beer cold!

One of the new changes for me has been the offer to be the Project
Coordinator for the next six months. It's a very challenging position in
a project of this size. Therefore, this has made this last week very
hectic for me in terms of trying to get my head around the current
project issues that encompass so many different program components
such as advocacy, logistics, malaria research, laboratory/technical,
education, counselling, VCT, TB, ambulatory care clinics, home-based
care and of course the scale out and up of ARVs (including access to
essential medicines). There have also been some interesting develop-
ments with a small flood of refugees from the Congo to one of the
islands where we operate a program.

In my new role, I still have time to be able to go out to the field. Since I have been involved clinically in many aspects of the program, I intend to have a hands-on approach as much as possible, especially doing adherence counselling for people on ARVs. We now have 29 patients on ARVs (2 died recently) with another 30 selected to start in the next 2 weeks so it's rolling along nicely. In many ways, we have just been doing the work without a lot of fanfare but we plan to do a story to promote the project with the advent of the 100th person to start ARVs.

All in all, life is good here; the people are great and the work rewarding.

Cheers, David

MAP OF ZAMBIA

Country Profile (2004)

Zambia Population: 10,872,000; Life expectancy: 42 years

MSF expatriate staff: 16MSF / national staff: 183

Stories From The Field Medicines Sans Frontieres, Sanniquellie, Liberia (May 2005)

- **David Murray, a nurse from Sydney, is a Field Coordinator for Médecins Sans Frontières' (MSF) programme in Nimba County, on Liberia's eastern border with Guinea.**
- Here MSF provides a variety of health services including HIV/AIDS, TB and nutritional care, community outreach and the training of local staff.
- Since joining the team in December last year David is beginning to get an insight into the Liberian culture and its people.

Hi Everyone,

MSF Base Sanniquellie, Nimba County.

The local people in northern part of Nimba County, belong to two main tribes. The Gio and Mano are Christians and linked culturally and historically. The other main tribe are the Mandingos, though most have either been killed through ethnic cleansing or fled to neighbouring Guinea. This occurred mostly during the latter half of the 14-year civil war that ended in 2003. The Mandingos are Muslims by faith and the many burnt out mosques and houses in town are a stark reminder of their fate.

The UN recently declared Nimba safe for refugees to return. There are approximately 15,000 Mandingos expected to return over the coming months. The UNHCR (UN High Commission for Refugees) in Guinea is facilitating this process and will soon start promoting voluntary repatriation. However, many Mandingos are still too afraid to make the journey home and I can understand why so many of these people are afraid. Many of the local people are critical of the Mandingos. MSF is watching this closely because, as they return, issues related to land, property rights and interracial marriage could ignite further violence in this region.

Most people here mix their Christian faith with a strong undercurrent of traditional beliefs including, witchcraft and other practices. Around this time of the year, there are many active secret societies, undertaking initiation ceremonies. There has been some talk of sacrificial killings and its hidden nature makes it very difficult to know whether it happens here in Nimba.

A photograph showing the devastation of buildings as a consequence of the Liberian Civil War.

Power and control is the motivation behind those who perpetrate such crimes and with the elections coming up, reports of these practices have been increasing across Liberia.

It is tropical here and the vegetation is thick, green and lush, with rolling, heavily forested hills. The social life is pretty limited but we have a great team and radio for news. Some of us go for walks in the early morning or evening as there are a number of pleasant walks around town. This gives us an opportunity to meet local people, talk to school kids and feel connected to daily life.

On the work front, many new things are now evolving and giving me a sense of accomplishment and hope that we can either build capacity or raise awareness on issues. Margaret, our new training officer from Australia, has been busy training Anthony, our new outreach worker. Margaret is setting up an Outreach programme that will eventually have 140 Community Health Workers and Youth Workers carrying out health education with a focus on maternal health and HIV/AIDS. The stigma associated with HIV/AIDS is enormous and we suspect that the prevalence rate is between 5 and 10%, maybe higher.

Help Us Find Our Parents. This poster was part of the Contact Tracing Program operated by the International Commission of the Red Cross (ICRC).

If all goes according to plan, HIV/AIDS care and treatment with anti-retroviral drugs (ARVs) will be fully effective from May or June. We plan to start voluntary counselling and testing (VCT) and prevention of parent to child transmission work next month. I think the outreach programme will be very effective. There are already signs that people are motivated to help their communities and are interested in attending workshops to gain further knowledge. However, traditional cultural practices such as male and female circumcision, family marriage, use of herbs (good or bad) and polygamy are rife and it will take a long time to change some of these practices.

Several new national medical staff, including an HIV/TB nurse, are being recruited in Monrovia to help support activities in our clinics and hospital. It is exciting but we have many hurdles to cross. We still have nurses in the hospital refusing to take out IV lines on patients who are suspected of having HIV. Most of these staff are nurse aides and their level of knowledge is quite poor. However, our expatriate hospital supervisor, and Amy, our doctor, have done a marvellous job developing the skills of the nurses' aides through improved ways of working and coaching.

Daily life on the main road, Sanniquellie 2005.

Overall, I feel that the Liberians are a strong people, very determined, resourceful and resilient. They have only known war, ingrained corruption and tribal conflict for a great part of their recent history. Many people here live in the hope of a bright future, though with an understandable undercurrent of pessimism. We will have to wait and see what transpires, but I am glad that I am here as part of this process, witnessing events and sharing the expression of hope with the Liberian people.

Cheers, David

Leaving Liberia, saying goodbye to the MSF team, September 2005.

Country Profile (2005)

Liberia Population: 3,261,000 / Life expectancy: 55 years

MSF expatriate staff: 12MSF / national staff: 170

Willen & Doen - Guest Author Wil Groot

Wil Groot is a very special friends and lives in Amsterdam, The Netherlands and we met some 15 years ago now. Wil has a special place in my heart and I call him my soul brother. We are kindred spirits who share a past life connection and are both Humanitarians.

When there is a will, there is a way and following my dream. . .

My name is Wil Groot and I was born in 1957, under the star sign of Sagittarius. My parents were Catholic farmers. I was number 14 in the row of 16, one mother and one father. I grew up with sharing, caring, and love, which has been always around and still is.

A picture of me with Wil Groot, taken in Berlin 2014 - at the Memorial to Homosexuals persecuted under Nazism.

In 1984 I was infected with HIV and was diagnosed at a later stage, because of my partner then, was too scared to tell me. In those days AIDS was a mysterious taboo about which people knew very little about. People didn't dear talk about it and because of the fear they were only whispering.

In June 2007, I was on the brink of finishing studying 6 years of cultural social development. Around this time, a friend of mine Leon visited me and asked me what I was going to do after my studies. I replied, "I don't know yet". He thought as an interesting read I might like a book called *28 AIDS stories in Africa*, written by Stephanie Nolan. Before I went to sleep that night I read one story about a woman, who had 7 children and 15 grandchildren. All her children died of AIDS. She had to take care of her grandchildren, of whom the eldest was a 15-year-old boy. The second grandchild, a 14-year-old girl was pregnant. The grandmother was very worried that she would have HIV as well.

That night I was dreaming that I walked on a dirt road with many black children playing, only children. I asked one of them, "where are your parents?". The kids answered, "They died of AIDS". Along the dusty road, I saw a broken down farmhouse. I told the children that I was going to make a house for them from what remained of it.

The next morning, I called my oldest sister Johanna and told her about my dream. I asked her what she would think if I would go to Africa to do some research to try and open up an orphanage for HIV/AIDS orphans. She immediately said yes, go for it. I had tears in my eyes when I read the story again and again. I made my decision after reading most of the book that I would go to Africa for 9 months (working as a volunteer) because my savings would be finished.

From that moment, my journey was like a rollercoaster ride. The friends and family in my life had lots of respect for what I was planning to do. They started to help and encourage me to arrange and organise benefit parties to raise money for a potential project. Well, that was easier said than done but I was sure that I would find on my path especially as my angels already know it. And so I did. After receiving various benefits from my extended network of family and friends, we needed to start a foundation due to tax reasons. The organisation and foundation we named *Willen & Doen*, in English *Will & Do*.

Wil with a group of children, Willen & Doen Project, South Africa.

In October 2007, I first moved to Bloemfontein. I started as a voluntary worker at *Our Place*, which is a centre for infected and affected orphans (children and adults). *Our Place* is a non-profit and non-governmental organisation which survives entirely on donations. The clients are people who have nothing and would quite often be homeless or from the gutter. I stayed there for 3.5 weeks and I was astonished by what happened there. In my first blog, I was surprised how in a short period of time it was read by more than 500 people.

It is not how much we have, but how much we enjoy, that makes happines!

Children sitting outside a mud hut. Courtesy Willen Doen Project South Africa.

A journalist friend of mine managed to get 7 articles published in one of the biggest newspapers in the Netherlands. This gave a lot of free and helpful media publicity for the children's home and helped immensely with our donations. *Our Place* was also active in the Transkei. Deon Mulder, the patron of *Our Place*, showed me around, and this helped me to learn so much about what was needed there. It was the first time in my life that I was truly confronted with poverty. Deon was also planning to start an *Our Place* in the Traskei but unfortunately didn't have the finances for it. However, he did have a broken down farmhouse, from which he wanted to make an orphanage because there were so many orphans in the Transkei. I told him that I would offer to help and the heartfelt stories that I wrote about my experiences along with the donations from Holland brought together the initial funds to start our building project. A week before I went back home I was putting the beds together. My first Mission was accomplished.

Following this time, I worked with many organisations as a volunteer and did research about AIDS and its impact on the economy of South Africa. During the time, I worked with the Salisian Institute and learned a lot about the life of street kids and ex-street kids in South Africa. They were such a source of learning and were so open to sharing their conversations and life experiences with me. Most of these kids ended up becoming my biggest friends. If I forgot my mobile or wallet, they would come running after me, screaming, "Master Wil, you forgot something!" Much of the social work I did in the Townships, especially talking with young men about HIV in the Shebeen was also a stunning experience. Nobody there had ever experienced a white guy who was so open about his HIV status. I worked with the Yabonga organization and I must say; it has also helped me immensely - in terms of being accepted - being a 50-year-old man, who still looked handsome and manly. They were amazed and would often ask how I could be 50 and living with HIV for 23 years. They'd often ask, "how did you do manage to do that?"

Wil marching in one of the protest rallies, South Africa.
Courtesy Willen & Doen Project, South Africa.

Another amazing experience was the Xenophobia there and the protest rallies which I actively took part in and wasn't scared at all. At the first rally in the Township Khayelitsha, I was with a handful white people. At the second rally in the Township of Nyanga, there was only me and a young Polish girl. We had ten young guys who protected us from the Salesian Institute.

I also visited the Transkei with a cameraman and a producer, who read my weblog and who wanted to make a documentary to sell to Dutch television as a way of raising awareness. They were volunteers like me. Willen & Doen interviewed some of the people who were politically active (on a small scale), about with community gardens and mussel projects. We interviewed Dylan Mc Garry, who did research about the impact of HIV/AIDS on rural children's reliance on natural resources within the Eastern Cape, South Africa.

What was so incredible, is that I witnessed how so many young children who survived from nature, because they were orphans or just didn't have food enough at home. They showed me around and taught me so much about what was good, and what wasn't. I learned so much about how poverty, hunger, malnutrition, and stigma impacted on their lives and how they developed skills around resilience, especially for survival. It taught me such a valuable lesson about how traditions and culture are still so embedded in society; yet education and guidance are still needed because the people are eager to learn and do it themselves.

I have spoken with so many young people over the years about HIV and AIDS, and I realise how so many still don't know the difference between them. I'd often get people asking what I was doing there and I would tell them I was working as a volunteer with projects. "What projects?", they would often ask. I didn't want to mention HIV/AIDS because I knew how stigma impacted on the local communities. I would often tell them that I volunteered at sport, dance, educational, agricultural, creative and health projects. They'd often ask me if I knew anything about HIV. I'd answer, "Yes, I do". The conversation would continue. "Can we ask you some questions about it?". I'd say, "of course, feel free to ask anything you like". "But 'meester' (which means teacher in Dutch) these are difficult questions", they'd respond. I'd smile and say, "Sure, ask any difficult question you like". "Are you HIV positive yourself?". Initially, I'd be so gob smacked as I didn't know how to answer and I was so surprised at how direct they were with their questions. I would then tell them that I'm 50 years old and have been positive since 1985. This would often lead to them requesting a meeting with me the next day which I'd agree to attend.

Later I realised how important it was to make people aware because there was so much denial and fear. I also came to understand that they were in a difficult situation because the closest place to get medicines was Mthatha (about 50 miles away). In addition, when you are taking medicine it's essential that you also need food. There was also a shortage of doctors and nurses and nurses were really needed.

Most of my observations and research during these early days, really made me aware that so much help is still needed, especially in rural and remote areas. People in these areas just need a little guidance and education around how to use the land as much of the land is so fertile e.g. if they can learn how to grow their own community gardens, they'd have enough food to feed their families plus have extra food to sell. Also because of poverty, many people have sold their cattle. In this situation, it only takes using a cooperative approach and providing a supportive environment to help move people from being passive (due to the barriers from fear and culture) to self-managing for themselves.

If you think about it, most households had lost family members, although they often deny this. Men also left the area to go searching for work in the mines; therefore, the women and children had to do most of the work. As you could imagine lots of children didn't go to school, mostly because of poverty and having to work. Many of the men were working in the mines for 11 months every year, therefore had little time at home. In addition, because so many men had girlfriends, it wasn't uncommon for them to come home infected with HIV.

I have also been active in the Townships around Cape Town, with different projects over the years and realise that there is a lot of good work being done. Many are still just small-scale projects, which support the communities. All I can say is that they do great work and provide support, counselling and education around HIV/AIDS as needed, but not everywhere.

I believe that South Africa is a country with a lot of possibilities. It can be a model country for the rest of Africa and the rest of the world. We only have to do it and make it work, because it needs education. It cannot only be done by politicians. The citizens of the world have to do it as well and help. Everybody has to help, and then we will have a prosperous future and a better life.

When there is a will, there is a way. It is a honour for me to share this with you.

Wil with a group of school children. Courtesy Willen & Doen Project, South Africa.

The ten years after . . .

Looking back at the last ten years, it seems as if I have been sitting in on an intercity train, with short stops. On my humanitarian path, I have learned a lot about life. For 8 years, it has been a rollercoaster ride fighting to raise money to help others and especially as a voluntary; it is not easy. I have always depended on others to help me including friends and family who volunteered their time. Raising money from foundations and institutions was almost impossible. It takes so much time and knowledge to get anything done. As a very creative and spiritual man, I managed to network with so many others on my path and they also helped me to achieve my dream.

My friends (mostly guys) would get dressed up as nuns and we would do performances together across Amsterdam. After each show, we would go into the crowd and collect money and sold little hearts (that were key-rings), made in South Africa. Also dressed as nuns, we would go to whatever festivals we could and sell wet kisses, just another way to raise money, all of which would go to Willen & Doen. I also worked together with various schools and we organised benefit parties and lots of shows, such great and colourful shows. The friendships that were developed within the group would stand the test of time. I believe over the last 10 years' thousands of people have walked with us.

Everyone has looked back at this time with amazing experiences and memories. It didn't matter if someone was gay, lesbian, black or white. Everybody was welcomed with open arms if they wanted to help. We have built two homes for orphans, which are self-sufficient and sponsored the Hospice for five years. However, it had to close due to internal politics as the male owner had started a new relationship with another man. The church involved (which was a big sponsor) didn't accept homosexuality as a lifestyle so stopped sponsoring it. Willen & Doen also opened a project in the Transkei, which included a preschool, a community centre, an orphanage and a permaculture vegetable garden. However, we did not get the permission from the local government to open the orphanage. It seemed that their social development policies ended up working against us.

Willen & Doen also financed three other preschools with money for vegetable gardens. Altogether we fed around a few hundred kids every day and created employment for 30 people of whom six still work for us. The projects which we sponsored and paid for the infrastructure are self-sufficient. Over the years we helped thousands of people.

Looking back, all I can say is that the Foundation that I started years ago represents key aspects of my values that I learned from my childhood. The most important lesson for me is that caring is about sharing. "If you do well to others then you will get nothing but goodness back". Nothing more; nothing less. If I look back at all the experiences I had over the last 10 years, I feel like I'm a billionaire.

The Statue of Christ, Rio de Janeiro, Brazil.

11

DIVERSITY IN LIFE

- ACCEPTANCE OF UNIVERSAL SEXUALITY AND CULTURAL DIVERSITY

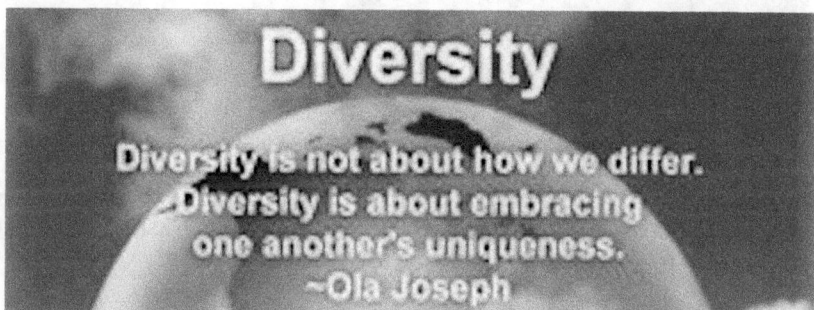

> *All of us who are openly gay are living and writing the history of our movement.*
>
> *We are no more - and no less - heroic than...Freedom Riders, Stonewall demonstrators, and environmentalists of the 20th century.*
>
> *We are ordinary people, living our lives, and trying as civil-rights activist Dorothy Cotton said, to 'fix what ain't right' in our society.*

— SENATOR TAMMY BALDWIN, USA

Australia - One of The Most Successful Multicultural Nations on Earth.

Australia is one of the most successful multicultural nations on Earth. More than seven million migrants have settled here over the past 70 years.

It's pretty impressive as a nation, and Australians on the whole; have come to love and respect the cultural diversity of our great nation. Australia has a solid history of taking immigrants, especially post World War II. We are basically a nation of Differents...

> **For all the Differents among us.**
>
> **Live Big.**
>
> **Live Bold.**
>
> **We need you.**

— GRETEL KILLEEN, AUTHOR, AWARD WINNING
TV HOST, COMIC, SOCIAL/POLITICAL
COMMENTATOR AND ZEBRA.

During the decade following the Vietnam War, Australia took more than 80,000 Vietnamese people many of them as refugees or what we call today "boat people". We opened our doors and our hearts and here we are recently voting in a conservative government based on a platform of "stopping the boats". It's quite ironic but sickening as it speaks to our lack of humanitarianism as a nation but not as a people.

This lack of humanitarianism is mostly fuelled by right-wing politicians in either party who promote ignorance and only know how to talk up fear and hate. Are we that stupid, I'd rather not think so but just short-sighted as a nation; as if we don't know any different. People who have Awakened don't hold these views. Fewer than 700 Australians reported Vietnam was their birthplace in the 1971 census, but that number grew to more than 80,000 15 years later.[46]

> We should indeed keep calm in the face of difference, and live our lives in a state of inclusion and wonder at the diversity of humanity.
>
> — GEORGE TAKEI

Bernard Salt, a well-known Australian social commentator, believes Australia can build a case to say that it is the most successful immigrant nation on Earth. He states the global community comprises 195 sovereign nations and if you take into consideration those nations who have a critical mass of ten million or more people; then in Australia's case, the proportion of our population born overseas is 28 per cent: almost seven million out of 24 million Australians. If you add the number of Aussies who have one parent born overseas, that proportion is closer to 40 per cent.[47]

These figures he says,

> Speak to a fundamental truth about the Australian people and nation. There is no other equivalent nation (meaning

with a critical mass of population) that has been as generous in absorbing migrants

— BERNARD SALT

SETTING MIGRATION PACE
Top 10 countries

Countries with more than 10m residents	Foreign-born population (%)	Population 2015	Population born abroad	Population born in country
Saudi Arabia	32	31,540,372	10,092,919	21,447,453
Australia	28	23,968,973	6,711,312	17,257,661
Canada	22	35,939,927	7,906,784	28,033,143
Kazakhstan	20	17,625,226	3,525,045	14,100,181
Germany	15	80,688,545	12,103,282	68,585,263
US	14	321,773,631	45,048,308	276,725,323
Britain	13	64,715,810	8,413,055	56,302,755
Spain	13	46,121,699	5,995,821	40,125,878
Belgium	12	11,299,192	1,355,903	9,943,289
France	12	64,395,345	7,727,441	56,667,904

Source UN

Setting Migration Pace Top 10 countries.

The only nation with a higher proportion is Saudi Arabia, where 10 million residents out of 32 million, or 32 per cent, were born abroad. But Saudi Arabia's foreign-born residents are guest workers who do not have the same sovereign rights as migrants.[48]

Australia's migrant proportion stands clear of other nations: in Canada, it is 22 per cent; in Germany, 15 per cent; in the US, 14 per cent; in Britain, 13 per cent. Our immigration story hasn't been without fault i.e., not being without ethnic tensions, division or racism. Nevertheless, we need to be proud as a nation, and to its credit, we have managed to do what no other nation has done. We have assimilated (blended into the greater urban mass) a great proportion of people within a short period of time, particularly since post-war Europe and recent economic booms.

When I talk about assimilating cultures, I refer to our ability to gently fuse together cultures, so that we grow with each other. By doing so, we take the best out of every culture and create something that is uniquely Australian, forever changing and subtlety new. Salt states that at the last census, 42 per cent of urban Sydney's population was born overseas. The proportion for New York, the great melting pot, is 29 per cent; for Paris, is 22 per cent; for Berlin, 13 per cent; for Tokyo, 2 per cent, for Shanghai, 1 per cent. **He says Australia stands apart.** Sydney stands apart. **We are different.**

Australia also has one of the highest permanent migration programmes in the world and remains at a ceiling of 190,000 for 2017-2018. The Department of immigration states that this is just over half our annual population growth per annum.[49]

Australia's immigration intake is approx. 14% that of the United States (which is approx.1.38 million in 2015). In literal terms, this means our immigration intake is approximately twice per capita that of the United States. Therefore, per person, Australia takes twice the number of foreign-born people in the USA. Some may say this puts upward pressure on our land and housing prices, especially in our largest cities. This may be true, but the positive benefits in terms of our economy and diversity in our culture far outnumber any negative ones.[50]

Our Most Ideal Path Moving Forward...

Our most ideal path moving forward is celebrating diversity in life!

What are the ideal features that a nation must personify to ensure that sexual and cultural diversity is respected and enshrined in our societies? There are only four things essential for our personal and global well-being. That is equality, civil rights, our freedom, and autonomy.

> The only queer people are those who don't love anybody
>
> — RITA MAE BROWN

Like Queerness itself, being seen as different by others at various times in our human history has resulted in people being denied their existence, succumbing to atrocious fear and persecution, but also having had fabulous times of celebration, enduring love, unity, and humility. This just means we are forced more than the average person to try and find ways to integrate and orientate ourselves in the world. Much like stealth we try and shield ourselves from the external dissatisfaction and judgement of others.

If you think about it, what has been the most dominant patriarchal force on our planet? Without question, it has been white-middle class men. They haven't had to view the world through a different lens thus taking everything for granted, sometimes with judgement and sometimes with hate. I say this with kindness as I am also such a man, except I'm a man who loves other men. In saying this, I just wish there were more people out there who have the courage to speak from their hearts and aren't ashamed to express anything meaningful or spiritual in their lives. In essence, we only create the behaviour and culture we model and therefore deserve.

It makes sense when you think about it, but once we all aspire to true gender equality; we won't view the world through a lens of difference, only a lens of commonality or universality i.e., the quality of involving or being shared by all people or things in the world or in a particular group (Wikipedia, 2017).

The brilliant colours of Diversity.

Our search for finding meaning in life often leads us back to discovering ourselves. We can bring about change by changing ourselves, and it's never too late. When the Government can create and change laws that govern our personal lives, how we live, who we love, our civil liberties and we are increasingly questioning the integrity of religion; it is imperative that we become more aware of what is sacred and spiritually important to us. Let's all celebrate the Queerness of life itself and stop perpetrating unwarranted, and outdated judgments, values, and beliefs. For we are all created equal, and we must ensure that this is enshrined in our most basic determination to create one global society, for the betterment of Humanity.

Two elephants each with only one tusk, they embody the imperfection of life and the unity, love, wisdom, strength and eternity of a diverse society.

The struggle for LGBTQI human rights

The struggle for LGBTQI (Lesbian, Gay, Bisexual, Transgender, Queer and Intersex) human rights are universal in the world and spans such a degree of acceptance from persecution (as in Chechnya, Uganda and with ISIS) to total freedom, to love openly as in most progressive societies on earth.

At least in 33 of Africa's 55 states, homosexuality is illegal. In Mauritania, Sudan and parts of Nigeria and Somalia, it can be punishable by death.[45] This struggle is essential for our shared Humanity whether you like or not. It's purely about human rights as opposed to the selfless right of right-wing individuals and government to control our destiny which is often based on an extreme religious view.

The Australian Government (including our Prime Minister Malcolm Turnbull) has been totally explicit in this, failing to speak out against atrocities towards LGBTQI people. Countries like Russia and their President Putin, are no better off in their treatment of LGBTQI people and especially their role in Chechnya. They took no interventionist action against the rising tide of brutality where hundreds of "suspected gay people" were rounded up, put in secret prisons, tortured and even killed by thugs i.e., the lowest of low-life men you could imagine. There's nothing manly and by no means, no pride in that, it's just men displaying the ugliest, abusive and evil side of their Humanity.

> Why is it that, as a culture, we are more comfortable seeing two men holding guns than holding hands?

— AUTHOR ERNEST J. GAINES

This is offset against a 50-year struggle for LGBTQI rights which

started with the Stonewall riots in New York City in 1969. Riots at the Stonewall Inn in Christopher Street, New York, marked the new beginning for homosexual liberation and the struggle for equal rights. Instead of seeking to be recognised according to the norms of the society around them, gays and lesbians fought for liberation and realisation on their own terms.

Woman Carnavale Rio De Janeiro.

In Australia, the 78'ers were the first group of gay and lesbian people to be arrested for holding a protest march for gay rights in 1978 which then birthed the beginning of the famous Gay and Lesbian Mardi Gras in Sydney. I had the pleasure of working with one of the most authentic and knowledgeable persons in the HIV sector in Australia, a beautiful man named Ian (Ross) Duffin. He works as a part-time Consumer Participation Representative in the former HIV service I used to manage.

Ross was one of the 78'ers, and we worked in the same building (the former Police Station in Darlinghurst now a health facility) where he was arrested in 1978.

Ross had lived in San Francisco when the HIV/AIDS epidemic hit and was also involved in the early response to HIV in Australia. As humble as he is, Ross has been one of the most inspiring people in my life. Besides being one of the 78'ers, you could best describe Ross as one the most intelligent and articulate men you could ever meet. Ross

A photograph of the famous singing Cowboy Times Square, New York City.

is a researcher, writer, an activist and as an Elder within our community, a beholder of a wealth of stories; a man whose story should be told.

In saying this, the events of the Stonewall riots and the 78'ers are seen within the context of the modern Gay and Lesbian rights movement, but one of the first Gay organisations was established in Denmark immediately post world war II. LGBT Denmark – *The Danish National Organization for Gay Men, Lesbians, Bisexuals and Transgender persons* was founded in 1948 as the main Danish LGBT rights organisation.

Their aim is to work for gay, lesbian, bisexual and transgendered people's political, social, cultural and workplace equality at every level of society. 1969 after applying for twenty years, they were officially registered as an association, thereby recognised by Authorities. In 1950 it already had close to 15000 members. [46]

> We seek to work against discrimination and to function as a dedicated lobby for the purpose of influencing lawmakers, for example in areas such as marriage, adoption, the artificial insemination of lesbians, and rights for transpersons.

— LGBT DENMARK

The Marriage Equality Postal Vote

The Marriage Equality postal vote was a farce! The Australian Government maintained a right-wing view of marriage when most other developed societies on earth moved forward to create constitutional change for equality. It's been totally futile and without excuse; especially when polls have indicated a majority of Australians supported Marriage Equality.

Marriage Equality Movement - it's bizarre that Australia was still debating the issue in late 2017.

The Government proceeded to hold a Marriage Equality postal vote, more as a delay tactic instead of addressing this important civil rights issue. In essence, it no longer became about our right to marry but everything else unrelated to Marriage Equality. In many respects, it turned into a public debate to prove our value and worth in society - our lives, relationships, identity, and worth!

What was most disconcerting is that our Prime Minister presides over the largest LGBTQI community in Australia (Division of Wentworth). Mr. Turnbull had the power to overrule this decision and allow his party to have a conscience vote. The cost of holding this postal vote was an estimated $121 million dollars. This money could have been better spent on addressing poverty, housing affordability, domestic violence or renewable energy. I believe Mr. Turnbull didn't have the courage and dignity to act in the best interests of his constituents.

During this time, I witnessed so many of my gay and lesbian friends (including myself) feel like they had become the victims of something much more sinister e.g. racism, homophobia, denigrating safe schools and same-sex rights to parenthood, raising children and our human rights generally. None of these issues had anything to do with Marriage

Equality. The Australian Christian Lobby and their supporters were very powerful, well-resourced and funded. Their attacks on social media using an "absolute fear" type advertising campaign, were inaccurate and outdated. The hard-line views held by our Prime Minister's party were actively promoting a potential racial, homophobic and political divide in Australia, like nothing we had ever seen before.

> *I hate the word homophobia. It's not a phobia. You're not scared. You're an asshole*
>
> Morgan Freeman

What added fuel to the fire, were many Australian churches which were so implicit in this. Their actions were callous and un-Christ-like especially in their support for an extended public campaign. The Christ I know would NEVER have acted in this way. Essentially, the Marriage Equality postal vote, "played out our lives in public". It was a cruel act of negligence that was attempting to set back any idea of social reform in Australia.

Our descendants will hopefully look back on this time with such disbelief and wonder how the world continued to discriminate against homosexuals, created such intolerance for transgender people, people from different cultural backgrounds and even women for that matter! I'd rather know on my death bed (whenever that time comes), I was remembered as someone who has made a difference in this world. If appeasing others for your own political gain makes you sleep better at night, so be it!

> When all Americans are treated as equal, no matter who they are or whom they love, we are all more free
>
> — BARACK OBAMA

Being The Only Gay in the Village

Being the only gay in the village is an experience that is deeply personal and resonates with me, especially in the early days when I first came out Gay in 1985. It seemed that I was "the only gay in the village" among most of my heterosexual friends and often, the first gay person that people had met. As far as I knew, I was the only gay person in my nursing group and on the whole, was generally accepted. However, I was often the barb of jokes from the boys - misunderstood and under-valued - all a part of the course back then.

It was the beginning of the HIV/AIDS epidemic and I usually had the same script in my head to explain what it was like to be gay, "I'm possibly not the first gay man you've ever met" and the script went on to explain, "no, neither person in a gay relationship plays the man or woman" and even for heterosexual men it often ended with, "hey mate, you're a pretty nice guy for the first gay guy I've ever met, but as long as you don't come on to me, it's ok". I couldn't help the feeling that this was often stated with such fear like they were walking with their back to the wall. The stigma Gay men experienced from Heterosexual men was particularly focussed on the concept of anal sex. Hence in my nursing days, the barb of jokes from the other guys was always sexual in nature.

> I think being gay is a blessing, and it's something I am thankful for every single day
>
> — ANDERSON COOPER

Move forward 30 years, so many heterosexual men I seem to meet now (whether they identify as men who have sex with men, bisexual, married or discreet) or from what their girlfriends or wives tell me; have experimented with their sexuality and/or their sexual practices. I find that empowering and also honest; that men can be submissive and open to experimenting with their female partners. There is nothing wrong with that, for what goes on in the bedroom is no one else's business, but it doesn't always stay there. In this modern age of cam sex, mobile phone videos, widespread access to pornography (especially for younger people) and the power of storytelling, nothing seems private anymore. The positive reframe for me is, I guess all men are created equal, we all get the same pleasure (leave that to your imagination).

> It takes some intelligence and insight to figure out you're gay and then a tremendous amount of balls to live it and live it proudly
>
> — JASON BATEMAN

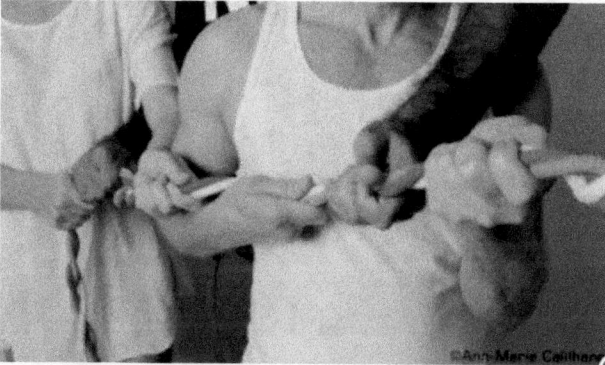

Our struggle is universal for we all seek acceptance to belong. We must all strive to pull Humanity out of the endless abyss - to Salvation. Ann-Marie Calihanna Photography 2016

The Final Frontier

The final frontier in terms of equality for many LGBTQI people and their supporters was about Marriage Equality. However, I'd like to think that there is so much work yet to be done. The final frontier for all of us, is about how we evolve our human consciousness, focussed on looking outward into the world (not inward) with a sense of greater social and global responsibility.

Some years after I first arrived in Sydney, I did some voluntary work for the Gay and Lesbian Legal Rights Lobby. I remember researching about gay partnership laws in Norway to develop a survey that could be used to ascertain our community views on this issue at the time. The Lobby was mostly staffed by lawyers, and I think I was one of the few non-lawyers at the time and although it was interesting, it had its own set of politics. I've always felt honoured to be of Norwegian heritage and even more amazed at how progressive they were as a nation when I first visited some thirty years ago. Even comparing Norway then to Australia now, they seemed to have left us light years behind.

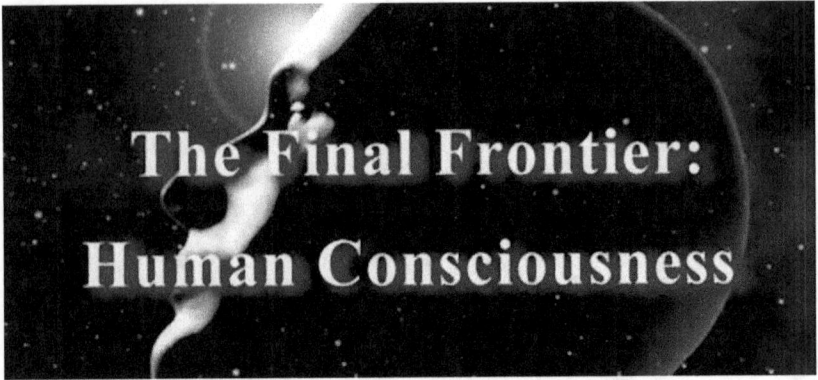

The Final Frontier: Human Consciousness

In the 1990's, I remember my brother saying stuff like, "I don't understand why your mob continues to protest", and I'd respond with, "We protest because we don't have equal rights, the same rights as you!". To his credit, he has evolved in his views and seems to get it now. Fast forward thirty years, Australia has made enormous gains in terms of equality. Although this wouldn't have been possible, without the LGBTQI community advocating, marching and fighting for change to hundreds of pieces of legislation over the years. This finally culminated in the acknowledgement of same-sex relationships, as part of our De Facto Legislation in 2008.

> The **law** requires that you and your former partner, who may be of the same or opposite sex, had a relationship as a couple living together on a genuine domestic basis
>
> — A DE FACTO RELATIONSHIP AS DEFINED IN SECTION 4AA OF THE FAMILY LAW ACT 1975

Our campaign for Marriage Equality drew to an end on Wednesday 15th November. **Justice was finally served with Australians voting for Marriage Equality, 62% for YES and 38% for NO.** The Australian Parliament finally passed the bill as law on Thursday 7th December 2017. It passed with 154 votes in favour and four votes against it (after almost 29 hours of debate and 118 speeches). I shared this my moment with mum and realising the reality of this struggle had come to an end; I gave mum a big hug and cried. Thirty years of debating, hoping, marching, protesting and yearning came to an end.

> Is the culmination of our agenda: *the coming together after a struggle.* It captures our aspirations for a fair and truthful relationship with the people of Australia and a better future for our children based on justice and self-determination...*they will walk in two worlds* and their culture will be a *gift to their country.*
>
> — ULURU STATEMENT FROM THE HEART

The passing of Marriage Equality into Law was a defining moment in Australian history. Guess what, nothing has changed; the sky hasn't fallen down and love always prevails over fear. Seeing our Parliament united gave me so much hope, that our great nation can achieve anything.

Let's build on this momentum and start the counter-revolution for change. It may seem impossible to achieve right now, but unity is deservedly much more exciting!

The beams of golden light are sharp and flickering like flames, illuminating the darkness of our struggles. Justice is honourable and gives us faith in the unknown. It always speaks to what is constitutionally fair and honest. Our bountiful land offers promise.

Our longing to fix 'what ain't right' in our world inspires so much hope. However, there are new struggles on the horizon. One such endeavour aspires to the exquisiteness of my being and is what is destined and rightful in our beautiful country.

The birth of our new nation and restoration of its soul is now in sight; it's what our self-determination is all about. It's what's rightful and speaks to the traditional owners of our land. It's time to flourish and renew the notion of the Republic of Australia, the great Southern land.

— DAVID SHAUN LARSEN

When all Americans are treated as equal, no matter who they are or whom they love, we are all more free

Marriage Equality Ambassadors Magda Szubanski, Ian Thorpe and Christine Forster on the Lawns of Parliament House in Canberra today. Picture Kym Smith

The Acceptance of Universal Sexuality

The acceptance of Universal Sexuality is something deeply profound. Being of a Norwegian heritage, I'm so blessed with very few "hang-ups', liberal tolerance, an open mind, sexual liberation and acceptance of diversity. It's something so innate in my DNA it's hard to describe, possibly the closest is how people identify with their Indigenous culture. I am very proud to share the cultural heritage of a land that has a long history of acceptance of gay and lesbian rights. It makes so much sense to me now when I remember my grandfather Vilhelm at the earliest age of 4 would give me a birthday card addressed to "Dear Daisy". It's a nickname my grandparents gave me but for him it was his way of being endearing and soft with his masculinity.

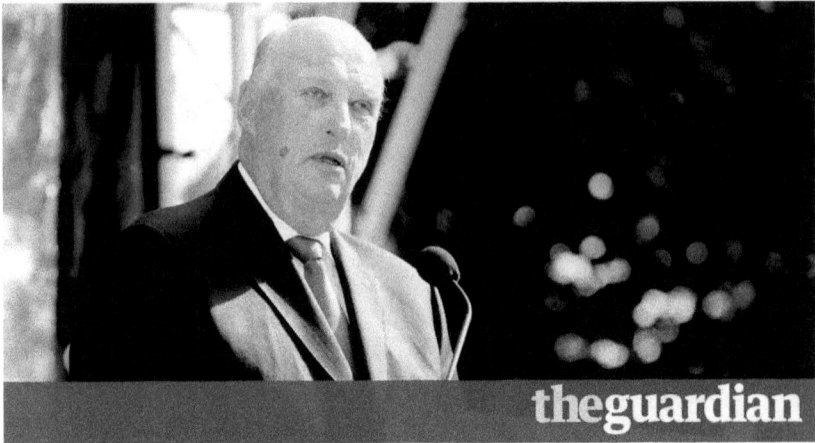

King Harold of Norway. The Norwegian King gave an amazing speech on love and diversity.

In 2016 the King of Norway in a famous speech to celebrate their cultural diversity said,

> Norway is a place for everyone, regardless of where they come from, their religious beliefs, sexual preferences or even their musical tastes. Norwegians come from the north of the country, from the middle, from the south and all the other regions. Norwegians are also immigrants from Afghanistan, Pakistan, Poland, Sweden, Somalia and Syria.
>
> **Norwegians are girls who love girls, boys who love boys, and boys and girls who love each other.** Norwegians believe in God, Allah, everything and nothing. Norwegians like Grieg, Kygo, Hellbillies and Kari Bremnes. In other words, Norway is you. Norway is us.
>
> — KING HAROLD OF NORWAY

This was said with such proud laughter and cheer from the crowd but left me so sad thinking; imagine our Prime Minister or Governor-

General of Australia saying that, it just wouldn't happen here. Hence, what does this say about our country and what it stands for? For me, it says a few things: -

- We are often very complacent as people;
- We are not always concerned about the welfare of those who are more disadvantaged or marginalised as people;
- We tend to feed our apathy or inaction around challenging political, economic, and cultural conditions.
- If we do care, we'd rather wait until the next election cycle to make a passive protest i.e., by then other issues have grabbed our attention.

On the whole, I embrace the U for **Universal Sexuality** (not being defined as anything). Universal sexuality is for anyone who doesn't want to be boxed into a category anymore, it speaks for the Universal sexuality of the 21st Century.

I truly believe that those people who feed hate, truly love nobody and in many ways, I'm so proud of the path I have walked and thankful for it every day. We all seek at some level to make a difference in this world, it's now time we make the effort together, to push ourselves to understand the world at large. It's about our solace and understanding.

Everyone has different ways of finding solace and understanding; for me studying Astrology and doing Astrology charts, has always been my unconditional gift for others. As someone who has always felt different, not only in terms of my sexuality but also spiritually; it has always been in my nature to question everything. Therefore, no wonder I have turned to the long-standing tradition of Astrology to find meaning and recognition. I may be gay or a man who has sex with men, but sometimes I prefer to be Queer who isn't.

David with Willen & Doen friends and volunteers - Nuns on a
mission to raise money for the Willen & Doen cause,
Amsterdam Netherlands.

It is through knowledge and truth that enable us to
understand our nature and the world at large. If ignorance is bliss, then who are we to complain about our sad
state of affairs. The affairs that decent, common-sense
people talk about.

However talk is cheap unless we strive to live meaningful lives, without distraction. If we bury our heads in
the sand, it forces us to see nothing but darkness. To only
find meaning in nothing.

Nothing but a care for the distractions of life that feed
our ego rather than our minds and spirit. As our senses
shut down, we end up cowering to others who can
control us, and they say everything you want them
to say.

It's numbing to the soul. We need to dream big; for our
moral protests are barely being heard.

See my friend, if we attempt to understand what is broken both inside us and out; our awareness can expand right to the horizon. But even then, we will not go far! It's only when we see that our wings are also broken, can we understand that we have the capacity to fly.

Through flight, we can soar and soar like angles in full flight. Their flight is our flight and once we truly understand this; we can become dancers on the world stage and possibly choreograph our next amazing journey through the tiniest eye of the Universe.

— DAVID SHAUN LARSEN

See when we fly, we can start to see many things that others cannot. Come and join me. What I see is a grand vision for the Great Southern Land. A nation that embraces our diversity, decent people who are searching for the deeper meaning to their lives and many people or souls with "with eternally deep eyes" striving to make a difference in this world but we don't hear of them, over the voices of our actors and sports stars. It's not their fault it's ours!

I have a lot hope for change, but it's tenuous. If we are to actualise the notion of self-governance as a Republic, it starts now. At its heart, I have great respect for the **Cultural Diversity of this great land, as it always has and always will be.**

An image shows the Indigenous Multiculturalism of Australia with 250 First People Nations.

12

MENTAL HEALTH AND SUBSTANCE USE

- RESILIENCE, THE USE OF DRUGS AND ALCOHOL AND THE SEARCH FOR RECOVERY

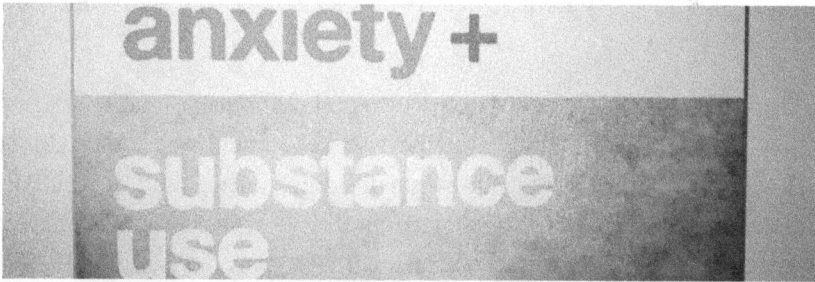

> *In this busy modernized age, it's easy to be blind to the light all around us. You see, there truly are real angels living among us that look just like you and I.*
>
> *If you pay attention, you can spot one because they're quite easy to find. They're the souls with the eternally deep eyes that always act like something is broken inside, but fail to realize it's just their wings.*

— SUSY KASSEM, WRITER, AND FILMMAKER

The Angels Living Among Us

Wow, I find this quote so profound!!! The essential purpose of this chapter is to raise awareness and understanding of two significant issues, our mental wellbeing or health and substance use in our society. In Australia, it is estimated that 45 per cent of people will experience a mental health condition in their lifetime and Australia has one of the highest rates of alcohol and drug use in the western world. Are we a nation of alcoholics? What does that say about us as a nation, our collective understanding and destiny, our self-esteem and how we respond as a society and individuals to those afflicted or most in need?

> **In richer countries...the biggest single source of misery is mental illness**
>
> — WORLD HAPPINESS REPORT, SEE CHAPTER 5

Every person has their own constructs and opinions around the definition of mental wellbeing and the use of alcohol and other drugs. However, too often people are stigmatised in society, and this results in discrimination, the formation of cultural myths, social exclusion, and judgement. Any person who deals with an acute or chronic mental health issue or misuses alcohol and drugs is still a citizen of our society, has their own lived experience or story in life, belongs to a circle of friends and family, and ultimately deserves our respect and compassion without judgement.

> Far away there in the sunshine are my highest aspirations. I may not reach them, but I can look up and see their beauty, believe in them, and try to follow where they lead
>
> — LOUISA MAY ALCOTT

Those who judge people with mental health issues and/or those who use and misuse alcohol and drugs, often forget about the fragility of life. Judgement of others is often based on a persons' own lived experience, intolerance of anything different and for many this may be founded on quite a narrow view of life i.e., whether a life of privilege or one's own societal status; ingrained religious doctrines; limited understanding of racial, cultural and sexual diversity; lack of awareness of those people living with disability and recipients of social welfare.

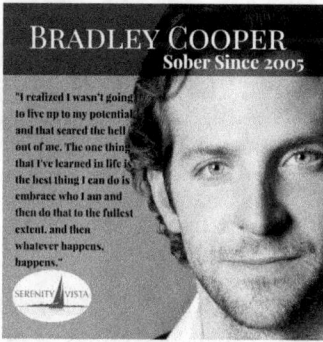

BRADLEY COOPER
Sober Since 2005

"I realized I wasn't going to live up to my potential and that scared the hell out of me. The one thing that I've learned in life is the best thing I can do is embrace who I am and then do that to the fullest extent, and then whatever happens, happens."

SERENITY VISTA

I often think about how fragile our lives are, how at any moment something can happen. Whether a sudden death, shock event or atrocity, accident, illness, trauma, relationship difficulties and breakups, betrayal, heartfelt mistakes and of course misunderstandings. Our mortality is a given, and without doubt, life can throw you many curve balls and at any stage. The bleating obvious is that as a response to these life events, we are all vulnerable to a mental health disorder and/or the use or misuse of alcohol and drugs.

My personal and professional journey

During my lifetime, I have experienced bouts of anxiety and depression and in the past treated with conventional medicine, although not the case now. In my mid 30's I went through a very dark, intense and depressive phase of my life that lasted for nearly 3 years. Depression is something that is so indescribable, because it is painful and the inner turmoil you feel is soul destroying, as it kind of eats away at you on the inside. For all appearances, you may as well be going through life like stealth because everyone else observes an altered reality compared to what you are actually feeling. I can understand why silence can be golden because you don't want to burden your loved ones with your negative dialogue, thoughts, and feelings. Although those closest to you might be able to notice personality or mood changes/swings, they can't see or understand the degree or intensity of the inner pain you feel.

As a society, it's far healthier that we are acknowledging depression and naming it for what it actually is, especially in men and with our Indigenous people. What's healthy, is that we are encouraging people to become better educated, seek help and ask for support. However, in reality, the act of reaching out especially with family

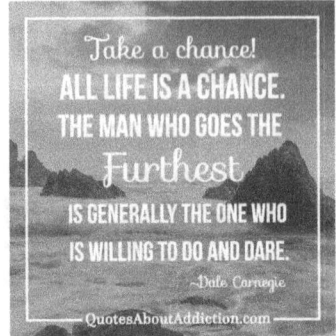

Take a chance! ALL LIFE IS A CHANCE. THE MAN WHO GOES THE *Furthest* IS GENERALLY THE ONE WHO IS WILLING TO DO AND DARE. —Dale Carnegie

QuotesAboutAddiction.com

and friends, can start to test their true kindness, patience, and skill in dealing with depression. Most people often want to project their own personal impressions and views about your life; whether what they see is functional or dysfunctional or a mix of both. This is the nature of the double-edged sword with depression. It requires a lot of commitment, non-judgement, and understanding to stick with your loved one in order to provide the long-term support needed until the person has the resilience to recover. More on that later but I have found Traditional Chinese Medicine (TCM) to be my preventative tool, not only to support my wellbeing but also support my long-term resilience and quest for recovery.

> The ultimate measure of a man is not where he stands in moments of comfort and convenience, but where he stands at times of challenge and controversy
>
> — DR. MARTIN LUTHER KING, JR.

Over the course of my adult life, I have also used alcohol regularly and experimented or used various drugs at periods of time such as

Cannabis, MDMA and Crystal Meth. So on a personal level, I understand about recovery and relapse prevention and have the lived experience; which now enables me to write about it. It takes a lot of courage to admit this, as many wouldn't. Yet I've been successful in life and achieved many things and walked a courageous path that many others wouldn't have even dared to walk. We all have our faults and weaknesses; so please leave your own personal judgment out of the equation. I've had an amazing life journey, and every experience has enabled me to grow. Some experiences such as alcohol and drug use have provided boundless opportunities for insight and transformational growth and some of the most addictive and self-hating experiences. Everyone's journey in life is uniquely different, judge only yourself and your behaviours for judgment itself are reserved for the unrighteous.

Our quest for drug reform in this country is not about encouraging drug use but is more about normalising what is already normal behaviour.

We can't always change human behaviour, but we can give people the help and tools to understand their behaviour, reduce harm and sooth the pain and suffering they may feel.

It's ultimately about removing the judgment and stigma created by those who believe they are more righteous than others.

— DAVID SHAUN LARSEN

Nevertheless, I have the professional and lived experience, and it's something to be treasured, especially when you rise to the truth - don't judge, scratch beneath the surface and there's a reason, a person with emotions and a past.

> There are a thousand hacking at the branches of evil to one who is striking at the root
>
> — HENRY DAVID THOREAU

I often think people like me don't need to walk the conventional path or straight line because we've walked it already.

The Universe is kind of initiating or challenging us (giving us a valuable experience) to grow and develop resilience. Viewing this through a spiritual lens, many Old souls or those Awakening I come across in my personal life, are always more sensitive in nature and quite often have experienced mental health and/or drug and alcohol themes throughout their lives. They also struggle to fit in, for they experience life through being different. The indifference people have towards one another is what is destructive. In many respects, they're the souls with the eternally deep eyes.

> *They're the souls with the eternally deep eyes that always act like something is broken inside, but fail to realize it's just their wings*
>
> — SUSY KASSEM, WRITER, AND FILMMAKER

"The priority of any addict is to anaesthetize the pain of living to ease the passage of day with some purchased relief."

Professionally over the course of my career, I have also been lucky working with many people who have experienced mental health issues and drug misuse, and it has given me an amazing insight and understanding around their lived experience and vulnerabilities. If we scratch beneath the surface you realise that there are many reasons why people use or misuse drugs and alcohol and it's correlation to mental health issues. Therefore, it makes sense that when you view these issues through a different lens, you start to develop compassion and a more complete understanding of that person's life, but that's only if you care to take the time. The various causes are many: -

- Childhood Trauma
- Post Traumatic Stress Disorder
- Grief and Loss Issues
- Abandonment from parents
- Relationship difficulties and breaks ups
- Sexual abuse and violence
- Stress and anxiety
- Poor self-esteem
- Peer pressure especially in teenage years
- Social isolation and discrimination
- Feeling of not fitting in and being different
- For some, it may even be escapism and adventure
- Others it might be the search for pleasure

" No-one can make you feel inferior without your consent

— ELEANOR ROOSEVELT

Remember life is fragile, and some people are more fragile much like an orchid, and they may not recover from the hard knocks. Do we blame the orchid? Or do we defend its fragility and have compassion for its existence and wellbeing. Within this construct, people also relapse as we are only human, and no one is perfect. So much of our ability to comprehend what relapse is about is intricately linked to the relapse prevention cycle.

Relapse prevention aims to try and reduce or eliminate drug use - the path through the stages of change is not smooth for many people. Initially, it may involve understanding your readiness to change just by being familiar with the stages of change. Contemplating change yet having ambivalence is a healthy start. Focussing on the meaningfulness of our social interactions, understanding our emotional triggers and the development of positive coping strategies all help.

Remember there is always hope from what may seem an ingrained cycle of addiction. Every person is different, what motivates them is different, and this takes time, commitment, and courage. It may take months or even years, but people with substance misuse and mental health problems *can* and *do* get better. It involves a lifelong development of coping strategies and skills.

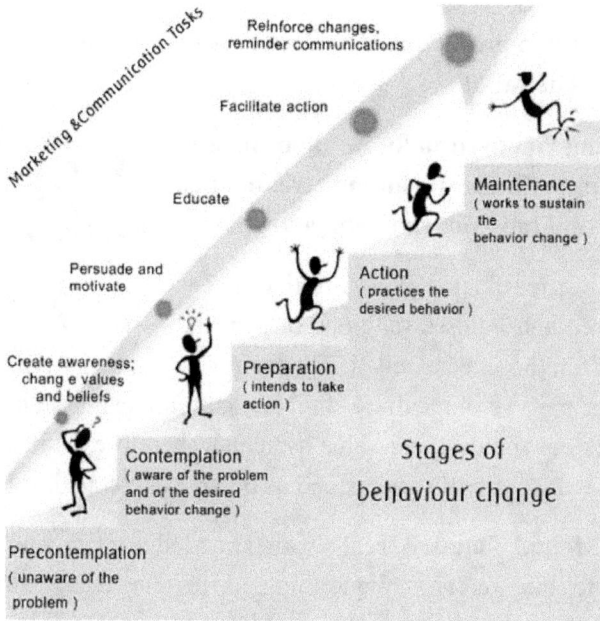

Stages of behaviour change.

> Good people are good because they've come to wisdom through failure. We get very little wisdom from success, you know... One who doesn't try cannot fail and become wise

— WILLIAM SAROYAN

THE PURPOSE of this part of the chapter is also to provide the reader with resources that they can access for further information. Three useful resources are included:

- **SANE Australia**
- **mindhealthconnect**
- **Cracks In The Ice - Crystal Methamphetamine**

DAVID SHAUN LARSEN

Fact vs myth: mental illness basics (This information is courtesy of SANE Australia)

Everything you need to know about mental health and illness including treatments, support, and how you can help yourself [51]

sane

AUSTRALIA

Myths are often related to a narrative that is both sacred and holds a religious or spiritual meaning for those who tell it. By their very nature, Myths innately become a part of our culture and our cultural expression then also influences our mindset and value systems. Therefore, Myths are often stories that are currently understood as being exaggerated or fictitious.

Fact 1: Mental illness is real - Our knowledge of mental illness is incomplete, but we can say one thing for certain: mental illness isn't laziness, attention-seeking, bad diet, mental, physical or spiritual weakness or a failure of character. Mental illness is illness, as real as cancer, diabetes, HIV and heart disease.

Fact 2: Anyone can develop a mental illness - There is no immunity to mental illness. Not everyone develops a mental illness during their lives, but anyone could. At least 45% of us will experience a mental illness during our lives. And that's just anxiety, mood disorders and substance addictions in people aged 16-85. Add in young people, schizophrenia, eating disorders, personality disorders and more and the figure is likely far higher.

Fact 3: At least 20% of adults are affected by mental illness every year - Anxiety disorders are the most common, followed by depression. A significant number of Australians are also affected by personality disorders, eating disorders, psychotic illnesses like schizophrenia, and more. Some people have more than one diagnosis, and far too many Australians go undiagnosed.

Fact 4: Four million Australians are affected by complex mental illness - At least 690,000 Australians live with complex mental illness

198

(CMI), but an experience like CMI affects the lives of many people around the person with symptoms. For each person with CMI, it's likely that five other people — families, friends, partners, colleagues and more — are affected. That makes four million Australians affected.

Fact 5: Some Australians are more likely to be affected than others: -

- Indigenous Australians experience much higher rates of psychological distress than the general population and lower access to mental health services.
- LGBTQI+ people experience very high rates of depression and psychological distress and are the most at-risk group in Australia for suicide.
- Mental illness is not more common in rural and remote areas than in cities, but rates of suicide are much higher, services are harder to access and stigma can be higher.
- One in seven children aged 4-17 have experienced a mental illness and over a quarter of Australians aged 16-24 are experiencing a mental illness at any given time. Many people who live with mental illness first experience symptoms during adolescence.

Identifying with one or more of these groups doesn't mean you will become ill. If anything it should empower the people around you to be more educated and understand that there is just a higher prevalence among these various risk groups.

Fact 6: The causes of mental illness are complex - There isn't one simple, obvious thing, like a virus or bacteria, that causes mental illness, and that makes the causes hard to work out. For some mental illnesses, like schizophrenia and bipolar disorder, it's possible to inherit a predisposition — a greater likelihood that you'll develop the disorder.

For others, there seems to be no genetic link at all. But even then it doesn't mean you'll get sick. The likelihood of developing a mental illness is influenced by a complex combination of genetic, neurological, developmental, environmental, socio-economic, cultural and life experience and other factors.

Fact 7: There's no link between mental illness and creativity - Experiencing mental illness doesn't make you more creative, and being creative doesn't make you more likely to experience a mental illness. Likewise, getting treatment for mental illness doesn't reduce your creativity, although the side-effects of some medicines can affect you.

What is Recovery?

This information is courtesy of mindhealthconnect (2017).

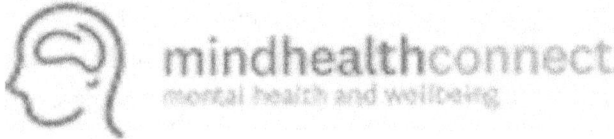

What is mindhealthconnect? mindhealthconnect is the easy way to find mental health and wellbeing information, support and services from Australia's leading health providers, together in one place. Supported by the Australian Government, mindhealthconnect helps you to find the information you can trust. Start now with the **Guided search or Mental Health A-Z** [52]

When you're talking about mental health, recovery is about living a satisfying life, in spite of facing mental health challenges. There are a range of services available that can help you do this. The first step is to see your doctor, who can give you advice and refer you to some helpful local services.

Recovery is about our ability to live a satisfying life, Equipped
with our resilience to face the challenges ahead.

What is Recovery? The majority of people who are diagnosed with a
mental illness recover, but it can be difficult to predict when, or to what
extent, you are going to get better. Recovery is about the whole of your
life, not just your symptoms. It involves:

- Finding hope, and developing your self-esteem and resilience
- Having a sense of purpose and meaning in your life
- Building healthy relationships with people in your community
- Gaining independence in your life.

Recovery is not the same as a cure. It makes sense to many people
because it concentrates on you as a person, rather than just a set of
symptoms. Recovery from using drugs and alcohol is still similar but it
is often just one part of a long and complex recovery process.

> When people enter treatment for a substance use disorder, addiction has often taken over their lives. The compulsion to get drugs, take drugs, and experience the effects of drugs has dominated their every waking moment, and abusing drugs has taken the place of all the things they used to enjoy doing. It has disrupted how they function in their family lives, at work, and in the community, and has made them more likely to suffer from other serious illnesses. Because addiction can affect so many aspects of a person's life, treatment must address the needs of the whole person to be successful. This is why the best programs incorporate a variety of rehabilitative services into their comprehensive treatment regimens. Treatment counsellors may select from a menu of services for meeting the specific medical, psychological, social, vocational, and legal needs of their patients to foster their recovery from addiction.

— DRUGS, BRAINS, AND BEHAVIOR: THE SCIENCE
OF ADDICTIONBEHAVIOR: THE SCIENCE OF
ADDICTION, THE NATIONAL INSTITUTE ON DRUG
ABUSE ADVANCING ADDICTION SCIENCE

Latest Resource

Cracks In The Ice - Crystal Methamphetamine

Methamphetamine use in Australia

Percentage of the population who used methamphetamine at least once in the 12 months prior to the 2013 survey (age 14 and over).

Australian average:
2.1%

NT: 2.8%*

QLD: 2.3%

WA: 3.8%

SA: 2.2%

NSW: 1.4%

ACT: 2.2%

VIC: 1.9%

TAS: 3.0%

*Estimate has a relative standard error of 25% to 50% and should be used with caution

Source: AIHW, 2013 National Drug Strategy Household Survey

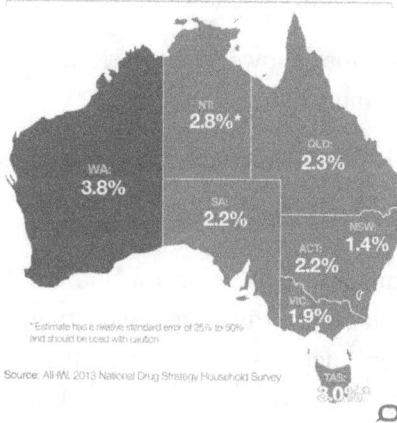

Facts and Community Toolkit - Cracks in the Ice is an online toolkit providing trusted, evidence-based, and up-to-date information and resources about crystal methamphetamine (ice) for the Australian community *(family and friends, schools and health professionals)*

Visit https://cracksintheice.org.au/how-many-people-use-ice

What is Resilience?

What is Resilience? From my experience, resilience is about our ability and capacity to recover from mental illness and/or alcohol and drug use and the various tools that you might use to assist with recovery and your wellness. Wellness for me is not that there is an absence of a mental illness and/or alcohol and drug use, but it's more about what you see as your quest for feeling a sense of purpose in your life. This is very dependent on your definition of wellness:

- What is it for you that gives you an overall sense of well-being?

- What is for you that ensures your optimal health and wellbeing?

- What is for you that allows you to achieve your desired equilibrium?

- What is it for you that allows you to prioritise yourself and ensure optimal self-management?

- What is the mechanism that enables you to advocate and participate in the delivery of your health care to ensure wellbeing?

> I have managed depression on and off for the last 30 years. Notice how I use the word 'manage'. I could say 'suffer from' depression but when you say 'manage depression' you actually have control of the matter...yes some days it is more unmanageable than others. However, you have to own the demon in order to conquer it and manage it; so it has fewer impacts on your day to day functioning.
>
> As for medication, anti-depressants et al, my opinion is that all these tablets do is suppress thoughts and emotions instead of trying to tackle them. Suppression just makes you feel worse. Hence, my alternative medicine includes going to gym, having a sex life, eat reasonably well and get creative with interest in art, gardening, music, etc. And oh yeah...my resilience is that I've come through life intact and every day I reflect on its fragility.
>
> — REFLECTIONS FROM SCOTTY A DEAR FRIEND
> AND KINDRED SPIRIT

I took this picture in Liberia in 2005, and it is so symbolic for me about resilience - finding the tools to help us survive and live life.

For tools on positive thinking, please refer to **Chapter 19: *Our New Hope** - A Toolkit for spiritual success and fulfilment.*

13

DIS-ABILITY

- PEOPLE WITH ABILITY WHO ARE BORN TO CHALLENGE OUR PERCEPTIONS ABOUT LIFE

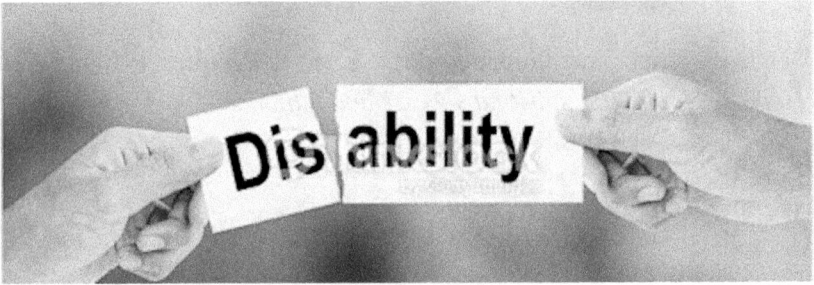

" It is a lonely existence to be a child with a disability which no-one can see or understand, you exasperate your teachers, you disappoint your parents, and worst of all you know that you are not just stupid.

— SUSAN HAMPSHIRE

PEOPLE WHO ARE BORN with or acquire a disability in life; I believe are often born to challenge our perceptions about life. Our society has not traditionally dealt with disability very well. Disability is any condition that restricts a person's mental, sensory or mobility functions. It may be caused by accident, trauma, genetics or disease. A disability may be temporary or permanent, total or partial, lifelong or acquired, visible or invisible.[53]

Demographics

• Over 4 million people in Australia have some form of disability. That's 1 in 5 people.

• 18.6% of females and 18.0% of males in Australia have disability.

• The likelihood of living with disability increases with age. 2 in 5 people with disability are 65 years or older.

• 1.8 million or 50.7 % of Australians aged 65 and over have disability, compared to 1 in 8 (12.5 %) aged under 65.

• 2.1 million Australians of working age (15 – 64 years) have disability.[52]

People living with a disability are still discriminated against in our society and often seen by people as being lesser able, intellectual and gifted. However, I'd like to think that this is changing. People with disability are often treated less favourably and discriminated against in terms of education, employment and accessing services such as healthcare and housing. They are more socially isolated than the average person and have less disposable income. I'd rather think of people living with a Disability, as People With Ability (PWA). So from now on this is the acronym I shall use unless referring to Disability in a traditional context.

Vale Jan Daisley - a Person with Ability

Jan Daisley is a person with ability and "A Mighty Activist". Jan was one of Australia's leading disability advocates who passed away in 2017. She particularly advocated for the rights of people with disability to live in the community and was a founding member of People With Disability Australia. Jan lived in an institution for 30 years and in 1993 as soon as she could communicate, she clearly stated that she wanted to move out and into the community.

Jan was determined to make an independent life for herself, despite many people saying that it was impossible. Jan enrolled in TAFE and obtained certificates in disability and law. She then went on to university to acquire a Bachelors of Education in Habilitation, then a Masters in Communities in Social Justice. She wrote and published three books, her autobiography "I hear more than you see", a sequel called "Rebels with a cause" and also a book about her experiences with disability support workers called "The Good, The Bad and The Unbelievable – Carers I have Known".[54]

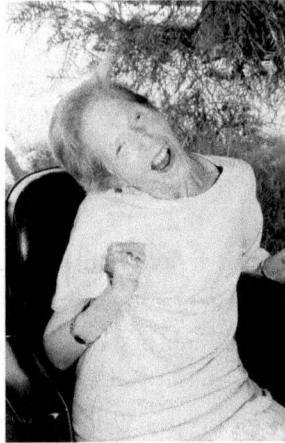

Jan Daisley

66 Since acquiring a disability I have worked very hard to assist other people to obtain their human rights, and their dignity of life, and I will continue to do this while ever I have breath in my body.

— VALE JAN DAISLEY, FOUNDING MEMBER OF
PEOPLE WITH DISABILITY AUSTRALIA PWDA

People such as Jan who are born with a severe disability such as Downs Syndrome or some other form of intellectual disability; I believe are often Old souls who have come into this world to teach us about unconditional love and challenge our perceptions of fear. As we move into the future, our society will provide many progressive changes and opportunities as opposed to challenges that will assist the lives of PWA immensely.

What the Future Holds

The National Disability Insurance Scheme (NDIS)

The NDIS is one of the most significant reforms in the health space in Australia since Medicare. Once rolled out it has the potential to be one of the most advanced Disability Schemes in the world and is a clear validation of the Aquarian energy that I believe Australia is embodying as a nation (or Republic) by 2023. For this reason, it is vital that the interface between the NDIS, Health and the broader community becomes better understood.

The Scheme will give people with disability in Australia with real choice and control over their lives. When the scheme is fully implemented in 2019, up to 10% of people with a disability – about 460,000 people are expected to receive a disability support package.[55]

Artificial Intelligence will be revolutionary for PWA - changing lives for the better.

The race for Artificial Intelligence (AI) dominance is fast expanding and will create a significant and powerful shift around how we live. For PWA, I believe it is going to be revolutionary. The possibilities are endless, and even our current sophistication with AI technology is already making an impact on people's lives. An example of this is the AI avatar which is helping people with disability to navigate through technology.

A bold Government foray into AI called the "Nadia Project", aims to help people navigate the NDIS through a virtual assistant. The development process for this project has been co-designed with people with disabilities, community groups, carers, academics, the National Disability Insurance Agency (NDIA) and the Department of Human Services.

AI has the potential to deliver critical services to the public however the "Nadia Project" has been stalled by the Government, amid concern by politicians and the bureaucracy who have been spooked by privacy fears related to the census and 'robo-debt' bungles (The Turnbull government bungle that issued robo-debt recovery notices to 20,000 welfare recipients who were later found to owe less or even nothing).[56]

It doesn't surprise me that such a project has been stalled by the Government. In many respects, this just represents another example where the bureaucratic forces of conservatism and fear are trying to resist the forward-thinking Aquarian energy that is coming in - radical change spearheaded by science, technology, and innovation. After 5 years of research and development, Nadia is the first commercial project to be launched with this technology. The Government uses excuses that it's early days and there needs to be more testing before it is unleashed on the public.

Sean Fitzgerald, chairman of the NDIA's Digital Innovation Reference Group is a quadriplegic from a bike accident 17 years ago. He said Nadia is a revolutionary program that could transform the lives of tens of thousands of people. He said there were many people with a disability keen to see Nadia enter her limited trial, adding there were thousands of would-be volunteer participants.

> The community is going to start asking more and more questions, and it's time to move on with things
>
> — SEAN FITZGERALD, CHAIRMAN OF THE NDIA'S DIGITAL INNOVATION REFERENCE GROUP

Oscar winner Cate Blanchett is the voice of Nadia, whose face and personality has been created by New Zealand artificial intelligence whiz Mark Sagar. His pioneering work on computer-generated characters for blockbuster movies includes Avatar, King Kong and Spiderman 2.

Cate Blanchett - The Making of Nadia

See it on YOUTUBE: Cate Blanchett - The Making of Nadia

> The more people with disability interact with her, the more she learns…It's all about trying to develop a voice that is positive, forward thinking and optimistic but also cognisant of the hurdles one needs to go through when you're living with disability…

It's a much more democratic, empowering way to deliver a service so that people can just get on with their lives. The liberating potential of this I think is really astonishing.

— CATE BLANCHETT - THE MAKING OF NADIA

14

HAPPINESS AND WELLBEING
- OUR MEASURE OF SOCIAL PROGRESS

Happiness is the meaning and the purpose of life, the whole aim and end of human existence.

— ARISTOTLE

Happiness cannot be traveled to, owned, earned, worn or consumed. Happiness is the spiritual experience of living every minute with love, grace, and gratitude.

— DENIS WAITLEY

How do we define happiness?

HOW DO WE DEFINE HAPPINESS? Well, that's the million-dollar question! I recently went to the world's largest conference on Happiness, called 'Happiness and Its Causes' which is held every year in Sydney Australia. Wow, I'd have to say it's the most amazing conference I've ever been to. I've been to two 'Happiness and Its Causes' conferences, the first conference was over two years ago. 'Happiness and Its Causes' is just so indescribable. It turned out to be the most uplifting and exhilarating conference, especially in terms of the meaningfulness it offers to the participant. It's well worth every cent!

"Happiness is that state of consciousness which proceeds from the achievement of one's values."

~Ayn Rand

Ven. Robina Courtin, Australian-born Buddhist

I have one of the fondest memories of seeing **Ven. Robina Courtin** (an Australian Buddhist nun) at the 2015 conference. The experience redefined my whole spiritual framework around Buddhism. Robina left me spellbound. She has worked with prisoners in the US prison system for 15 years, and even the Dalai Lama never thought that she would become a nun. In 2000, she founded the Liberation Prison Project, a project which works to help transform prisoners' lives, so they may cope with incarceration and deal with the fundamental reasons why they turned to crime.[57]

> Positive states of mind are natural to us. They are at the core of our being. They are what define our mind. They are what we really are
>
> — VEN. ROBINA COURTIN

Little did I know, Robina had given me one of the most amazing insights around my spirituality - even Buddhists can fight for what they believe in because if it comes from the **Right Intention**, then spiritually, it's perfectly fine.

Illness and Our Aim for Wellness

Illness and our aim for wellness are variable from person to person. When we experience illness or sickness, our focus is mostly on wellness. More than likely, each of us will draw upon our personal experience, mindset, and resilience when we are going through illness or suffering. A clinician or doctor's focus is more about diagnosis, curing, and treatment at all costs. There is a meeting of two perspectives, the professional perspective versus personal (rather than using the word patient) perspective. Sometimes they are in synergy and other times not.

One of my dear mentors is a beautiful woman called Dianne Nyoni. Dianne is a heterosexual woman living with HIV. She was diagnosed late with HIV because the health system missed several opportunities to diagnose her when she was sick, simply because they never tested her for HIV. Dianne is an amazing woman, a mother with 4 children and is a well-known HIV activist, public speaker, consumer representative, and writer; with a vast wealth of experience in counselling, domestic violence, and storytelling. I first started working Dianne professionally earlier in 2017, when she was employed as a part-time Community Engagement Officer in the HIV service I managed. A few weeks after Dianne started work, she was diagnosed with stage 3 invasive breast cancer and over a period of 8 months had numerous cycles of chemotherapy, surgery and radiation therapy. Dianne is so courageous, and I am honoured to include her story in my book. Her determination and strength to manage her illness with such dignity and respect are what exemplifies the meaning of our aim for wellness. She is currently in remission. **Find out more about Dianne. Visit: diannenyoni.com or her story on Youtube Pozhet Dianne.**

> Through storytelling, I champion change for personal growth.
>
> — DIANNE NYONI

Our health system is a complex beast, focussed primarily on disease and risk models. It is a web of bureaucracy, politics, array of different professional groups and power structures. At times it's messy, hard to comprehend and even harder to navigate. We spend very little money in Australia on community and preventative health and this only fuels the demand for more disease/risk focussed care and investment.

There are also many dimensions or influences that affect wellness, and these include things such as: -

- Environmental - the conditions in which we live and where and how we live.
- Financial - our capacity to earn an income to provide for ourselves and our families.
- Intellectual - our ability to comprehend, understand and use logic.

- Creative - an expression of our most innate creative abilities and tendencies that feed our soul.
- Occupational - our need for work, and what we strive for in terms of our achievement and identity.
- Physical - our ability to undertake physical exercise and its influence on our wellness and health.
- Social - the need for social connectedness and personal meaning in community and society.
- Sexual - the casual or intense pleasure and satisfaction that comes from sexual relations with others.
- Emotional - the ability to cope with the swings of our emotions from joy and ecstasy through to sadness and depression.
- Participatory - our level of confidence around the co-design of our health services whether through advocacy roles, consumer participation, community engagement, representation on boards/committees or even working in voluntary roles.
- Love - our ability to function and experience loving relationships both whether conditional or unconditional.
- Spiritual - our understanding of existence itself and the deeper meaningfulness of life.

> *Whether living with disability, HIV or experiencing some other chronic disease or trauma, all people are the beholders of their stories.*
>
> *Many of us have experienced discrimination and suffering at the hands of others because of their limited awareness and consciousness. And sometimes this has been demonstrated through the brutality of war and terrorism.*
>
> *If Jesus Christ (or Buddha) lived today, he would stand in awe, as a testament to people's stories and suffering. He would have still sacrificed his life today on the cross for the purpose of alleviating the suffering of mankind.*

It really makes sense, one of the greatest things an evolved Old Soul can do, is come to the earth plane to raise the consciousness of mankind by showing us our darkest, deepest and hatred flaws or fears.

Where is our Jesus (or Buddha)? Maybe he or she is walking the earth plane right now. God forbid because we need him or her for the sake of our planet and our human survival.

— DAVID SHAUN LARSEN

I hope this might inspire or serve as a testament for those who so deeply wish to share their stories and fill their life with service to others.

The Victim Mentality

The victim mentality is not healthy. I understand this concept well, as I have played the victim role in the past. Pisceans know how to play the victim well. It makes sense to me, not to be a pacifist and turn the other cheek, all the time. In your personal life, when you're dealing with people you know who may seem irrational, critical of you/others and just plain frustrating to be around; sometimes you just have to ask the Universe for help: -

"What the fcuk", I just can't deal with how YOU are behaving today; my compassion cylinder is running on empty. Please Universe, give me the strength and understanding to deal with them/this situation".

In this type of situation, if the behaviour is not warranted, it's perfectly okay to set boundaries or challenge it, "I really find your comments and behaviour disrespectful. If you value anything I have to say, then you need to also compromise and see my point of view. Only YOU can create the change that YOU need in your life to be humbler and respectful of others".

So in other words - stop playing the victim role. At times we need to get out the violin and pretend to play a person's favourite piece of music while saying, "It must be dreadful for you that you've had to endure such a terrible thing like that". Anyway, I can't play the violin; I only pretend to. Therefore, "in a nutshell", it's hard to feed the victim mentality and I'd rather not. However, if you have some insight, interest in change or patience; I'm sure we can learn to play the violin together!!!

Dear friend Scotty Carson

I can look back on my life and it was this complete internal evolution. Constant wish to understand the truth; constant looking. Searching for it. Definite.

At the same time pursuing what I wanted. Doing what I wanted. Trying to get happiness. Trying to see these two together. This was always what pursued me. More than the wish for security. More than the wish for happiness and things.

I'm not saying I don't like things; it's just that this is what drove me in my life. And lots of up and down. Completely crazy, manic-depressive, fighting with people, dramas, relationship dramas, angry dramas — this is my memory of my life.

Then I met these lamas and a whole new phase of dramas started and that's the last 30 years, the hardest years of my life.

— VEN. ROBINA

Happiness is about those special moments. Xmas celebrations 2016 with my mum Astrid, Janet her partner Ralph and son Ben and his friend. Janet is writing a book at the moment - she's been a beautiful friend and support.

The World Happiness Report

In April, the first *World Happiness Report* was published as the result of a United Nations initiative on happiness and well-being. The Report provides a landmark survey of the state of play around global happiness and also ranks countries by their level of global happiness. Governments, Organisations and Civil society around the globe are increasingly using happiness as a measure of social progress and to assist in policy-making decisions.[58]

The OECD has now committed itself,

> To redefine the growth narrative to put people's well-being at the centre of governments' efforts

> — OECD, JUNE 2016

The first full-day World Happiness meeting was held in February 2017, in the United Arab Emirates. This meeting was part of the World Government Summit. Now on March 20th, we have launched World Happiness Day. A direct summary of *World Happiness Report is* presented below: -

> **Norway tops the global happiness rankings for 2017.** Norway has jumped from 4th place in 2016 to 1st place this year, followed by Denmark, Iceland, and Switzerland in a tightly packed bunch. **All of the top four countries rank highly on all the main factors found to support happiness: caring, freedom, generosity, honesty, health, income and good governance.**

Their averages are so close that small changes can re-order the rankings from year to year. Norway moves to the top of the ranking despite weaker oil prices. It is sometimes said that Norway achieves and maintains its high happiness not because of its oil wealth, but in spite of it. By choosing to produce its oil slowly, and investing the proceeds for the future rather than spending them in the present,

> **Norway has insulated itself from the boom and bust cycle of many other resource-rich economies.** To do this successfully requires high levels of mutual trust, shared purpose, generosity and good governance

These are all factors that help to keep Norway and other top countries where they are in the happiness rankings.

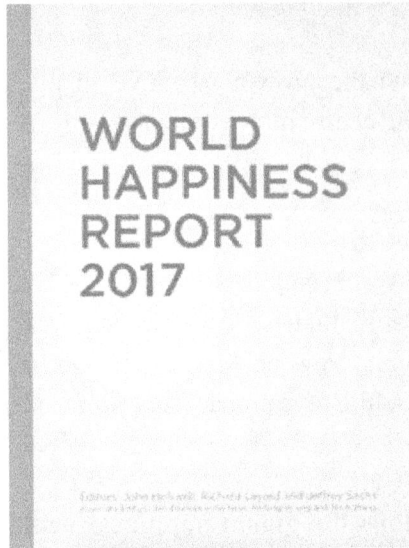

WORLD HAPPINESS REPORT 2017

All countries in the top ten also have high values in Six Key Variables, used to explain happiness differences such as:

- Income
- Healthy life expectancy
- Having someone to count on in times of trouble
- Generosity
- Freedom
- Trust

The latter is measured by the absence of corruption in business and government. Here also, there has been some shuffling of ranks among closely grouped countries, with this year's rankings placing Finland in 5th place, followed by the Netherlands, Canada, **New Zealand, and Australia and Sweden tied for the 9th position** (having the same score).

Happiness is both social and personal

This can be seen by comparing the life experiences between the top and bottom ten countries in this year's happiness rankings.

> **This year's report emphasises the importance of the social foundations of happiness**

— WORLD HAPPINESS REPORT, SEE CHAPTER 2

Scotty my kindred spirit

There is a gap between the two groups of countries, of which 3/4 of differences are explained by the six variables, 1/2 due to differences in having someone to count on, generosity, a sense of freedom, and freedom from corruption.

The other half of the explained difference is attributed to GDP per capita and healthy life expectancy, both of which, as the report explains, also depend importantly on the social context.

> **Happiness has fallen in America / The USA is a story of reduced happiness.** In 2007 the USA ranked 3rd among the OECD countries; in 2016 it came 19th. The reasons are declining social support and increased support and increased corruption
>
> — WORLD HAPPINESS REPORT, SEE CHAPTER 7

These same factors that explain why the Nordic countries do so much better.

However, 80% of what The Report calls, "variances in happiness across the world" occurs within particular sets of countries. For example in richer countries - the differences are not mainly explained by income inequality, but by differences in mental health, physical health, and personal relationships:

> **In richer countries...the biggest single source of misery is mental illness**
>
> — WORLD HAPPINESS REPORT, SEE CHAPTER 5

Income differences matter more in poorer countries, but even their mental illness is a major source of misery. Work is also a major factor affecting happiness (see Chapter 6). Unemployment causes a major fall in happiness, and even for those in work the quality of work can cause major variations in happiness.

People in China are no happier than 25 years ago

" — WORLD HAPPINESS REPORT, SEE CHAPTER 3

The *World Happiness Report* chapter on China contrasts the sharply growing per capita income in China over the past 25 years with life evaluations that fell steadily from 1990 till about 2005, recovering since then to about the 1990 levels. They attribute the dropping happiness in the first part of the period to rising unemployment and fraying social safety nets, with recoveries in both since.

" **Much of Africa is struggling. It tells a much more diverse story**

— WORLD HAPPINESS REPORT, SEE CHAPTER 4

The Africa chapter, tells a much more diverse story, as fits the African reality with its greater number and a vast range of experiences. But these are often marked by delayed and disappointed hopes for happier lives (see Chapter 4).

Bhutan's Gross National Happiness Index

In 1972 Bhutan's then king Jigme Singye Wangchuck declared gross domestic product was not a meaningful measurement for wellbeing and said the country should instead look at gross national happiness (GNH).

What started as a loose philosophy about how the country should develop became more concrete over the following decades, until 2008 when GNH was formally enshrined in the constitution.

Along with the creation of the GNH Centre and a GNH Index, this philosophy became a formal guiding hand for the government and its policy development.[59]

Learn more at YOUTUBE: Bhutan's former Prime Minister Jigme Thinley explains what GNH means

> We look into the developments through the lenses of society and happiness. We measure the conditions of happiness and we say, OK, if there is increase in the conditions of the people in terms of happiness conditions, then yes, we have developed.
>
> We don't look into technology or infrastructure for that matter as a means to see how we have developed.

— SAAMDU CHETRI, GNH CENTRE'S EXECUTIVE
DIRECTOR

A Microment of Happiness, Berlin 2014

The GNH Centre considers four key "pillars": environmental conservation; good governance; sustainable and equitable socio-economic development; and preservation and promotion of culture. It then breaks this down into nine "domains", which are interconnected. The nine GNH domains are:

- Living standards
- Education
- Health

- Environment
- Community vitality
- Time use
- Psychological wellbeing
- Good governance
- Cultural resilience and promotion

Lastly, it conducts research and uses indices to monitor whether there is an improvement in these areas.

My final thoughts on Happiness

Serenity such a beautiful Concert Hall, Sydney Opera House

Happiness is not something that you seek or buy but rather what I call, "a feeling of being content, in flow with life and living in the moment". I believe Happiness is very much connected to one's sense of spirituality - by this, I am not talking about religion. The more you are dedicated to and living on your spiritual path, a greater sense of synchronicity starts to occur in your life. It's not something that we can sustain or prolong, but it's just a state of being that is so indescribable and pure. Often associated with this are Micro-Moments of happiness. These are pure states of happiness and positive emotions that may only last for a second of time, but you experience the awareness and blissfulness of the moment. Micro-Moments of happiness also offer us inner strength, recharge our souls and validate our resilience and ability

227

to become something much greater than the sum of us. So what are some examples of Micro-moments of happiness:

10 Micro-Moments of Happiness

Maria Rodale reports in a recent study, "that people are happier and more resilient when they enjoy micro-moments of positive emotions in their lives talks". Maria lists her top ten Micro-Moments of Happiness[60] here:

1. Morning coffee on my couch outside. All it takes is 15 minutes for the caffeine to kick in, but in the quiet morning when the birds are singing and the sun is rising, I feel grounded and ready to face a brand new day.

Maria Rodale - top ten Micromoments of Happiness

2. A fresh morning hug from my just-awake daughter. She's a late sleeper, and there is nothing like pulling her out of her crib and burying my face in her still-warm neck and having her nestle into my arms... Lord knows she won't hold that still again until the day is done.

3. An email from a friend. Especially if it's someone I haven't heard from in a while or someone I've just been thinking about. Especially if they aren't asking me to do anything, but just saying hello or sharing a story about their lives. That's why Facebook is so much fun.

4. Finding good micro-greens at the farmer's market. You have to get there early. And the farmer in the stall knows what I'm there for. I can see his face lighting up as he scans the table to see if there are any left. They are so tiny (micro!). So tasty, so delicate and fresh. I love them.

5. Something good to eat. It doesn't have to be fancy or fabulous. In fact, something simple is usually best. But there is nothing quite so momentary-happiness-inducing as the taste of something good — like a fresh, off-the-bramble wild black raspberry, or bread still warm from the oven.

6. A package that I forgot I had ordered that shows up on my doorstep. Happens all the time. Some people have joked I need a loading dock at my house (don't worry, I shred the boxes to use as mulch in my garden). But living out in the sticks of Pennsylvania, I rely a lot on mail order (although less than I used to). Those surprise deliveries are like Christmas all year round.=

7. Birds, other animals, and goofy kids. The groundhog that can't make up its mind which way to run as I pull in my driveway...the bird that bonks its head on a window, but is fine...seeing where your pet poops every morning to claim his or her territory. Nature (kids included) is everywhere, and always brings a little smile.

8. A nap (and all that might ensue from that). It's rare, but so lovely. Even better if it's raining or snowing. I love my bed.

9. Crossing things off my list. I'm a list-maker, partly because the act of crossing something off it is so delightful. The other reason is if it's not on the list, I probably won't remember it. A day that's done with a long list crossed off is awesome.

10. A story with a happy ending. It could just be a story in the local paper, or a story you hear from a friend. But most likely for me it's a romance novel. Nothing beats that flush of happiness when the book is done and all is well and they live happily ever after. I don't care if you think it's corny, it works! And it works for millions of women and a handful of men who read those books.

> We are fragile creatures, and it is from this weakness, not despite it, that we discover the possibility of true joy.
>
> — DESMOND TUTU, THE BOOK OF JOY: LASTING

HAPPINESS IN A CHANGING WORLD

Sunlight Yellow Angel Feather

Happiness awaits!

The Angels ask that you feel "happy and optimistic". There are bright days ahead for you!

Happiness awaits! Sunlight Angel Feather: The Angels ask that you feel "happy and optimistic". There are bright days ahead for you!

15

LIVING, LOVING, AGEING, AND DYING

- THE TRUE ESSENCE OF LIFE

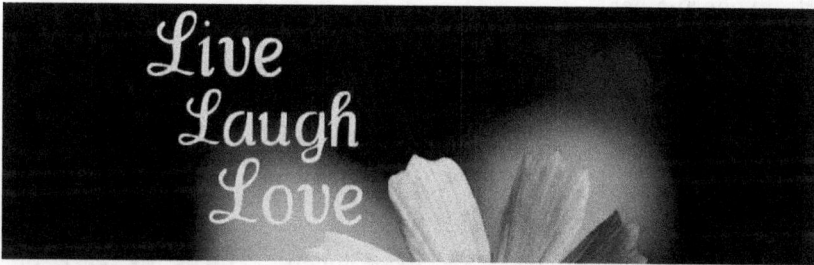

> *There is only one law in the universe that never changes - that all things change, and that all things are impermanent.*

> *Because the dying also are unable to help themselves, we should relieve them of discomfort and anxiety, and assist them, as far as we can, to die with composure.*

— SOGYAL RINPOCHE, TIBETAN BOOK OF THE
LIVING AND DYING

Scared To Be Lonely?

SCARED TO BE LONELY? At the very start of life, we are born so innocently and come into this world with no responsibilities; but alas we then go through a series of pre-conditioned ways of learning and being taught how to live life, depending on our religious, cultural, societal and familial upbringing.

Some of us were lucky to be nurtured, and our creativity caressed with love and understanding. Some of us may have been unlucky to be bullied as teenagers and truly endured how harsh life can be, but somehow we survived that. However, for some of us, we have experienced what it's like to fall in love and feel the tremors of two hearts beating. Maybe like fools in love or possibly even soul mates which foretold our strong attraction and how we couldn't bare to be apart from one another.

Often our relationships are tried and tested, and some of them end up magnifying all our purest flaws and imperfections. On occasions like this, we possibly wonder why we ever stay in such relationships and keep coming back for more. Was it real or was it perhaps something not so real, a dream? Maybe we preferred the illusion of what it could've been or just so scared to be lonely. Perhaps it's what some call unconditional love, something much more significant than what we can understand or want to understand. Maybe it's something undefined and possibly something so unreal, we end up questioning our faults, our whole existence and even lose our minds in the process.

It's only those Awakening and Old souls that don't take life for granted. All we truly know is that the sun is shining today, tomorrow and the next day and even then the weather may be unpredictable. Life itself is finite and perishable, and everything else is temporary. In essence, what we genuinely come to understand is how fragile life is and how this determines what we hope for the most out of life. At the end of life, it is only our mortality that matters and the value of our purpose. However, a life lived with exceptional purpose is profound.

We truly need to treasure every moment, for it may not come again particularly not in our current incarnate form.

> Do we need somebody, just to feel like we're alright? Even when we know it's wrong, been somebody better for us all along

— SCARED TO BE LONELY MARTIN GARRIX & DUA LIPA LYRICS

My beautiful dogs Gracie and Parker

All Communities have an Ugly Side

All communities have an ugly side and contribute to creating our culture, but we can also change it by challenging others. I feel that the Gay community perpetrates some of the most extreme forms of discrimination in our community. This includes outwardly saying things such as "no fems", "no Asians", "no Trans", fatties, "no oldies", "masculine only" and never mind age discrimination. Many become invisible as they age "only into younger", "no one older than me" or vague cut off points such as 38, 45, 50. It's not very endearing! I've not experienced a great deal of discrimination in my life, from family, friends or associates whether 'coming out' being gay in the 1980s; losing a partner from AIDS in the 1990s and becoming HIV positive in 2010. On the whole, the most significant discrimination I've ever encountered has been from my community.

The narcissism, judgement, racism, self-entitlement, and disrespect of others seems to run very deep in our culture and psyche. It's horrible! Social media provides endless opportunities to support this as people hide behind fake profiles, headless torsos, or being muscled or toned to perfection. We still discriminate on HIV status; sexuality (some men's dislike towards lesbians); men not respected by some women as feminists; Prep use and whether someone is Transgender. Many have open relationships yet disclose to others that they are breaking their predefined rules; make excuses that we are discreet, bisexual or socially awkward; some say they dislike Asians or Indians but when you ask why it usually comes down to vague responses such as skin colour, "slanty" eyes and smell. We also judge others for their drug use as if they are more enlightened (they say you can or can't use, but they do) and think they are immune to any fragility in life - yet we all are!

So many younger people are either ignorant or choose not to know about our history, and what others have done before them to fight for the rights and freedoms they so enjoy today and often take for granted. Nevertheless, the older I get, I struggle more with the notion of an LGBTQI community; as it means so many different things to many different people e.g., for me, it's more about relevance and meaning. I can see why some people would ask, "why would you associate or tolerate this when it has such an ugly side?". I don't want to be identified anymore with an acronym that defines my sexuality. I see this time as an opportunity to be something much more Universal, in everything and everyone.

> Life's too short to waste on selfish or vacuous type people. We must never feed other people's egos - it should be avoided at all cost.
>
> — PROVERB

In many ways we are so influenced by what we see around us, who we associate with, our upbringing - family, sex, culture, traditions, sexuality, etc. We don't need to publicly display our discrimination toward others for we become no better than anyone else and will lack any ability or power to evolve and grow as souls. Society needs more depth, spiritual insight and respect for others and especially our Elders (our role models) for they have great wisdom that we need to treasure as a community - however you define that. As people, we interpret the meaning of community differently, and each of our interpretations is so broad; therefore each of us will explain or define it differently.

A photograph of me dog walking - volunteering at the Hervey Bay Adoption Centre

My only hope is that Mardi Gras in Sydney becomes a parade that eventually celebrates our Universal expression of sexuality in all shapes and forms. Maybe the 40th anniversary in March 2018 will be the foundation for this. I also know some people will criticise my views for what I have written, but I accept that. What I write about is a significant issue with society as a whole and all human beings. We are no different really! I choose to challenge this as an individual otherwise the only other option is to extoll the virtues of our culture with all its flaws. If we take on board all the negative criticism from others, then we only validate their unwarranted belief and are not true to ourselves. I just don't have the energy for that! I'd instead try to find my solace and make the world a better place to live in and as always, believe in making the Impossible, Possible.

Finding solace in life is about surrounding yourself with like-minded people, your kindred spirits. I also love animals, especially dogs. The love of many animals is unconditional. I choose to live in Hervey Bay now as I want to live in a community that values older people (like my mother) and occasionally visiting friends, and family interstate and overseas is a pleasure. I also get joy out of visiting more enlightened communities and societies in the world, as it helps to provide that benchmark for what is missing in our society.

What I found so touching the other day was reading an article in the local newspaper where two Paramedics, Danielle and Graeme, were called out to take an elderly lady in her 70s to the palliative care unit to die. However, her dying wish was to see the beautiful ocean here for one last time; it's like the Bay was calling her. The paramedics lovingly granted her wish and in transit took her to the esplanade and propped her up on a chair so she could savour its beauty; the pier and the expanse of the whole bay right across to K'gari (Fraser Island). She stated to them, "I'm at peace, everything is right". Graeme went on to say that if the rocks weren't there, he would have got into his jocks and carried her down into the water; instead, he got a vomit bag and filled it up with sand and water so she could feel the sand and smell the ocean water one last time. This gesture is what I call a loving act of kindness; it's the kind of the stuff you get here. That's the kind of community I want to be a part of, as Graeme stated, "We don't take time to take in the smell the roses and look at the beauty around us".

> *This world would be a whole lot better if we just made an effort to be less horrible to one another*

- Ellen Page

Walk the Path Least Travelled

Walk the path least travelled, its easy to spot because it's the path of the fallen angel, the angel with no wings. It looks lonely, you can't see the footprints of others, but deep down it beckons you and instils fear and trepidation. Just know the footsteps of our ancestors have been there before, they're asking you now to take the wings that are rightfully yours and fly. When we buy into the resultant myths about life and its conditioning; it potentially challenges our sense of purpose and place in the Universe. We likely lose out on the richness and wealth of personal, familial, social and cultural opportunities to grow and

The Older Soul always walks the path least travelled

develop as people or souls on a more in-depth spiritual level. In reality, this limits us from living a life with purpose. Instead, we end up conforming to whatever societal values prevail, preferably "living lives" like most other people - it's easier to walk the path that most others travel. Why wouldn't you?

The path of least resistance is always more comfortable, but it doesn't get you where you want to be. It makes sense, why would you walk down some alternative path that looks lonely (as if it's less travelled) and doesn't give you the safety, security, and predictability we often crave. Life gives you some of the most exceptional opportunities by throwing yourself into the unknown or void i.e., walking the path least travelled. It's heartbreaking and dispiriting to end up leaving this life with journeys untravelled. It's so easy to end up living a life full of regrets, but you're never too old make amends, even if it's for the smallest of virtues e.g., a minor act of kindness can indeed make a difference in a person's life.

As the philosopher and writer Thoreaux once said, we live "Lives of Quiet Desperation". When faced with challenges in life that seem difficult, uncertain or full of despair; we ultimately are faced with two choices. We either can embrace the moment with a sense of love and endearing tenderness or oppose it with fear, hate or judgement. In other words, we either make excuses why we can't do something or think about all the possibilities that can come out of it. Often when I review back in my life, there are some cherished moments and personal qualities, I thought I'd never experience or grasp in life. These have mostly originated from my fear, self-doubt or self-esteem issues i.e., not feeling confident about my abilities. However, I have proven to myself that anything you put your mind to can be achieved. Therefore, what seemed impossible in the past, has become possible. Here are a few examples: -

- Experiencing unconditional love
- Writing a book on spirituality
- Becoming a Humanitarian
- Finding my Norwegian family
- Guiding the way for others to be themselves
- Understanding resilience and recovery
- Knowing and understanding authority
- Knowing the difference between power and influence

Reflect on What Matters - Make the Impossible, Possible

Reflect on what matters - make the impossible, possible. Here are two of those moments when you know you are "meant to be here". I don't remember, but the story goes when I was six months of age, my mother was bathing me one night, and my father came home drunk. He came into the bathroom and thought he'd help my mum with bathing me and started throwing me up in the air. I guess in his drunken state he thought it would've of been a bit of fun. However he lost grip on me and in a sudden shock event, my mum reached out and caught me just seconds before my head was only a few inches from the hard tiled floor. Lucky me!!!

At 3 years of age, while visiting my Grandparents; mum was with Grandma having a coffee, and I supposedly wandered into the nearby bedroom. In my wisdom, I saw a pair of scissors and thought that I'd start cutting the light chord. Luckily, Grandad thought he'd come looking for me, and just as he entered the bedroom, he heard a loud bang sound. The shock of the electricity must of self-propelled me against the wall like a loud thud. Amazingly, I wasn't hurt, and all that remained was just a frayed smoking chord and I a bit dazed.

What take from these early experiences in life, is that that life is frag-ile; death can happen at any time. I feel somewhat equipped to write about death and dying as I've sat at the bedside of an untold number of people when they have died. The gift comforting those who are dying is something special, and I often see life and death in the reverse of what we are conditioned to believe i.e., basically we celebrate birth and mourn death. I'd rather think that we have it around the wrong way.

Imagine we are born and as we start to have the realisation of life and things around us; we may start to realise the circumstances surrounding our birthright: -

- Where we are born.
- The parents, siblings, and family we are bound to.
- The culture of the life around us.
- Our innate wisdom of the things we know.
- The disability, limitations and self-esteem issues that we may experience.

Have we chosen these circumstances for whatever karmic reason or not? Maybe so, maybe not, but if you think about it; it's quite logical that choice and destiny could very well co-exist together. Whereas death, on the other hand, is an upsetting time for most, as we experience varying levels of grief and loss for the person/s whom we have loved and honoured. I'd rather see death as the moment we go home and return either to our heavenly sphere, enter another parallel Universe, become one with the Universe or reunite with our spiritual families across this amazing Universe (which is my preferred belief). I feel the moment of death is a time of deep reflection; seeing all our life events pass by in a flash. It is a time when we assimilate everything that we have ever done, and we

Enjoying a train ride in Berlin

inevitably process it with such insight and learning. It, therefore, holds a strong karmic influence over our next life and the creation of its roadmap. This moment becomes the reference point for how we want to live our life again, however profoundly bound by our karmic actions and deeds. What a fantastic opportunity life offers us!

If you imagine tomorrow is the last day of your life, how do you think you would face your death and would you be satisfied with how you've lived your life? Would you be satisfied with whom you are, how you've made a difference in the world, the value of your relationships and the quality of life you have lived? Would you end up dying with lots of regrets in your heart or reflecting on how you could've done some things better? In short, how would you answer these questions:

- How did I live my life?
- How did I love?
- Did my life matter?

As you reflect on your answers, how do you feel inside, what does it feel like? Is there a well of joy that comes up or is there some disconnect, discontent and maybe a sense of you feeling scared. You might have butterfly's in your stomach or that feeling of being at peace (especially in those moments when you are still and aren't thinking). No one person has the answers to everything, but collectively we can dream big and make anything possible. We just need to believe in ourselves, challenge our fear and ask the Universe for courage. The revolutionary idea of only one woman or man can seed a thousand possibilities. Empowering and enabling others to act is what inspires hope, to dream big and achieve the impossible.

> There is only one thing that makes a dream impossible to achieve: the fear of failure

> — PAULO COELHO

My friends Ross and Karen - Healer, Traditional Chinese Medicine Practitioner, Physiotherapy Ph. D. TCM: http://www.lotushealingarts.com/

The Questions that Matter

The questions that matter is something that most nurses in our profession think about quite often. Nursing has given me the wisdom to deal with death, face the learning it has afforded and help others to pass on. Maybe this is akin to hidden talents, knowledge, and skills that are so deep and spiritually meaningful. I just know about death and dying. It's like something I've experienced many times before but do it with such honour and privilege. Being a nurse is a privileged position. Any position of privilege, if used with the right intention enables, your innate gifts or skills to shine, especially when opportunity meets your talent. In times when we shine, we just know that we are in synergy with life, if we choose to see it.

Synergistic situations create immense opportunity, often without expectation but the bar is high. In essence, life has given me enormous opportunities to practice my craft i.e., experiencing death and dying both personally and professionally. Most of us want to know that our lives have had some meaning and if not; then at least a feeling of being at peace with how we have lived and experienced life. What is the value of being human if we don't reflect on how our lives, our work, and relationships provide meaning in life; so that we truly live, love and matter?

I believe there are only three things that people focus or reflect on when they are dying. In the last days or weeks before you die; I can guarantee your inner self (depending on your level of awareness and insight) will spend time exploring and evaluating the following:

1. The Value of your Relationships? Will you think about the immense moments of joy and pleasure you've had with your friends and family or about the missed rare moments, regrets and painful experiences? Some of us may not have any or little insight regarding our actions towards others, which is sad, as our souls will accumulate this karma. Those with deep insight will know that the Universe is scanning your life across every event, meetings with people and the value of your connections with others (much like when a computer scans for viruses, we get a warning or message). Therefore, the Law of Cause and Effect comes into play; we ultimately have choice around our actions. The value of this is that the Universe is asking you to accept the responsibility for your actions and how it feels. Maybe it could be about the conversations we didn't have, the isolation we felt, missed opportunities to meet someone (especially when our paths crossed) or just the emotions we felt when we thought of someone in that passing moment.

World AIDS Day Panel 2014. Pictured on the back row, from left: Bill Bowtell and Nic Holas. Pictured on the front row from left: Abby Landy, Myself and Sebastian Robinson. November 2014

2. Did I make a Difference in this World? Most people when they faced with death reflect on this. They often dwell on the things they've set out to achieve and accomplish. They might ask, "why didn't I do the impossible (however you define this) it seems so logical to me now" or "it's so obvious to me now I can't believe I've wasted all this time focussing all my energy on that (however you may perceive it)". In essence, there may be a range of personal questions you may ask here; I have just thrown in some examples of what they could be. Only

YOU will know whether YOU have a made a difference in the world, no one else but YOU.

3. What was my legacy? I know this is something that my first partner Michael most questioned. Many of us will ask questions about our legacy i.e., how others remember us by what we have left behind. We will all do this to varying degrees but just through different lenses in which we have lived life. For some of us, it will be about the importance of property and security; for others, our 'legacy' will focus on the children we have left behind, and for many others, it will be about whether our existence has meant anything and is not forgotten. The last one is quite common as we most often focus on the fear that our loved ones will not remember or "forget us". In reality, we will all be forgotten in time unless history has a way of recording or telling your story. Even then history has a way of altering or distorting things.

> If you cannot stop yourself from getting angry, then at least get angry about things that matter
>
> — AMIT KALANTRI

Holding My Man

My first partner Michael Wayne Garnam who taught me about the meaning of unconditional love. Bless you "my boy wonder" you were my soul mate and a true spiritual warrior of the highest order.

Holding my man. Is our understanding of unconditional love the ultimate life lesson? It's indeed one of them. I nursed my first partner Michael Wayne Garnam when I was a nurse at St Vincent's Hospital in early 1988. After a brief interlude together, I headed off to Europe with tears in my heart; not knowing I was in love. I travelled to Germany first and stayed with a lesbian friend Sigrid, who shared an apartment with three or four other lesbians in Potsdamer Straße, Berlin. For a young gay man, it felt foreign, not so much for being around women but more the language barrier and cultural fit. I did learn a lot of things especially knowing about the Trümmerfrau, the women who rebuilt cities in Germany and Austria, out of the rubble in the aftermath of World War II.

I only stayed in Berlin for a few weeks; with much yearning in my heart, it would turn into a flame of restlessness. I decided to head off to Oxfordshire, England to stay with my dear friend Andy. He lived in a little village just near the White Horse on the Hill. It's a highly formed prehistoric figure; formed into the shape of a horse, carved out of deep trenches filled with chalk rock. Andy was a farmer, academic and linguist (he could speak well over twenty languages and is still learning more languages today) and among many other accomplishments served as a Deacon in the Russian Catholic Church. I only stayed with Andy one week, as he could sense my sadness and the abandonment I felt.

My dear friend Andy, 2017

I always remember his wise words of wisdom "David if you feel such strong feelings for Michael it's not going to serve you any purpose to be here; love is something that is so special. Why don't you follow your heart; call him right now and tell him that you want to come home". At that moment, I did, and Michael was so excited to hear my voice. Within twenty-four hours Andy drove to me Heathrow airport and had me on a flight home to Sydney. Michael greeted me at the airport, I was home, and we spent four and half glorious years together.

That's how we met, and I often reflect back to the moment when he died on the 31st August 1992; as this was the time I learned about the meaning of unconditional love. Michael embodied it. Most relationships are somewhat conditional, with varying degrees of transactional obligations, emotions, fear, and love that are interwoven in the mix and spanning a spectrum of function to dysfunction.

Our relationship was great at the start, although a little uncertain with a mixed bag of emotions (both love and hate); two completely different people who came together for four and a half years to share our lives together. The only difference was that he had HIV/AIDS and in those days, every day seemed precious as there was a lot of confusion and uncertainty; given that death could strike any moment. Michael was a foreign exchange dealer and worked for The Bank of America. Michael's father died early in his life and his mother Wilma was on a veteran's pension, so had to raise her five children on her own. Michael always had a curiosity for life, and certainly lived life to the fullest like every day was his last. Even before he got diagnosed with HIV in 1985, he had travelled to every major continent on earth including Africa, Russia (on the trans-Siberian railway) and South America.

It's by no design fault that I have included Michael's picture twice in this book, in two different chapters. It just felt right!

Michael was a larger than life figure, with an infectious laugh and zest for life and quite blunt to say the least. He was a pure Aries; fiery, passionate, self-determined and independent. You either liked him or not, and he didn't give a shit what anyone thought about him. Given my sensitive nature, poor self-esteem and lack of confidence, from the very start; I took a back seat in the relationship. Possibly my search for spiritual meaning in life made it hard for me to live in the real world and he was just the complete opposite - ambitious, flamboyant, and fearless and loved adventure. When we argued Michael would often say that, "Your halo will come down and strangle you one day". He was half right, but I'd rather think of it as a metaphor for me being a fallen angel of some sort. Michael always said that when he got sick, he'd do himself in. However, when the time came, he chose the complete opposite path and became the spiritual warrior.

When Michael's health started to decline, I knew it was the beginning of the end. It was that frightening dread of not knowing what would happen next and I'd often wonder how I'd cope and question why me? In the midst of it, all I knew was that my man was eventually going to die. Nonetheless, I knew his love for me was the thing that enabled me to find the inner strength to go on. Michael endured long periods of sickness over nine months with a debilitating illness caused by Mycobacterium Avium Intracellulare (MAC). MAC symptoms are similar to TB and are one of the AIDS-defining illnesses. It causes a person to have fevers, diarrhoea, malabsorption (difficulty absorbing nutrients from your gut), as well as a loss of appetite and weight loss. Michael certainly had all these symptoms and needed regular blood transfusions due to anaemia from the toxic HIV drugs.

During this time, I also was working full-time as a nurse on a rotating roster in the HIV unit at Royal Prince Alfred Hospital. My mother and Michael had an exceptional bond, and she would make regular trips down from Brisbane to support both of us, mainly when he was sick in the hospital. Often I would surprise Michael with her unannounced visits. When I would walk into his room, my mother would be following me; not far behind, visibly in my shadows. Michael's smile was endearing, and my mother loved him so much. At the end of his life Michael was skeletal, and after three long weeks, when he was in and out of consciousness, he died. I always remember that moment, as he was Cheyne stoke breathing (the breathing that often happens when someone is dying, and it's nothing like portrayed in movies). We often gasp for every last breath. I shared this moment with my best friend Kevin by my side. Michael's mother Wilma arrived just minutes later, but she was relieved not to see him die. So as I always say, when people are dying, they choose the moment of their death.

My "Holding the Man" moment is different to the one told in the book of the same name. Michael and I planned his funeral down to every last detail including the music, eulogy, flowers, priest, and venue. We had the White Ladies carrying his coffin and an openly gay Catholic priest doing the service in the Penshurst Catholic Church, in the southern suburbs of Sydney. There were well over a hundred people if not double that number at his funeral; a mix of extended family, our friends, his school mates, a group of older ladies from the Penshurst Catholic club, some hospital staff and his work colleagues from over the years. I sat in the front row with his mother Wilma and during the service; it was acknowledged that I was his partner and that Michael died from AIDS. It's how Michael wanted it, and it was a testament to the kind of person he was, loved by so many. There was no shame, fear or hate; only love for this most beautiful man. Later that day after the wake, a group of his closest friends including my mum went down to Neilson's Park, lined up along the beach and threw Gladiolas into Sydney Harbour in memory of "my wonder boy".

> Maybe we'll meet again in another life. Maybe we're better in another paradise.
>
> Maybe we will meet again. Maybe we will fall again. In another life...

— ANOTHER LIFE AFROJACK & DAVID GUETTA

Reconciling the Past - Liberates the Future

Reconciling the past - liberates the future, sounds like an old adage. How can we become the great beholders of our destiny if we do not learn from the past?

> Living in the moment is much like the zero degrees of separation from our past and our future.

— DAVID SHAUN LARSEN

It commands us to be present at the moment knowing that each degree of separation from our past intricately links to each degree of separation from our future. Reconnecting with my Norwegian family seemed impossible all those years ago, much like 99 degrees of separation.

I knew in my heart that there must be a way to find out whom my family was; all I vaguely remembered was where Grandad was born, what ship he sailed on and that he had four daughters. Without email, it was challenging, but the pleasure one gets from writing and receiving letters now seems like a dying art. I initially contacted the Norwegian embassy, and they sent me a document titled, 'How to trace your ancestors in Norway'. It provided a lot of helpful information but nothing that enabled me to do anything useful with it, given the distance of living far away in Australia. One day after much deliberation, I thought to myself, why not write to one of the Norwegian newspapers? I thought it would be a long shot, but I ended up writing to a newspaper called VG in Oslo (Norway's capital and largest city). In my letter, I asked them how much it would cost to have my letter transcribed into Norwegian and published in their newspaper. A few weeks after this, to my amazement, VG wrote back to me with a copy of my letter translated and published in their Saturday's readers section with the heading 'V.A. Larsens Familie'.

Letter to VG with a description of my Grandfather - V. A. Larsens Familie, 29th February 1992

When I saw the newspaper clipping that VG sent to me, I was filled with sudden joy and just knew the Universe was intervening in some way. A few weeks after this, I received a letter in the mail from Unni, the oldest of my Grandad's daughters. The letters that followed from all the sisters were humble and sincere and provided an enriching cultural exchange for me at the time. I discovered that my Grandad's first wife Dagmar had to clean train carriages at night to support the family and it seems Unni, as the oldest sister took on the role to help support her sisters and her mother later in life.

What a strong woman Dagmar must've been, as it wouldn't have been a comfortable life. If anything it would've been a very hard and tough life for her and surprisingly, I often think about Dagmar with much admiration. I will never know her, but maybe our paths crossed in some distant past life; who knows I can't explain why I think about her. However, I have never questioned why my Grandad left Norway; I guess some things are meant to become what they are meant to become. As Norway was occupied by the German's during the war, it must have been a tough time for everyone. It's a distant reminder that war in itself, is traumatising and futile in the end.

I finally met my Norwegian family for the first time in 1993. It was truly a joyous moment in my life and on many levels, I believe it was a healing experience for the whole family i.e., a reconciliation with the past. I know that the future holds a wealth of new experiences and untold connections with Norway, as I am in contact with my cousins Britt and Arne. I'm very proud of my heritage. Mum eventually made the journey to reunite with her sisters in 2004 after many years of writing letters. Unni was ten years old when her father left Oslo for the last time, and she has now passed away. Bless you, Unni, I often think of you and have the utmost respect for my aunts Mary, Irene and Grethe and their families. Mary is now in a nursing home and well cared for by her family.

Dear David

> I am known with your article in a Norwegian newspaper. It was big surprise to me and my sisters.
>
> As far as I can see, your grandfather is my father. The dates and the names in the birth certificate (also mentioned in the newspaper) are correct.

He was married to my mother when the 2nd World War broke out, but during and after the war we all lost contact. My mother searched for him after the war. She knew he was signed off in Melbourne, and she also knew he was married again. But no contact from my father.

She died in 1979 a short time after her 75th birthday.

We are four daughters. I am the eldest, born in 1928. Then there is Mary, born in 1930, Irene born in 1935 and Grethe in 1938…

I write only this for the moment. If you want more details, we can write more later.

We should like to know how old my father was, what he was working with and if he was in good health in his elder days. If possible can you send us a picture of him as an old man.

Will you give our kind regards to your mother.

Kind greetings to you too.

On behalf of us 4: Unni

— LETTER FROM UNNI LARSEN 10TH MARCH 1992 -
RECONCILING THE PAST

Discovering One's Identity in Life

Discovering one's identity in life is a lifelong process. There are three crucial stages that all people go through in life regarding understanding and building our formed identity. I frame these stages using an astrological interpretation or others may find this corresponds best with other well-studied stages of life. Someone who walks the path least travelled in life will always have life experiences that reflect their journey which is entirely different to the majority of people; who feel it's easier to walk the path most travelled. If you walk the path most travelled, it doesn't enable or trigger you, to get you out of your comfort zone.

Astrologically, the first stage in life is what is called the Saturn Return. It's like a coming of age (or reaching adulthood for the first time) or the first time in life you understand who you are as a person. A Saturn Return is literally that; the planet Saturn completes a full revolution around the Sun, returning to where it's located when you were born. This takes approximately 29 years. Saturn is the great initiator. Around the age of 27 most people go through a process of self-questioning "Who am I?" or "Where am I going in life?". In the 28th year of life, a significant life event always happens for every person, depending on what lesson/s the Universe needs to initiate or teach about life. If you have deviated from your life path, Saturn just gives you the ability and tools to get back onto your path.

The next phase of life is the mid-life transits or 'mid-life crisis' as we'd alternatively coin in life (as an expression). The person knows deep down that something has to change, and they wonder how or what? Some people will end up feeling physically exhausted during a combination of midlife transits (especially if additional transits to personal planets get involved, and they often do). A very compelling question during this time usually is,

> When will this end for me? It's like I'm being tested or asked to do something I have never done before.

This phase in life starts as early as 37 until 43. It's the time in life when the Universe is asking you to truly understand where you are going in life (what is your life destiny OR purpose?) and act on it if there is work to be done (your new life phase). There's an old African expression which says that "if you haven't got your life together by 43 then you are less likely to in the future". I'm kind in my interpretation of this expression. Not that it's impossible to get it together, but it's just that it's going to be so much harder to at a later stage in life. But nothing is impossible without the blood, sweat, and tears you put into it.

The next phase between the ages of 52 to 58 is a crucial time in life. Th Universe is asking you to evolve or rise into your next phase in life, where you are meant to experience life at a higher or deeper spiritual level. It may be a time when you may very well reinvent your whole life. Possibly change everything about who you are as a person, where you live, the work that you do and even the friends or associates you surround yourself with. You can see why this is a much harder time for those who never used the opportunities from their mid-life transits to develop insight, grow or open their awareness.

My dear friends Mark, Peter and of course mum, Astrid popping her head up in the picture. Taken Boxing Day Dec 26, 2016.

Discovering the True Essence of Love

Discovering the true essence of love is unpredictable, and so many of our life experiences will influence who, how and the situations; in which we search, stumble across or be receptive to love.

There are many forms of love and our relationships forged with family, friends, lovers, and others are varied. They are all very different in terms of their connectedness, expression, values (including cultural and spiritual) and conditions that we place on them. In many regards, social media has taken over how we engage and meet others and the mediums in which we used to use; such as face to face social meet-ups, seem to be a thing of the past.

Ultimately, what are we all looking or aspiring for concerning love? We are all very different by our physical appearances, race, sexuality, soul evolution and other perceived features, such as masculinity, femininity, etc. Some of us are open to experiencing, learning and exploring new pursuits and social interactions and some of us are not.

If you're an Older type soul, Brianna Wiest describes 12 reasons why Old Souls have such a difficult time to fall in love.[61] It may diminish your prospects regarding potential partners, but that's the value of asking the Universe for what you want. Ask, and you shall always receive. Say to the Universe,

> At this stage in life, I deserve nothing more and nothing less.
>
> — DAVID SHAUN LARSEN

1. Old Souls have a powerful sense of their identity. Often this is isolating for them as they know exactly what they want and don't want a partner, and what works and doesn't.

2. Old Souls tend to be more sensitive than the average person and have more insight into the deeper meaning of things. This sensitivity can be to their detriment concerning feeling and over thinking. Don't overthink it because your sensitivity can break the ideal notion of what that relationship can be, especially if you haven't had the opportunity to establish a strong foundation.

3. In the meantime, you might find yourself involved in strong karmic type, 'twin flame relationships'. These are relationships that

you are meant to be in, i.e., they are meant to be, what they are meant to be; enjoy them for what they are and learn from what they offer you.

4. You often feel that you have a higher purpose in life. You may feel or think that this is a sacrifice at the expense of potential partners - these people may only distract you from achieving what you are here to do.

5. Often you will not settle for anything less than what you ask the Universe. You may meet potential partners who tick so many of your boxes, but you just don't feel that special something. You'd rather be alone but not lonely.

6. This deep sense of connection with others may attract many lovers who are fascinated with you, but few bring a sense of spiritual compatibility or meaningfulness. This is challenging and always will be, but the Universe is asking you not to give up hope.

7. You may find that you are less inclined to use the conventional ways of meeting people as you see them boring. Online dating may not come to you naturally or go out to a bar is also less appealing.

8. You often attract people who need healing (not love) maybe you might even think that you are a sexual healer of some sort or seek that type of healing expression. Hey!! Old souls always need to help others. Just take it as your sense of duty to evolve and as a child, be in awe and surprise for what comes along.

9. Older soul types aren't that interested in dating if anything they find it inherently exhausting. They can't feign their disinterest or instinctively say what the other person wants them to say for the sake of it. They get bored pretty quickly and get more stressed by the whole process as opposed to seeing the "fun" in it. They can't hide their emotions if they're bored it shows.

10. Old Souls have high standards. They expect a lot from themselves. Therefore, they expect a lot from their partners. Accept that you cannot

change others. Just don't write the other person off because they're imperfect!

11. We all have baggage. However Old Souls often find that they've had to do more work on their baggage, possibly more so than the average person. Old Souls have this innate need to understand their inner self because of the challenges they've had to face. We try to understand the baggage, what it looks like, how heavy it is and the surprise of why certain things are in it! Like a mirror, some of this can re-manifest in close relationships.

12. We also feel fear, as intensely as we feel love. The degree in which we feel love is proportionate to how we experience or feel fear. In other words, as much as we love; we feel the fear of losing it. This is just what Old Souls do; we experience the polarity of life far more deeply than the average person.

We All Age and Die

We all age and die, and if you think about it, every amazing story that we have ever told has the potential to touch countless lives. Our older people are our 'elders' the beholders of many stories, and we must respect and value their wisdom. It would be to our detriment as a society if we chose not to because once our Elders die, this knowledge and understanding are gone forever. Our modern society is increasingly isolating older people and creating an environment of social isolation and loneliness. How some people respond and view an older person is by devaluing and discriminating them; showing impatience and disrespect; exhibiting frustration and seeing them as lacking knowledge. It is a travesty if we value the beauty of youth over the wisdom of our Elders; for all of us age whether we like it or not. Being physically young has the advantages of youth but not the wisdom that comes with age.

> Old places and old persons in their turn, when spirit dwells in them, have an intrinsic vitality of which youth

is incapable, precisely, the balance and wisdom that come from long perspectives and broad foundations

— GEORGE SANTAYANA

Two frames of a picture of my two best mates Kevin Redmond and Anthony Templeton - the second picture was taken 10 years after the first in 2007.

Our youth and beauty culture feeds our obsession with ego. The more we become obsessed with it; the more we lose regarding our capacity to develop ourselves on the inside. Our outer obsession with looks and body can be at the expense of developing our inner self. If we place too much emphasis on looks and body, this imbalance or distortion will subtlety destroy us. Societal infatuation with this also manifests inter-generational trauma; so deep in our psyche, most people aren't even aware it's happening. False greed and ego are driving it, and this distraction can potentially be at the expense of our connectedness to life, it's stories and the interwoven threads it offers us as human beings. Do we need this and is this the legacy that we wish to pass on to our next generation/s?

Our Media (which is just full of Corporate beasts) is one of the guiltiest perpetrators. Besides feeding us every type of reality television to the point of overkill; the images we see on TV is mostly of botoxed people, faces without expression. If we feed our thirst for beauty and perfection, wrinkles and expression lines become our enemy. The alternative is frosty and cold without the warmth and surety that our imperfection provides. That's what the power of the media does; it's a lethal weapon to keep people stupid. Slowly we get dumbed down and don't question. This unwieldy power then becomes a form of Government and Corporate control. Who can we then trust? However, you can change this by challenging the youth and beauty culture that permeates our society. Social conditioning can have harmful impacts on our community and therefore challenging it; requires the courage and determination of the spiritual warrior.

> They are our storytellers – our elderly is meant to be those who share the secrets of wisdom and knowledge of life with our youth

— CAMERON DIAZ

Don't be scared to age; let's embrace our ageing process with dignity. ACON in Sydney has a project called LOVE which aims to create better conversations and improved social engagement for older lesbian, gay, bisexual, transgender and intersex (LGBTI) community members.62 I think the idea and notion of this is something that is so pertinent to all older people no matter what our sexuality. Ageing is such a defining part of our lives; why not make it something that is a cause for celebration and love.

I always say every line and expression on my face tells a story. The character expressions that come with age are charming and have indescribable features in so many ways. If we become cloned to look the same then how boring will life be for all of us. Our innate spiritual essence will disappear with the stretched faces of people searching to be something that they are not. Maybe as some us start dying inside, we will finally resist the forces and discover the new youth of Age. One of my role models is Annie Lennox, and she has been a strong advocate of growing old gracefully and a member of Purple Clover. Purple Clover is a site for people over 50 who have no sense of age. It encourages people to explore how we live today, what we've learned from the past & how to navigate the future.

> There's this youth culture that is really, really powerful and really, really strong, but what it does is it really discards people once they reach a certain age. I actually think that people are so powerful and interesting - women, especially - when they reach my age. We've got so much to say, but popular culture is so reductive that we just talk about whether we've got wrinkles, or whether we've put on weight or lost weight, or whether we've changed our hairstyle. I just find that so shallow.
>
> — ANNIE LENNOX, DEC. 25, 2014, PURPLE CLOVER

Let's finally stand up for Older People. We need to embrace our ageing process with dignity, and LOVE. Love who you are, and just be happy and content with yourself; especially as you get older. If you're conservative and set in your ways, or rather a little less risk averse, so be it! Maybe you're a bit kooky and eccentric, or even a bit radical; there is nothing wrong with that. We need that energy to counterbalance things, so why not celebrate it! No matter what, you're wiser and more mature, and that's heart-warming. I recently chose to live in Hervey Bay, Queensland to be closer to my mum as she ages but also to move to a community that values older people. There is kind and caring energy on the Fraser City Coast that is indescribable. Although it is the gateway to K'gari (Fraser Island) and home to the Australian whale migration, it's an energetic centre unlike any other in Australia. It's not a place where older people come to retire or die; it happens to be something much, much more. It's a fresh, energetic centre that embraces its community roots and offers a new and evolving city of art, creativity, education, healing, hospitality, innovation, nature, tourism and tranquillity.

A picture of me at dinner with my beautiful friend Heather - such an intelligent and gifted women and such an inspiration in my life!

Death and Our After Life

Death and Our After Life, really none of us know when we will die. In Buddhist philosophy, the most significant thing we will all do in our lives is our death, and we all die, just as we are all born. Most people avoid the conversation because they find it depressing or it distracts us from the joy of the moment. Upon reflection, I do think we have it around the wrong way. Death should be a celebration of a life lived, and perhaps the acknowledgement of our next journey to come. Given that we will all die, why don't we reflect more on the importance and value of our lives now? It's not that hard to stop and sniff the roses and get excited, feel the passion and laugh the way we do (embrace your inner child). We are now at a crucial time in our evolution, not only as human beings but also with the synergy of our planet. These are defining moments; our consciousness is being asked to evolve not only to actualise our destiny but also for the sustainable survival of our planet - Mother Earth.

Elogy for Wade

> As I lay on my bed in the early hours before daybreak. My heart ached with the knowledge that you were gone. My higher self knows there is no separation. Yet in spite of this, my whole being cried out in disbelief.
>
> The universe has called me *again*. But this time I responded kicking and screaming. How can my beloved universe play such a harsh cruel game?
>
> To take my first born, the love of my life, my stars, my earth, my world. All I could see was darkness. And then through this darkness you came to me. At first it was hard for me to bear, to know you had crossed to another realm but it gave me hope.
>
> It gave me love, it gave me strength, to know that your spirit lives on, and that our bond of love is forever and there is no separation.
>
> To know, that beyond my suffering something beautiful exists. Through my aching heart these secrets were revealed. So I responded to the universe's call, knowing I would encounter much darkness along the way.
>
> As I crossed over that threshold I could feel a higher force guiding me into the direction I needed to take, and it was through an open and grateful heart that I was able to feel my beloved universe embrace me again.
>
> And in my moments of deep spiritual reflection, I witnessed the Angels kissing and caressing me with the healing power of their love. And then it was time, to graciously let go of my sacred journey and return home.

My heart both broken and strengthened by love. I had been transformed, never to be the same. And as I looked back with open eyes and open heart I know it has all served its purpose.

I can now hear our beautiful mother earth's heart beat and feel the light and love that surrounds me. I now have a profound sense of peace and tranquility. And the most wonderful of all, I can now *always* hear the universe whispering to me, "I love you"

— JANET MURRELL, AUTHOR, AND COUNSELLOR

(A ELOGY FOR MY SON WADE WHO PASSED OVER 25/5/2008).

When our human consciousness is being challenged or initiated; in many ways, it forces us to question the value and quality of our lives. What's it all about? It's also a reminder to **never put off until tomorrow what we could do today**. Do you ever ask who you really are and what your name really is? Do you ever ask what is important to you as a person, not your career? Do you ever dream of doing something different and ask why you can't make it a reality? Do you ever ask if only I had more time, more money, more opportunity or the confidence, ambition, and commitment to succeed? Do you ever say what you really think but hold back because you fear judgement or being laughed at? How do you define happiness and ever wonder about its causes? These are all healthy questions to ask and the more you ask these type of questions, the more you will start to grow. When you commit yourself to your spiritual path, your inner voice will only become more perceptive and stronger. Once you discover "this is who I am" moment in your life, you will finally have the courage and realisation to forge something different. It will set you forth on a new path of discovery. This is your "true path" or "roadmap", and every day you will be blessed with the compassion and will to succeed in fulfilling your spiritual destiny.

This chapter has sought, in a limited way, to explore just one thread within the big picture of life. But living, loving, ageing and dying is the most encapsulating and significant thread to understand. There are many complex factors at work here, and I don't claim to have all the answers. Otherwise, I wouldn't be living. We live in a world of rich diversity and resources; but we live at a time of growing economic disparity, hardship, and fear. There isn't anything more important than valuing life, laughing and loving. The theme developed in this chapter has focused on some key features, what I call the "**archetypal features of life**". The things that hold control over us and our destiny and that of the human life cycle of birth and death.

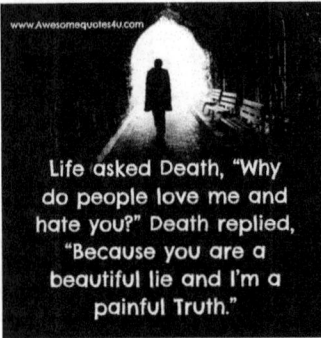

Life asked Death, "Why do people love me and hate you?" Death replied, "Because you are a beautiful lie and I'm a painful Truth."

Have you ever wondered about your After-Life? Imagine how many breaths you have breathed in your whole life. Hold that thought and imagine if one lifetime was just one breath? Within the entire realm of our continuous existence, life would be over in only a few seconds. Do you know the average healthy person breathes less and less as we age, and as we approach death? Just before death, our breathing gets progressively deeper and sometimes faster. In essence, when we die, we gasp for our last breath but this moment is also our release into the After-Life. I define the After-Life as,

> **What is it for YOU that makes YOU understand the deeper meaning of YOUR After-Life and YOUR After Existence, no one else's, but just YOURS?**

> — DAVID SHAUN LARSEN

16

AWAKENING THE SPIRIT
- LIGHTING THE FLAME OF CONSCIOUSNESS

"Dear Mother Goddess,
From the moment I awaken I can see the flame.
It flickers with beauty and knowing, and I am open;
My thirst for spiritual knowledge becomes a quest and devours me.
It seems endless, untold and for the most part, life seems unfair;
For the Universe is truly testing and initiating me into the unknown.
It's lonely at times, and I often can't see the light at the end of the
tunnel;
But somehow the journey gives me the resilience to live and survive.
Truly humbled by what I don't know, yet amazed at what lies ahead.
As hard as life may seem, my heart has faith, an inner strength;
And a greater sense of being and intuitive understanding.
For I realise more and more, that I have deep insight;
And see things that many others do not see.
I give gratitude and thanks."

- David Shaun Larsen

Our Spiritual Coming of Age

AWAKENING the Spirit is best described as our spiritual coming of age or as I'd like to say, "lighting the flame of our spiritual consciousness". This Awakening point is midway between our ego nature (or attachment) down one end of the spectrum and spirituality (or meaningfulness) down the other end. **One end is about attachment and ego, and the other is about non-attachment and spirit.** One end of the spectrum shackles us to our limitations while the other end of the spectrum liberates us to evolve. We can either treasure our older more evolved Souls (our Elders) or push them away.

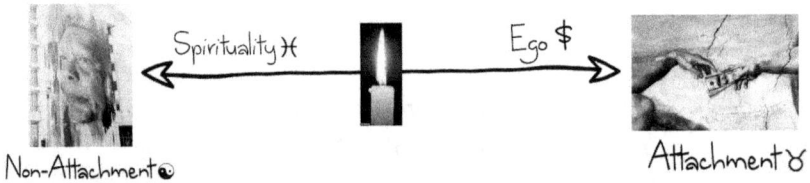

A picture representing the spectrum of our spiritual journey from our ego nature to the right to spirituality to the left. The candle is symbolic of our Awakening moment.

When we reach the Awakening point, we become immersed in the experience and start to see things with new eyes. It enables us to become more aware and understand the connection we have, not just to nature but to the cosmos. We begin to grow in maturity and are more likely to appreciate the Buddhist teachings about the impermanence of life, suffering and the wisdom of selflessness. These teachings reveal what it means to understand the deeper meaning of life and not neglect our wider wisdom perspective. The Awakening time also manifests with a deeper connection to reflection, meditation, and solitude, as a path to find the necessary fearlessness to grow.

When we Awaken, we now have enough collective experience to challenge our ego nature; and start to counterbalance life with a more dedicated focus and commitment to the spiritual path ie., that stirs passion and seeks to explore the deeper meaning, truthfulness, and value of life. The midpoint of this spectrum is our Awakening point, however, unfortunately, it may take many years for some people to transition across it. For many others, they just find it too hard and cower back to what they know best. It's important to not predominantly stay in your ego nature for too long because if you haven't got it together by your midlife age; it's just so much harder and more of a struggle later on. But never say never!

When we consciously decide to break free and light the candle, we have taken the first step. This is the most courageous act, for it endears us with the responsibility to challenge our ego nature. As we move forward, we find that we have more courage and most of our decisions are made with the right intention. But sometimes even when we break through, we can also end up feeling a little broken. Respect that we are all broken in many ways, and no one is perfect. This is something that our inner child can fix, especially with the right influence of people to guide us and heal our wounds. Being open to this process also enables us to then become the wounded healers.

Christ the Redeemer (statue) at the summit of Mount Corcovado, Rio de Janeiro, south-eastern Brazil.

How do you know when you are Awakening?

How do you know when you are Awakening? I attract many people who are going through this stage in their spiritual life, and I believe a critical mass of Humanity is about to Awaken over the next five to seven years. You'll know when you are Awakening; as you start to evaluate or review your whole life, friends, career, purpose in life and what's important to you and what's not. Your inner voice or intuition becomes stronger, and you also become a lot more sensitive at this time. The types of people you meet are different, yet they have the same thing in common. They are often people who are more sensitive, empathic, generally non-conformists and seem to have this innate ability to guide others or empower you to do the same. People are more likely at this time to understand what it is like to have a teacher in their life. The people or teachers you start to meet at this time also open you to things that are a little unusual and different and sometimes at first damn scary. Some may even say kooky and alternative, but they certainly hold views that you never thought you'd ever entertained; especially when you look back on your former self.

What's most important at this time, is that you have the personal resolve to keep yourself true to your convictions and newfound path in life. However, around this time, it is also normal for people to blow out their candle and resume the same old pattern or status quo with life. It's difficult when loved ones you've known all your life just don't seem to get you anymore and start judging your decisions, behaviour and new friends. Remember they are just projecting their own fears. The other end of the spectrum can be quite frightening to some and others just throw themselves at it no matter what comes along; much like a kid in a lolly shop. There's no prescriptive process, but ultimately we will all have the same outcome. Some of us will vacillate at this time, and others will thrive! All you need to know is that it's okay to blow out your candle but trust me you will relight it again when you are ready; just take your time. Eventually, you will just keep your flame alit; so have faith, the Universe is asking you to grow, so embrace it the best way you can.

Courage and Teachers

When did I truly Awaken? I'd say my Awakening occurred when I was 29 (although reading my first book on Buddhist philosophy at 19 was enlightening). However, I found once I committed myself to the spiritual path, the Universe asked me to Awaken even further. In many respects, this establishes and promotes the concept, that there are various stages of your Awakening process i.e., you either experience a quickening of events or subtle levels of development as you evolve. I feel I have experienced the latter with life.

Lighting the flame feeds your spiritual consciousness, and sets you forth on a path of untold intuition, wisdom, higher meaning and understanding in life

Although I have been on a spiritual path for most of my life, my Awakening was life-changing because this was when I met my first teacher, Kerrie Redgate. Kerrie was a Buddhist and an Astrologer, and I initially went to her for an Astrology reading i.e., of my Astrological Natal Chart. I was quite naive, as I didn't know much about Astrology. Like most people, my awareness was limited to sun sign columns in newspapers. I remember my first reading with her went for 3 to 4 hours. Afterwards, I was quite speechless. How could this lady validate everything about me and also have so much insightful understanding of my life? She did this by professionally interpreting my natal chart but also gave me the necessary tools such as book authors and titles; talked about her life experiences and suggested other ideas and strategies for spiritual fulfilment and success.

Teachers come into our lives every day, and some are truly selfless in their actions. One example of a selfless teacher was a Registered Nurse who I worked with when I was a student nurse working in the operating theatre at the Queen Elizabeth Hospital in Adelaide, probably circa 1985. I was assisting this theatre nurse with a patient who was having major brain surgery, and she asked me to swap positions so that I could assist the surgeon directly. It was such an amazing experience and selfless act, seeing (first hand) a surgeon about to use mild suction, using a suction device on an open area of the exposed brain.

The surgeon asked for a gauze pattie (cloth) to be passed to him, and he gently placed the pattie on the exposed brain tissue before applying the suction tube. Something so complex seemed so simple, yet logical! It made sense, if you'd applied suction to the exposed surface of the brain, you'd end up sucking out the delicate neural tissue. Argh logic prevails, it's so powerful and a valuable lesson that has always remained with me. However, I read in a recent

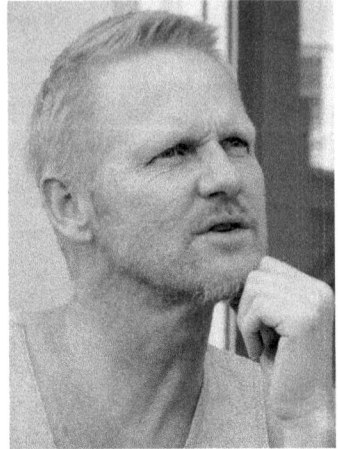

A picture of me deep in thought possibly one of those lightbulb moments

research paper, that suggested contrary to their aim; patties actually adhere to brain tissue and cause damage during removal.[63] The article goes on to say; "to mitigate possible adhesion and neural tissue damage, surgeons should consider regular irrigation (application of water) during neurosurgical procedures". I guess the moral of the story is, "don't just rely on using a gauze pattie; when you apply suction to the brain tissue during major surgery". The other way to look at it is - knowledge, mindfulness, and experience of time, affords great wisdom; for we have much greater insight around not only what we do and how we do but I also why we do it?

Out of your Comfort Zone

Being Out of your Comfort Zone often goes hand in hand with an Awakening experience. It seems that the nature and value of each experience possibly become more extreme and extraordinary; the greater we evolve along with our spiritual path.

I truly believe some things in life, you're not meant to understand, until well after the event. Sometimes, you may even question whether they were moments or events of stupidity or smart wisdom. One event I remember so vividly as a young boy, was when our family was nearly home after a long car trip (some 2600kms) from Adelaide to Mount Isa. We were close to passing though Camooweal (only 189 km to Mount Isa) but the Camooweal river was flooded, like a raging torrent. It was during the infamous wet season, and the waterline was above the meter reader on the road. My father in his wisdom decided to get our car towed by a road train.

> Move out of your comfort zone. You can only grow if you are willing to feel awkward and uncomfortable when you try something new.
>
> — BRIAN TRACY

The driver of the road train hooked our car to the back of the road train with some cable, and he proceeded to cross the creek. Of course, our car started moving or actually floating, and water came seeping through the bottom of the car very fast, actually gushing in. I thought OMG we will either make it across or sink.

I remember putting my hand out the passenger window and could feel the water splashing right up my arm. Then water was so furious and would soon start gushing in and swallow us all. What made the situation worse was seeing a coach bus washed to one side of the river and another car floating further downstream. At this moment, I wondered if this was a smart move or just plain stupid, but we managed to get across to the other side. The car was still functioning so we could resume the shorter part of the trip home. Looking back, I think it was smart wisdom thanks to my father. It wouldn't have been possible to wait out the floods as Camooweal was on the other side of the river, so we would've been forced to make the long journey back to nearest town, Tennant Creek (some 600 km away).

Picture of me at the Devils Pool standing on the edge of the Victoria Falls, Zambia / Zimbabwe border 2004

" Do not let your fire go out, spark by irreplaceable spark, in the hopeless swamps of the approximate, the not-quite, the not-yet, the not-at-all. Do not let the hero in your soul perish, in lonely frustration for the life you deserved, but have never been able to reach. Check your road and the nature of your battle. The world you desired can be won. It exists, it is real, it is possible, it is yours.

— AYN RAND

Writing this book is a classic example of being out of my comfort zone. There has been some fear and trepidation in terms of self-publishing, but ultimately my hope is to make the world a better place. I feel that I'm a writer at heart and on occasion have got great pleasure from others who have been inspired by what I have written. Story-telling is so powerful! For me, this journey is ultimately about being selfless and true to myself; especially in terms of my own and ongoing spiritual awakening process.

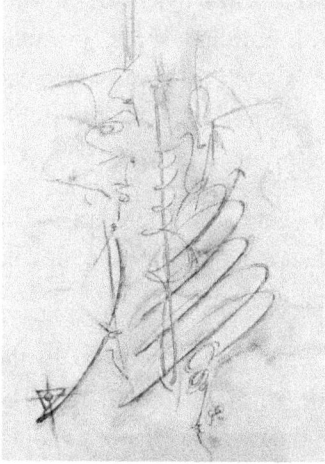

The personalised drawing was done by a lady who I studied Astrology with, in 1994. It portrays a spiral of gold light representing my kundalini energy spiralling upwards sparking at my Crown Chakra

It takes courage to be out of your comfort zone and stop hiding behind the veneer that limits our ability to grow and challenge ourselves as human beings. It is my intention that this book Awakens others to some deeper insights that I have observed or witnessed in life. This also takes immense courage to speak and put it out there. In French, they use a word called témoignage. In essence, it's our ability to witness indifference, make others understand what it means and speak out i.e., either in private or in public as a vehicle for change, challenge and/or protest.

" Lighting the candle is very much about re-connecting people to Awakening to their true self.

It's something so personal, awe-inspiring and in synergy with your own life purpose.

— DAVID SHAUN LARSEN

The Seven Energy Centres and their role in Awakening

George Kinder who is a renowned Buddhist teacher and Harvard-trained certified financial planner discusses money in the context of the seven energy chakras of the body. Kinder postulates that our beliefs, attitudes, feelings and physical responses to money are entangled in these various energy centres. I'm just presenting his views basically as another lens through which to view the overall Awakening process, especially for those who still see life only through a money lens. Kinder's book, ***The Seven Stages of Money Maturity***, is filled with practical information, market-tested, wealth-building skills, personal success stories, and spiritual guidance.[64] It's such an invaluable read and guide for those who want a richly lived life.

1.   Innocence (base chakra) - The childhood state we are born in, devoid of any concept of money.

2.   Pain (second chakra in the middle of the abdomen) - The discovery that we have more money than some and less than others, and that work is necessary to make a living.

Our souls evolve each lifetime; death is only like the sun setting then we are reborn just like the sun rising.

3.   Knowledge (third chakra just below the navel) — the intellectual task of learning financial techniques such as saving, budgeting, and investing.

4.   Understanding (the fourth chakra, the Heart)— the emotional work done in coming to terms with feelings around money, such as greed, envy, and resentment (which are rooted in pain).

Kinder writes that when we are able to relate to money increasingly from the heart or fourth chakra, we begin to see our money from a wiser context. **The possibility of personal transformation that we experience at this stage is not dissimilar to our Awakening process.**

❝ Now we understand the larger world and see the emotional consequences of our monetary decisions within its rich tapestry. We are able to recognise it as an agent for personal transformation.

— GEORGE KINDER, THE SEVEN STAGES OF
MONEY MATURITY

5.   Vigour (the fifth chakra, the Throat) — the energy (physical, emotional, and spiritual) that must be expended to reach financial goals.

6.   Vision (the sixth chakra, the Third Eye) — the direction of Vigour outward toward the health and welfare of communities, with or without a profit motive.

7.   Aloha (the seventh chakra, the Crown) - the compassionate goodwill that allows one to use money to perform acts of kindness without expecting anything in return.

Using these Seven Stages will help you understand how even our encounters with money and more importantly, in life in general, is a step toward further Awakening. This underlying philosophy basically teaches us about one of the most important relationships, not only the relationship we share with others but the relationship we share with ourselves. At our most evolved point, it is always the spiritual warrior who will find it so natural to serve something much greater than oneself.

Me in a Microlight high above Victoria Falls overlooking the Zambezi River in Zambia 2004

17

REPUBLIC OF AUSTRALIA

- THE EMERGENCE OF A 21ST CENTURY NATION

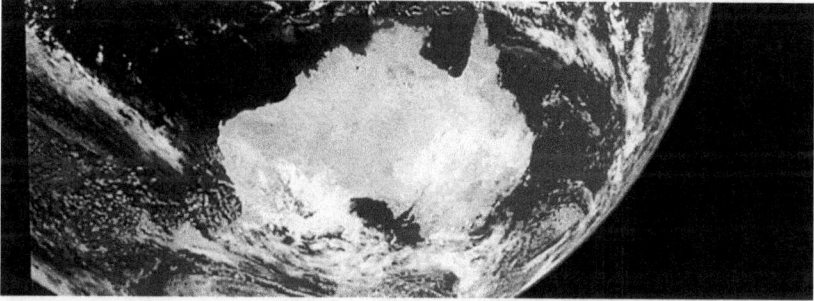

" There is no greater agony than bearing the untold story of what our great nation could've become. If we hold it inside us; we miss out on the immense opportunity to teach future generations about our vision for Australia.

If our next generation doesn't hear our stories, they will see us as much greater fools than what we think we are. Our future generations know that they eventually become the great beholders of our stories and destiny...

— DAVID SHAUN LARSEN

How do we describe the emergence of a 21st century Nation? There are many ways you could describe this process, but I'd rather think the emergence of a 21st century Nation describes the distinct attributes of the nation that we see Australia becoming today and over the next 5 years. This is opposed to the nation we birthed at Federation in 1901. I believe there are three distinct elements that define our modern nation, much like a trinity of energy.

A map of Australia incorporating our Aboriginal colours: Black – represents the Aboriginal people of Australia. Yellow circle – represents the Sun, the giver of life and protector. Red – represents the red earth, the red ochre used in ceremonies and Aboriginal peoples' spiritual relation to the land.
newsroom.unsw.edu.au

As a nation, we have an identity or that part of us that defines us as people and what we aspire to achieve in life and work. **This is what I call our nation's spirit.** We also have an emotional heart or that part of us that embodies our emotional feeling as a nation. This is what I call our nation's soul. Lastly, we have a persona or character, which very much describes how the world sees us as a people and a nation. This is our nation's personality vehicle or outer world identity.

If you think about it, Australia is a country that has found its modern identity through a range of attributes such as punching above its weight in terms of science and humanitarianism; experimenting with new ways of doing things; fighting to preserve its environment; embracing computers and technology with a fervour and not to mention our sexual diversity and multiculturalism. Also like our flora and fauna, our geographic isolation has created something a little bit different when it comes to celebrating its dance music culture; rock bands, cabaret, forging its identity through cinema and interactive light displays such as 'Vivid'. We also exhibit extreme apathy towards our current nanny state and political system. All these features describe our obsession with being different and unique (what I call Aquarian in nature).

However, our nations' soul speaks to something very different, our inherent ability to reconcile the past and heal deep emotional wounds. Our nation's soul is the spiritual essence of who we are and our connection to the land; something so profound and ethereal, thus represented so symbolically by our Indigenous people and their cultures. The Oldest Continuous Spiritual Culture on Earth, that's something mighty to be proud of and celebrate with such joy and passion.

A photograph of the Australian Parliament.

The persona or character of our nation in many ways, defines how the world sees us as a nation e.g., such as when we finally emerge as a Republic. We are seen as easy go lucky, optimistic and always coming to the aid of others when there are disasters, emergencies or war (the great rescuers). We always fight for the rights of others; love our freedom and are also characterised by many things such as our love for sport, gambling, horse racing, respect for truth and wanting fairness for all. We also don't want our politicians to give us the simple facts, for we are not that stupid. We want our politicians to tell us the detail and the truth; it's as simple as that.

The Australian Counter-Revolution - 2018-2023

Wake up Australia, the undercurrent of the Australian Counter-Revolution has started and will only escalate. In effect, it commenced in late 2017, with our postal vote for Marriage Equality (and possibly earlier last year with the Uluru Statement). The Marriage Equality postal vote has nothing to do with Marriage Equality but has everything to do with where we stand as a nation, in terms of our maturity, sense of justice and appetite for change.

Play Your Part in Creating Change for Australia

This will be followed this year or possibly next by our first recession in 27 years since June 1991. This recession will be significant for Australia, possibly quite severe and will happen under a Liberal Government. I always see recessions as great levellers, as they force us to look outwards rather than inwards. In times of recession, everyone knows someone who is doing it tough, and we can no longer rely on the old industries or ways of working e.g., mining, agriculture, and property. A recession is a catalyst for change, that births new innovative industries or ways of working.

I believe this change will be centred primarily around computers, science, technology and innovation and structural changes on a scale that we have never seen before i.e., green technology, new scientific discoveries, carbon tax, greater environmental protection, political uprising (reclaiming our civil liberties and transforming our political institutions) and many other revolutionary grass-root and innovative changes around how we live. This will also lead to massive societal changes or shifts in our national psyche; not only around the way we think but also view ourselves in the world. In many respects, it will enable us to transform ourselves as a nation, out of the "me me me" culture that we have created over the past 27 years of economic prosperity.

Therefore, what we become and how we act as a nation, will be more focussed towards the greater good of Humanity in contrast to our self-obsessed, patriarchal and inward-looking qualities as a country. But I believe more and more people will have the courage to challenge the system. During this period, we will reconnect with our egalitarianism as a nation; focus more on a fair and equitable sharing of resources and wealth. There will be an escalating shift towards the left of politics that will be revolutionary. The emergence of far-right extremism in Australia will be put to bed, as Australians will finally see it for what it is i.e., a racist, conservative, and backward thinking ideology that no longer serves any purpose for our great nation.

Other key events that will most likely play out, will be a movement for legalised euthanasia in most states, the legalisation of medicinal cannabis and the likelihood of drug reform in Australia. This will become a major reform for our nation, similar to Portugal or Norway, using a health centred approach. Finally, we will wake up as a nation and start dealing with our alarming drug and alcohol issues and escalate the fight against domestic violence, as a matter of urgency.

The Rise of the Great Southern Land, Outback Mount Isa, Queensland

The Drug Reform agenda will:

- Spearhead the decriminalisation of recreational drugs.
- Introduce drug testing at rave/music festivals.
- Put an end to the use of sniffer dogs.
- Increase access to free drug rehabilitation treatment.
- Change our perceptions around drug use, not as an addiction but as a disease.

We will not eliminate the black market but it is likely to substantially reduce in its size, free up the court system, and people will be able to seek treatment without discrimination and fear of stigmatisation. Sites such as **www.realmedicine.com.au** will spearhead access for people living with acute and/or chronic pain; seeking the expert advice of practitioners who prescribe medicinal cannabis in consultation with their doctors to help manage their symptoms.

How politics plays out is uncertain, but I think we will see the emergence of new left-leaning political parties. Thanks to our compulsory voting system; a new leader will emerge. This leader will be someone inspiring like Bernie Saunders in the USA, who will be able to inspire the nearly one million Australians under 30 who have never registered to vote. Most people do not realise that funding to the Australian Electoral Commission has been cut, so they have little capacity to follow up on people who have never registered to vote. The Australian Government knows this because if they all turned out to vote, they could change the course of our next election overnight. Our youngest people tend to be more left-leaning by nature. Therefore, it's common sense that they are the future force of change - Our New Hope.

We just need to stop burying our heads in the sand, and I'm optimistic that the counter-revolution and the forces of change will do exactly that. This change will be about building momentum, and we will finally reach a critical mass of people who will accept nothing less than the will of the Australian people for constitutional reform.

The Republic of Australia - January 26th 2023

I envisage that Australia will choose to become a Republic by February 2024 (either February 12th 2024 or January 26th 2023). Most people cannot possibly imagine how it could happen so soon but it will happen, trust me!

I am by no means a psychic and let me preface this; my predictions for the future are based on a number of lenses I use to observe patterns with behaviour, ideas generation, energy resonance and mind sets, including: -

- Simply being intuitive and observing and looking for the deeper meaning behind things. It's then just a matter of connecting the dots and seeing patterns.
- Forecasting and scenario planning, one of the tools I use in relation to ideas generation and channelling concepts. I also test concepts and ideas with others which is another source of validation.
- Energy resonance which is about mapping past, present and future universal energetic influences.
- Using my skill of clairaudience i.e., ability to perceive messages through sounds (music) or words from outside sources, when I'm spiritually connected in one with the Universe.

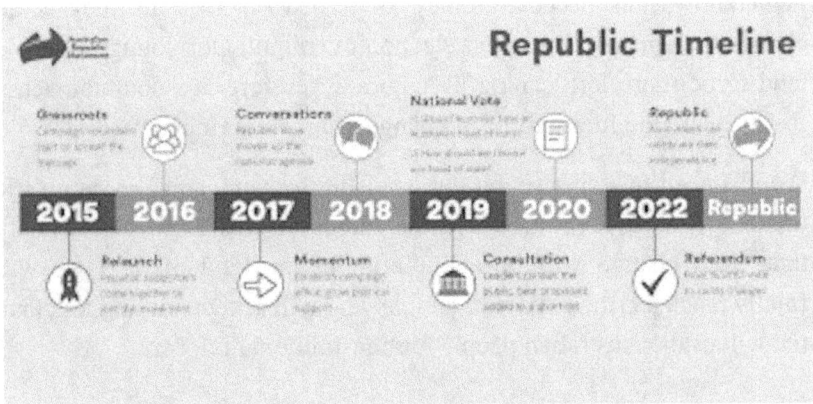

A timeline from the Australian Republican Movement. It is possible!!! This image by no means shows my affiliation with any organisation.

The birth of our modern nation will not only be a product of the counter-revolution, but also a series of events that forces us to determine how our own destiny plays out. This will be a time of great self-determination for our Nation. Likely events include:

- The deep recession that we are destined to have (approx. 2-3 years). This will also be a catalyst for more Australians "Awakening".

- Massive shifts in terms of global financial markets, leading to further instability and unrest in the world.
- Rising right-wing extremism in certain countries, unfortunately including the USA (with the exception of some states like California and New York).
- Most likely with much sadness, the death of the Queen. This becomes a catalyst for change in itself; with conversations escalating around the debate for Australia becoming a Republic.
- The passing of the media mogul Rupert Murdoch. This will symbolise the loss of his personal grip on our media.
- Extreme climate change events associated with Global Warming and the USA leaving the Paris Accord - this legal process will take four years to complete and would lead to an official exit on Nov. 4, 2020.
- Immense influential change with greater numbers of our younger generation becoming more politically astute and challenging our outdated and prevailing patriarchal systems.
- As more and more people Awaken, this reaches a critical mass of people by 2020-2021, that becomes the catalyst for evolutionary change for our nation. **Change without Revolution.**
- The possible nuclear threat from North Korea and the likely questioning of our alliance with the US.

I fear that Australia will possibly become a nuclear target for North Korea, with a devastating attack being played out. This or some act of similar proportion will be the fundamental shift for Australia (not only the damage it will cause to our environment but on our psyche as a nation). The USA will most likely not come to our aid and possibly, more surprisingly China will. This will only place a greater emphasis on how Australia traverses the US / China relationship, with much diplomacy and care. The only solution for us is to declare neutrality in the world, much like Sweden and Switzerland did in Europe during the 1930s. Do you get a sense of history repeating itself? Most likely!

Sir Henry Parkes envisioned the idea of a Federation of Australian colonies but died in 1899, two years before his dream coming to fruition. In the footsteps of my triple great, grandfather; I see a vision for the birth of a new 21st century Australia, and it's one of the grandest visions one could ever imagine. However, what is central to this vision is the need for constitutional change, when our Indigenous people are proclaimed at the heart of our new constitution. The eventual transcendence of their culture will be the greatest gift to our new nation.

Australia's future holds boundless opportunities, why not walk along the jetty as far as the horizon. See for yourself, imagine the unimaginable!

> We seek constitutional reforms to empower our people and take a rightful place in our own country. When we have power over our destiny our children will flourish. They will walk in two worlds and their culture will be a gift to their country.

—ULURU STATEMENT FROM THE HEART

Uluru Statement from the Heart

In the lead up to the looming changes that will occur in 2023/2024, most Australians living and working overseas will see the writing on the wall. I predict over the year leading up to, and soon after Australia becomes a Republic, the Australian diaspora will mostly come home. The Australian diaspora refers to the approximately 1,000,000 Australian citizens (approximately 5% of the population) who today live outside of Australia. Most of these people are based in Europe and Asia and their return home, will help seed and fuel the innovative enterprises our new nation needs; providing an injection of cutting-edge ides, new ways of thinking and working.

Our immigration intake will stay at the same level, if not increase further due to escalating political instability elsewhere and rising public support for embodying our humanitarian spirit as a nation. In addition, our immigration intake over the next six years will see an additional 1,200,000 or more new Australians immigrate here, who will consist of many more enlightened types. Watch our immigration patterns for yourself and see who comes here, you will be surprised. This will also influence our counter-revolution and everything else leading up to Australia becoming a Republic.

Australia will not only birth the world's most modern nation; we will also become a nation that embodies the global force of the future energy to come, that will influence the world over the next 15 years following 2023/2024. Humanity and 2024 will become more about our survival, how we influence the world and the survival of the planet.

In my third book, I plan to write about Australia's future role in the world; a nation with global influence, fulfilling its true purpose and destiny…

Maybe we need a new way of viewing DOWN UNDER don't you think? It's all about perspective.

18

HUMANITY AND 2023/24

- OUR OPPORTUNITY TO EMBRACE THE NEXT GLOBAL SHIFT

Humanity is now forced to understand its true nature, challenge its ego and become what it truly deserves to be in the Universal order of things. Forced on our knees looking for the answer, this will be the Global Shift that finally evolves our consciousness.

There will be a shock event unlike anything Humanity has experienced before. Out of the chaos, pain and revolution will spur new endeavours, a world of endless opportunity that seeks to drive Humanity to new frontiers, never possibly imagined before.

— DAVID SHAUN LARSEN

What About Us?

WHAT ABOUT US? At this time in our human history, we are increasingly becoming aware of something much deeper Awakening in us. This is simply about our quest or search for meaning in life, and a fair go for all. Where we have greater control over our destinies, as opposed to the control, greed, and mistrust of Government and Corporations e.g., corruption, unanswered questions and plans that end in disaster.

> Without a global revolution in the sphere of human consciousness, a more humane society will not emerge
>
> — VACLAV HAVEL

This is about our civil liberties and freedoms, giving us greater control over:

- The lives and the decisions that affect us.
- How we care, love and raise our children.
- The health and well-being of the people we love.
- Our right to choose who we love, without discrimination.
- Our right to choose the place and time when we die.
- Our right to indulge in whatever makes us happy without hurting the welfare of others.
- Enabling our Indigenous people to be granted the constitutional recognition and reform which is the right thing to do.
- How the land we love is used; the national parks, the marine sanctuaries and protecting the environment above all else.
- Our right to come to the aid of those misfortunate and **ensure safe passage to this country because we can.**

Are you ready? The next Global Shift will be the most significant for our planet, which will most likely result in a shock event of a scale like no other. It will be the Global Shift to transform humanities consciousness, evolving us into a more humane society. It's going to be our coming of age and a time when Humanity's direction will be focussed towards the future.

A picture of a possible flag for when Australia becomes a Republic. I predict the date January 26, 2023.

It will be a future with a global network of communities and a predominant liberal society that is open-minded, progressive and unconventional. Government, Corporations and Financial Institutions will collapse and become a thing of the past, replaced by new Global bodies and systems advancing science, environmentalism, computers and technological endeavours. Things such as green technology, geo-spatial innovation, quantum commuters, digital media, energetic resonance and artificial intelligence will drive this change.

> **We are searchlights, we can see in the dark.** We are rockets, pointed up at the stars. We are billions of beautiful hearts. And you sold us down the river too far...

What about us?…

We are problems that want to be solved. We are children that need to be loved. We were willing, we came when you called. But man you fooled us, enough is enough.

What about us?…

Sticks and stones they may break these bones but then I'll be ready, are you ready? **It's the start of us, waking up, come on.** Are you ready? I'll be ready.

What about us?…

I don't want control, I want to let go. Are you ready? I'll be ready. Cause now it's time to let them know. **We are ready**

— PINK LYRICS - "WHAT ABOUT US?"

Most people whom are "Awakening" or already have "Awakened", instinctively know or feel deep down inside that that some type of change is coming. They're also becoming more aware of their power, sense of truth and justice and true purpose on this earth. Therefore, we need to experience or undergo this immense transformation for the ultimate benefit of Humanity.

The series of shock events will possibly result in a global conflict on a massive scale, environmental destruction, technological revolution (impacting on the planet in a radical way) or germ warfare leading to possible extinction. The people and nations that survive or transform from the initial chaos, will be faced with either two options, the choice to evolve or revolt. How this plays out will be entirely dependent on how resistant we are to change, due to traditional, cultural and societal limitations.

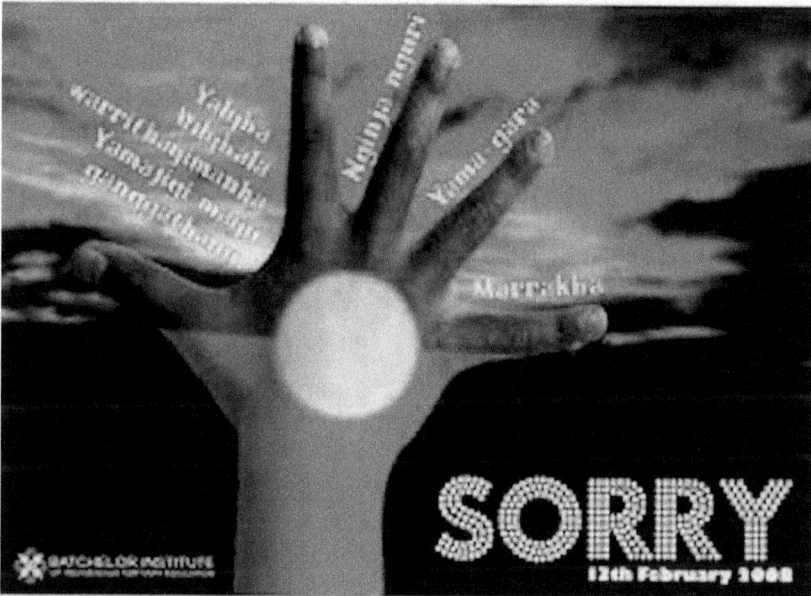

> " The world is changeable, and its ability to change is so fragile that a single person can be responsible for it

— A.J. DARKHOLME, RISE OF THE MORNINGSTAR

The radical transformation of civilisation

The radical transformation of civilisation, as we know it, will lead to the emergence of:

- A radical change in our political concepts and systems - new movements will emerge appropriate for the 21st Century, based on the individual pursuit of liberty as the primary political value.
- A new global world arrangement, eventually advancing Humanity to the stage where I believe we will be invited into the self-discovery of other worlds and advanced lifeforms (not the other way around).

- Advances in science and technology on an unprecedented scale; including quantum computers, digital transformation, and artificial intelligence.
- Radical transformation of Disability services such as the emerging NDIS - read on further in this chapter.
- New forms of leadership emerge - change and thought leaders, who are able to inspire and captivate the public with their visionary ideas and new perceptions.

Future city: What will Adelaide look like 20 years from now in 2036? Source Sam Kelton, The Advertiser, May 15, 2016

- Greater acceptance of cultural diversity, including "global multiculturalism" and sexual experimentation, diversity and liberty - a movement towards Universal sexuality.
- Communities will advance and merge as intersectional adapters and become more networked. However, communities will be primarily motivated by various ideals, principles and values, adopted at the time ie., our primary way to teach and impart cultural norms & truth.
- A generational shift will be in full force as millennials and Gen X grow older and become more politically astute and

herald evolutionary change around the notion of purposeful work.

- Educational systems are likely to transform into a technology-driven world with an array of virtual learning possibilities; with an emphasis on science and social learning, humanitarianism, ideas generation and change management.
- Advances in science will further propel aviation into new realms and herald a new era for space exploration (2030 onwards…). Australia will rapidly develop and transform its Space Industries.
- New technological advances and discoveries in medicine, healing therapies and treatments will emerge, based on complex systems using genetic and energetic resonance for healing (most pharmaceutical medicine will eventually become obsolete by 2034).
- Australia will become a Republic most likely before 2024 and fulfil its destiny to take on a more significant role in the world i.e., the world's most modern nation and Aquarian in identity (January 26th).
- A world of endless opportunity will drive Humanity to new frontiers in Space from 2039 onwards (frontiers never possibly imagined before).
- The global shift from 2039 onwards will be the time Humanity makes the impossible, possible; bound only by our imagination. This will herald an awareness of other civilisations and worlds far advanced than ours.

> " If humans are still around after a massive catastrophe, they may look back and think it a grave dereliction that we did not do more to reduce existential risk. But if humanity is gone, and there is nobody left to deplore our era, that doesn't make us any less deplorable.
>
> — NICK BOSTROM

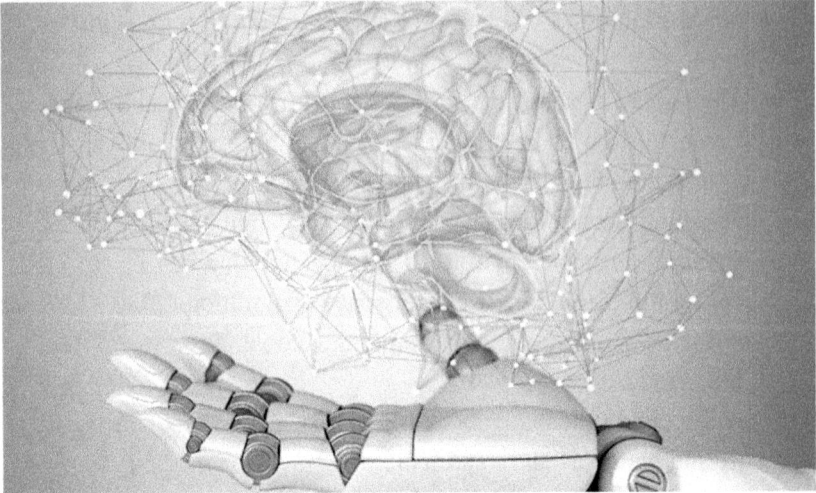

The Power of Cognitive Technologies to Change UX, Businesses and BGO
Software. Search by image cognitive technologies

It's also by no design fault that there are many people living today with exceptional purpose, who I believe are destined to create, invent and lead the way through the coming times. IN some sort of way maybe it's the Universe's grand design for helping and supporting Humanity through the changes that are coming. Those who are able to "tune in" to the vibrational shift will adjust, and "ride the wave" into the future. Those who cling on to old ways, patterns, and teachings of the past will increasingly find things "working against them" unless they are open to change altogether.

Australia - A Nation Embracing its Geospatial Future

Despite having a small population relative to its geographic size, Australia punches well above its weight on the global geospatial stage. Niall Conway in his article for GiS Professional provides an impressive overview of the Australian geospatial industry, its active community, as well as the many geospatial initiatives which are taking place in the land Down Under.[45]

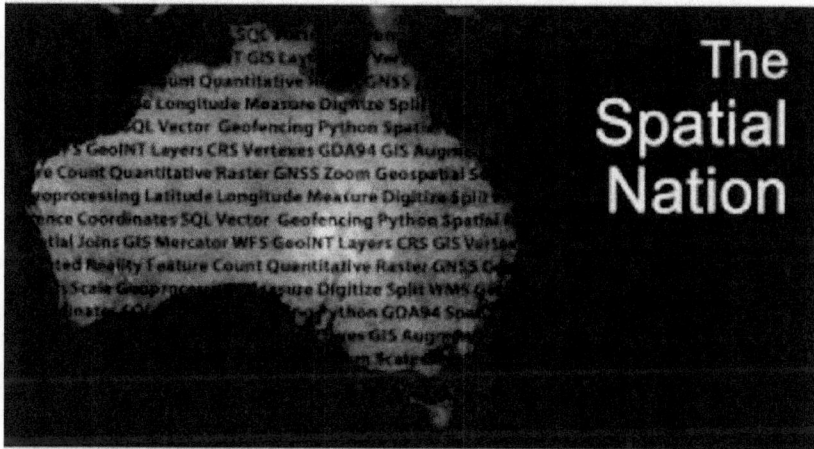

A map of Australia The Spatial Nation

Conway highlights the following key features: -

- As a land with a long, rich history of maps. A complex web of migration routes known as Songlines was used by our Indigenous people for essential seasonal migration. By sharing Songline verses with one another, other tribes would be able to navigate the unfamiliar landscape by reciting the borrowed verses, thereby ensuring their tribe's survival.
- The success of the Australian geospatial industry has been driven by a strong history of investment by industry leaders in order to protect the nation's natural and man-made wealth.
- The Australian geospatial community, together with the space sector, provides direct employment to approximately 100,000 people.
- The country boasts a thriving geospatial community which receives strong support from many local bodies and active representation on a number of international bodies.
- An indication of our country's emerging status on the global geospatial stage was the hosting of an international conference

in Sydney this year attracting industry leaders from around the world.

- The geospatial field presents many opportunities; a notable example is Campbell Newman (the former Premier of Queensland) who has focussed his attention on agricultural robotics as an attempt to scale up Australia's attempts to become the 'food bowl' of Asia.
- Nevertheless, the Geospatial industry is not without its challenges. There is a skills shortage; not having enough graduates study surveying, spatial and software development courses.

The race for Artificial Intelligence (AI) dominance

The race for Artificial Intelligence (AI) dominance is fast expanding. Tech companies are leading the way with companies paying huge salaries for knowledge and expertise, including in academia. This is going to create a significant and powerful shift around how we live; possibly everything from driving cars and providing manual labour (including dangerous jobs) to even cyborg technology and diagnosing an illness without the need for a doctor. China's third-largest technology company Baidu has just announced artificial intelligence as its major focus, including driverless cars.

Soul Machines (a Kiwi startup) AI company focuses on creating 'emotive' machines and has revealed its first virtual assistant named, "Rachael".[48]

Rachel is an avatar created by two-time Oscar winner Mark Sagar, who worked on the blockbuster movie of the same name. He states that his aim is to make man socialise with the machine, by putting a human face on artificial intelligence.

It potentially opens up a whole new paradigm around how we relate but I ask this one key question, will AI ever possess the ability to feel and possess the innate wisdom of the human soul?

See it on YOUTUBE: Soul Machines' 'Digital Humans'

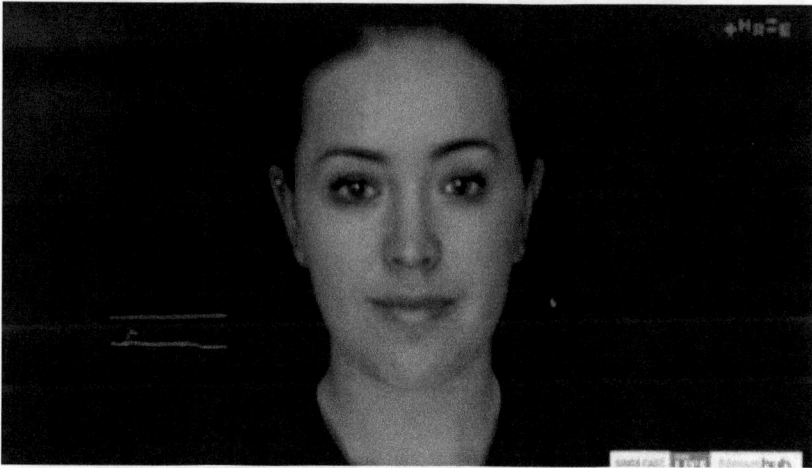

A Youtube picture of "Rachel" - Soul Machines an Artificial Intelligence company, focuses on creating 'emotive' machines and has revealed its first virtual assistant.

> So what we are doing with Soul Machines is trying to build the central nervous system for humanising this kind of computer

— MARK SAGAR, SOUL MACHINES

View of Australia and Earth as viewed from space.

" In the true heritage of our Aboriginal people, may we pay our respects to the traditional owners of this land, our Elders both past and present who have walked on this most beautiful and sacred earth!

It's not our intention to take anything for granted; your invaluable teachings and seamless actions haven't been in vain. Your suffering and devotion to evolving Humanity has always been in our best interest and always will.

Forgive us, for we do not know any better and have mercy on us, for we are yet to see your divine energy. Humanity now offers you thanks and praise and the realisation and certainty of hope for our future.

— DAVID SHAUN LARSEN

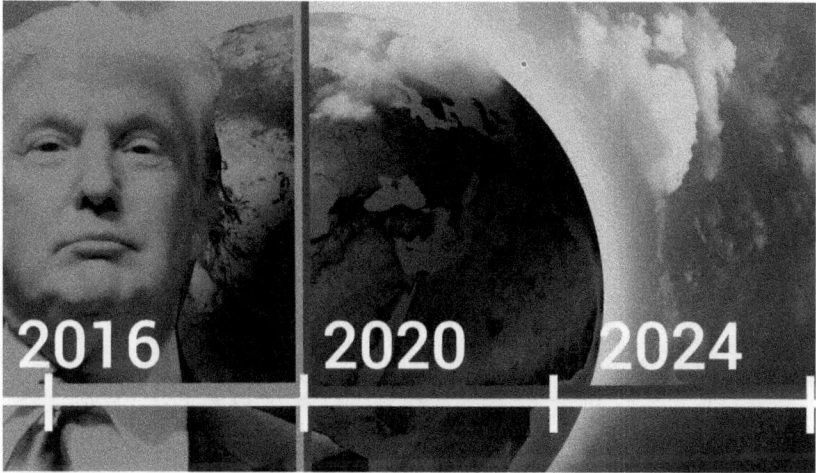

New frontiers, never possibly imagined before.

19

OUR NEW HOPE

- A PRACTICAL TOOLKIT FOR SPIRITUAL
FULFILMENT AND SUCCESS

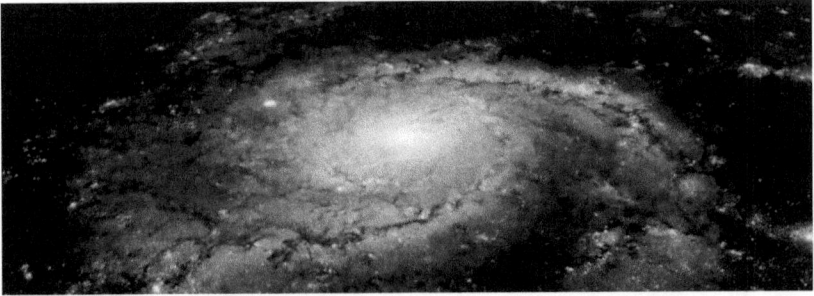

> *Your playing small does not serve the world. There is nothing enlightened about shrinking so that other people will not feel insecure around you. We are all meant to shine, as children do.*
>
> *It is not just in some of us; it is in everyone, and as we let our light shine, we unconsciously give others permission to do the same. As we are liberated from our fear, our presence automatically liberates others.*
>
> — MARIANNE WILLIAMSON

The Moon Landing

THE MOON LANDING, in 1969, was a surreal moment for Humanity, as we first set foot on the moon. It was our New Hope and a defining moment in our world's modern history. Neil Armstrong declared his famous words, "That's one small step for man. One giant leap for mankind". It was also the first time Humanity saw a true reflection of itself, as media images were beamed live. The earth appeared as a tiny rock, so far away and just hanging out there in the vast sphere of space. The Evolutionary Intention of this moment signalled an important shift for Humanity. This was our "Awakening" to our connection with the Cosmos. In doing so, opening the door to understanding, for the first time, the Universal Law of balance and harmony.

> This world is but a canvas to our imaginations.

> — HENRY DAVID THOREAU

This moment also connected us to our authenticity as human beings; it was now logical that Humanity had the potential to step deeper, into the realm of outer space. Our New Hope is, we will finally have the realisation that we don't need to conquer space but be passengers; learning to understand its nature, be in immense awe of its beauty and appreciate the Universal Laws it may prescribe to us. What is significant, is Australia's important role in the creation of this moment in history and what it forbid for the future.

The Parkes Radio Telescope, 'the Dish', played an integral role in getting the television pictures of man first walking on the moon to the world. The Parkes Telescope was chosen due to its size (being 64m in diameter, it had seven times the sensitivity for collecting signals). The Parkes Radio Telescope was recognised as a world leader in radio astronomy.[67]

When the actual day arrived, there were a number of significant hurdles that the Dish had to overcome in order to transmit the signals.

As there was a change in the mission schedule, the moonwalk was rescheduled to begin later than originally planned at 4.20pm AEST. This meant Parkes was to become the primary receiving station.[67]

> The conditions at the time here were terrible. Just moments before the moonwalk began; a violent wind squall hit the telescope. The Dish was fully tipped-over at its most vulnerable when it was hit by two gusts exceeding 110km/h, and that actually made the telescope slam back against its zenith axis pinions causing the tower to shudder and sway.
>
> The astronauts may very well have been on the Sea of Tranquillity on the moon, but it was most definitely the ocean of storms here at Parkes at the time. For the first eight minutes of the broadcast, NASA switched between the pictures that were being received by Parkes, Honeysuckle Creek, and Goldstone, before finally settling on using Parkes' signal for the rest of the two-and-a-half-hour moonwalk.
>
> Just as Buzz Aldrin switched on the TV camera, they were able to pick up the signal. What started off with Parkes perhaps not getting any pictures, ended up with them getting the entire picture and the majority that the world saw. And all this happened during a wind squall.
>
> — JOHN BOLTON, THE DIRECTOR OF THE PARKES OBSERVATORY 1969

It was a great moment in the history of Australia; we allowed the world to witness this most remarkable event with the greatest possible clarity. As John states, **"It really is something that Australians should be proud of"**.

Beyond the Black Stump of Eternity

Succeeding at Becoming More Spiritual

Sometimes, succeeding at becoming more spiritual; we do not need to do more things, we just need to give up on some of the outdated ways of doing things and refocus our energy on the new ones. Although every person has a different definition of spirituality, there are certain things I believe are universal or relate to "Universal Law". There are over billion-trillion stars in the Universe clustered in over 100 billion galaxies. Imagine if there is an intergalactic community of civilisations, far more evolved and intelligent than ours. It follows logic they would not reach that level of spiritual evolution if they were barbaric and used the forces of destruction and evil to create their civilisations or societies. Some may say, unlike other civilisations, such as ours. We still invest in war and terror like no different time in history. How could we be responsible for anything or any living thing for that matter, beyond our known frontier of space?

So how do you think they would live and act? It is certain they would prescribe to a set of "Universal Laws" that maintain balance and harmony. This is not dissimilar to how progressive societies on earth use law for the advancement of equality and our civil rights. I remember the eminent and Honourable Michael Kirby once talking about the importance of gay marriage in Australia and its subsequent law reform, "law sets a precedent and behaviour change follows". What this infers, is that Law sets the standard for what we want our society to become. Once achieved, the old behaviour changes. In thirty years' time, we will look back and wonder why we spent so much time debating issues such as Marriage Equality; especially when our country remained so resistant and far behind many other nations.

305

A photograph of a sunset taken on a boat to Ilha Grande, Brazil.

There is also a lot written about Universal Laws and searching the Internet you will find an abundance of these from seven, twelve or more. I am just using the ones that make sense in our daily life and the order these appear is done with a sense of purpose, as I find they tend to build on one another, much like building blocks. And lastly, I'm certainly not proclaiming to give you a new list of 'Ten Commandments' for that is not the purpose of this book.

If you do your best to prescribe to these Universal Laws, you will become more spiritually aware; not only in your day to day outlook but in your fulfilment of life and success i.e., achieving and living the life you're meant to have with the greatest sense of gratitude and kindness. Applying these laws in your life sometimes work with great success and sometimes with failure and criticism. But like everything it requires dedication, practice, and a bit of faith i.e., being open to the unknown. How can we truly know something's value or worth if we don't give it a go?

My only word of advice is to experiment for yourself, but like everything we become good at, you need to put in the effort or the hard yards. In saying this, nothing in life is set in concrete for choice and destiny work together. Investigate it for yourself and find new ways and terminology to use these Laws, in a fashion that suits you. In principle, there's nothing wrong with creating your own set of Universal Laws, as long as it resonates with you and is done with the right intention.

A Practical Toolkit for Spiritual fulfilment and Success

1. The Law of the Body, Mind, and Spirit - Balancing the Healthy Lifestyle Trinity.

"Take care of your Body. Challenge the Mind. Nurture your Spirit" — *David Shaun Larsen*

If you want to fulfil your spiritual destiny or you'd rather think of it as the life that you're meant to live, everything starts here. I deliberately don't spend much time writing about the topics or things where there is already a wealth of information and knowledge. My intention is to write about everything I know, in the hope the reader is able to find new ways of thinking around **balancing the healthy lifestyle Trinity i.e.,** the Body, Mind, and Spirit.

Take Care of your Body

There are only two basic things you need to keep in mind:

- **Maintain a healthy diet** but don't give up on everything that you enjoy. The body gets enormous pleasure from the foods that you intuitively like, but like they say, everything in moderation. There are so many dietary fads that come and go but follow your instinct because our bodies are all different, what works for one may not work for another. Being vegetarian is probably one of the healthiest diets you can have.
- For the adventurous, explore Ayurveda and the foods you can eat based on your body type e.g., Kapha, Pita, and Vata.
- _Tips_: daily Tumeric, Apple Cider Vinegar, Lemon, Cayenne Pepper is a great tonic. Using lemons and their juice in water is a good alkalinising agent and turmeric and cinnamon on their own are great herbs to use on a daily basis (just mix one teaspoon daily in smoothies). Brazilian nuts are also highly nutritious with many essential minerals including selenium._

- **Undertake physical activity** that you enjoy e.g., aerobic exercise, cross fit, walking, gym, swimming, kayaking, surfing, sport, and dog walking. It takes some trial and error but the hardest challenge here is making it happen as routinely as possible. Don't beat yourself up though if you waver from your routine; the golden rule is to just start again but mix it up or try something different.

Lastly, don't feel overwhelmed and take courage, start with your foundation first, get your body's health right. Then work on achieving a healthy mind and spirit, and remember small steps, every day is a new day. No one is perfect.

tcmaustralia.com.au

Challenge the Mine

HERE ARE A FEW VALUABLE TIPS: -

- **Access to professional counselling** is always beneficial for any emotional issues and/or just talking therapy with trusted friends, mentors, sports coach, work colleagues, etc. The key words here are the people you can build a rapport and trust with. Therapy always helps, especially for any childhood trauma; post-traumatic stress situation; grief and loss, drug addiction, suicidal ideation and relationship difficulties.

- **Using Mindfulness Practice and Reframing** in daily life. This is probably one of the most important things you can do. I used to always be such a negative thinker. Examples would be, "This always happens to me" or the tendency towards catastrophism in everything i.e., thinking of the worst-case scenarios all the time. Thinking positively helps you to manifest what it is you want to become. It'll also give you greater power to challenge any self-criticism and negative thinking.

- **Mindfulness is** the human ability to be fully present, aware of where we are and what we're doing, and not being overly reactive or overwhelmed by what's going on around us (https://www.mindful.org/about-mindful/). Mindful is a mission-driven non-profit. Mindful is the voice of the emerging mindfulness community. It's the place to go for insight, information, and inspiration to help us all live more mindfully.

- When you constantly fall into the trap of self-criticism and negative thinking (which develops into negative thought patterns over time), you can start to take on the victim and martyr role. However, you can easily fix this but it requires a lot of mental dedication and focus. What I have found useful is using my Buddhist practice of Mindfulness - as a way of starting to identify the negative thoughts or patterns, capture them in your mind and then try your best to reframe them into a positive.

- Also, try some of the Mindfulness Apps that are available to download. Smiling Mind is great! Smiling Mind is a not-for-profit organisation that works to make mindfulness meditation accessible to all.

- **Reframing** is a framework in which you simply reframe negative experiences and thoughts and turn them into a positive. It's often hard to do at the time, but even afterward you'll start to realise that you can reframe any negative experience or thought. I even reframed my whole childhood experience. The "woe is me" attitude can consume you, "I have such a terrible father, why can't we be like other families who seem more functional and what right does he have to destroy my childhood and upbringing?". The reframed experience is, "big deal I had this dysfunctional father. However, how amazing is it, that I have this most beautiful and supportive mother in my life who have been there for me and held the family together, when some people may not have had either parent there for them". Try it; you can reframe anything, it's just about having "the glass is half full" mentality as opposed to "the glass is half empty".

> We cannot, in a moment, get rid of habits of a lifetime.
>
> — MAHATMA GANDHI

Nurture your Spirit

Nurturing your Spirit is so important, and few of us know how do it right, or we just don't take the time to try. These types of therapies or practices also help with our body and mind.

Welcome to beautiful Hervey Bay.

- **Quiet time out,** sitting somewhere quietly in nature or by the sea is often one of the most nurturing activities. I love sitting on one of the empty chairs, that are nestled all along the boardwalk at Hervey Bay (pick your choice they're all different and I've given up counting how many). It's so serene, this vast bay of majestic ocean at your feet, that connects you to something much greater. Words cannot describe the feeling of pleasure this gives, all I know is that the mother whales will return to seek a safe haven here to have their baby calves. That says something in itself.

- **Meditation,** there are many meditation techniques and practices which people can research. It is not the purpose of this book to influence you with any particular practice or technique. Maybe start with simple meditation apps that you can download. There are many on mindfulness practice too.

- **White lighting the body,** sit quietly and use a meditation technique that you like or even as you stand or wash under the shower if you find this suits you better and white light your body. It's simple, just imagine a beam of universal white light travelling down through your crown chakra (head) and let it flow through every part of your body (like standing under water) cleansing away any negative emotions, thoughts or energy. This technique will always cleanse your aura and body. Hey, you can even white light your car or house to ask for protection. I've used it many times, and I know it works. Just try it.

- **Traditional Chinese Medicine (TCM),** one of my favourites and I have used it as my preventive medicine on and off for over 20 years now. With a history of depression and anxiety in the past, I have not had any mood-related disorders in the past ten years since I have been actively using TCM. I have acupuncture monthly and take herbs daily. In TCM no one is in a perfect state of health and we all have our imbalances. If ten different people experience acute or more often chronic depression in Western Medicine, you will possibly be given a type of anti-depressant.

- In TCM you'll probably find that those same ten people will all have different diagnoses based on their imbalances. It's amazing for any digestive issue, nervous system, mood, stress, and fertility condition. **But even if you aren't sick, it's just about maintaining wellness.** In addition, I'm not espousing to use this as a stand-alone medicine both Western and TCM medicine have a place and role to play in optimising our healthcare.

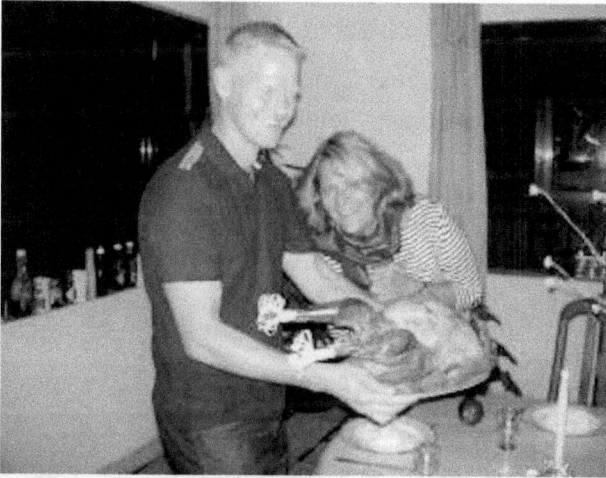

A picture of me with my dear friend Colleen. She's an amazing woman, a true Humanitarian who has been such an inspiration in my life (she's now retired living in Denver Colorado). We worked together both in Liberia and Iraq.

Other therapies to consider include:

- **Smile and use Humour** (so healing, natural and everlasting)
- **Reiki** (channelling Universal energy).
- **Spiritual Healing** (laying on of hands).
- **QiGong** (traditional Chinese practice using exercises and tools to improve energy flow within the human body).
- **Flower Essences** (such as Arizona Desert Essences, Australian Bush Flower Essences and NZ Flower Essences).

- **Yoga** there are many yoga techniques, and practices try it out, if it's not for you, then try something else.

Lastly, don't feel overwhelmed and take courage; start with your foundation first, get your body's health right. Then work on achieving a healthy mind and spirit, and remember small steps, every day is a new day. No one is perfect.

---

2. The Law of The Cosmos, "Understanding and Working with the 12 Universal Energies" - The Importance of Astrology in the 21st Century.

Astrology provides one of the greatest spiritual gifts that the Universe can provide as a toolkit for our survival in terms of its ability to interpret or validate our nature, predict future influences and ultimately transform our lives. However, the people who condemn it and are opposed to it (often using the reasoning of logic and science) often fail to see that it actually is logical and works. They don't even want to bother to learn or understand it in any way. It's a very complex craft, and although science doesn't see it that way, it's only because science is not yet that advanced to be able to explain it; so of course, it's classified as a pseudoscience for a good reason.

Humans have an innate need to find or search for the meaning to life and some of us the deeper meaning of its existence. We all seek meaning in something, whether our beliefs, religion, the media, nature, education, and relationships. We also create our own understanding of the things we observe around us and look for signs that point to the way forward. Often when we are in a dire situation, we look up to the sky or heavens for the answer. It's the heavens that I look to for my innate ability to frame life through an astrological lens or sense of understanding of the world. Studying one's birth chart can be a liberating experience, especially for those who are receptive to it i.e., those Awakening. On the other hand, for those Older / Old souls (like Princess Diana), they have an innate understanding of it and see it as a very enlightening process. It not only gives us the basic tools to understand our human nature but also clarifies all the various contradictions that we grapple with in everyday life. Often these contradictions are things we experience internally but also defend externally through our external environment such as relationships with others and the day to day set of circumstances we find ourselves in.

A picture of an astronaut, Astrology, and the earth - courtesy pixaby.com.

I love the logic of Astrology, and it's actually quite complex in terms of its mathematical equations and interpreting the various effects of planetary angles. Astrologers use the exact same measurements that Astronomers would use to calculate the movement of planets in terms of their degrees and minutes. Any twelve-year-old child could learn or grasp the concepts of Astrology with ease, for it's that easy. Although Sun sign Astrology is as popular as ever, it cannot be simply reduced to Sun signs, which only indicate very little about an individual. Sun sign Astrology takes a very ancient and scientific craft to the lowest understanding possible, without really getting anything meaningful out of it.

Every person's Astrology chart is always divided into 12 houses which are just hypothetical points where the sun would be at 2 hourly intervals at the moment of your birth. Most people don't even know that there are 12 forms of Sun sign expression just as there are 12 forms of Moon sign expression. The Sun and Moon are very much like our Yin and Yang cannot co-exist without each other. They are synergistically connected much like day and night and hot and cold but represent our spirit and soul identity. Therefore there are actually 144 different qualities of Sun sign expression and 144 different qualities of Moon sign expression, which is pretty amazing and that's still only giving you a very basic understanding of Astrology as a science.

> For far too long, *genuine* Astrology has been regarded as an 'occult science' known only to a privileged few.
>
> I believe it is now time to 'rebrand' this superb *language of consciousness*, — a **Mind-Brain interface** — I've been clinically refining for the past 30 years.
>
> This new system uncovers your *intrinsic motivation* for living, describes our *Exceptional* **Life Purpose**, exposes the *source* of any deep **self-sabotage**, connects you to your **inherent Compassion**, gives **any career** a **humanitarian** focus, and can also **be of value** to . . .
>
> Kerrie Redgate

See it at Kerrie Redgate - Astrology & Reincarnation on Conversations With Robyn.flv

3. The Law of Polarity, Our Soul Evolution - Everything has opposites; it's the Spectrum of Life.

The Law of Polarity is simply that; everything has opposites, it's the spectrum of life. As stated in previous chapters **the spectrum of life is about attachment and ego at one end and non-attachment and spirit at the other.** One end of the spectrum drives us to shackle ourselves to our limitations while the other end of the spectrum liberates us to evolve.

An aboriginal interpretation of Yin and Yan.

Extreme fanaticism permeates our human condition at every turn; it's the pure force of the Ego that separates us and uses aggression and hate and is constantly in our face. Enlightenment is the opposing force (purity of spirit) that works to unify and is subtle, compassionate and unconditional. They polarise each other!

It's really about the polarity of life that exists in everything that we see, and no one can doubt the existence of it!

In seeking the deeper meaning of life, Older Soul's experience a deep tension between the polarity opposites of our "Soul Evolution" spectrum. This is just what Old Souls do; we experience the polarity of life far more deeply than the average person.

4. The Law of Change, "Your Choice and Destiny" - Being Out of Your Comfort Zone.

The Law of Change states, **"There's one thing we can be certain of in life, and that is change itself"**. The Awakening Soul knows this and starts to seek out the "Out of your Comfort Zone" type of experiences in life, and for others, it's either the Universe's way of initiating you to evolve or speeding up your soul's evolutionary process.

Me sitting on a donkey dressed in a traditional Kurdish costume in Erbil, Iraq 2006.

Older Souls know that **"Choice and Destiny Work Together"**, they are synergistically connected. Although we may have a predestined roadmap (however planned or vague it may be), we still have choice around the decisions that affect our lives. The "Awakened" soul starts to develop more awareness around this and realises that certain people come into your life for a reason. However, they still have a choice as to what they may do with that meeting.

The core essence of this teaching is understanding that we cannot control everything - release yourself from the things and situations you cannot control, and focus on the ones you can. No-one is perfect, and know that sometimes, the only thing you will be able to influence is your attitude towards others.

> Some things are up to us, and some things are not up to us

— EPICTETUS, STOIC PHILOSOPHER

5. The Law of Fulfilment, "What will be, Will Be" - Become what you are Meant to Become

The Law of Fulfilment simply asks the soul to learn to live with acceptance of **"What will be, Will Be"** and be open to the forces of change when the timing is right. Some things in life are just predestined. Therefore, accept your path in the world but be vigil and become what you are meant to become in regards to your roadmap. Enabling and empowering others to act is a dynamic part of this karmic influence.

To actualise The Law of Fulfilment, the soul needs to be attuned to understanding Karma (which I have not discussed here). Karma is the **Law of Cause and Effect**. Karmic influences do not require activation, as these powerful Universal forces are influencing us every waking minute of the day i.e., what you give out will come back to you threefold. At the highest vibrational level, it nourishes our destiny. At the lowest vibrational level, it offers the reverse effect i.e., sorrow and misery.

> Always feed the spirit and walk the path of the spiritual warrior. The spiritual warrior is the courageous one and

walks the path least travelled because it speaks to solitude and meaning. Although this path is fraught with much difficulty and challenge, it always leads to immense joy in understanding Universal abundance and happiness.

If you always feed the ego, your soul never gets the opportunity to be nourished. Only the defiant ones walk the path most travelled because it is alluring and speaks to self-focus and distraction. However exciting this path is, it provides nothing but emptiness and eventual misery. The misery of never fulfiling your destiny.

— DAVID SHAUN LARSEN

Sunset over Sugar Loaf Mountain, Ipanema, 2006.

Attuning to one's karmic energy isn't something we do; it's something we are.

6. The Law of Focus, "The Force of Success" - Focus Only on the People and Things that Matter.

The Law of Focus asks the soul to activate its mental power of commitment which is indispensable. It requires a soul to be present in the moment, attuning into their strong mental focus and concentration to work effectively. Successful people know how to use this energy well, as they're often driven with strong deter-

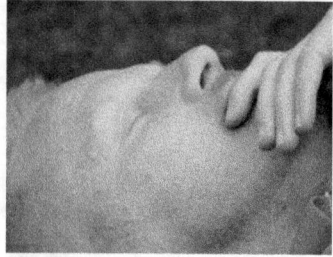

A picture of me reflecting.

mination to succeed. They focus on one thing at a time and exert power or force at any cost.

The Law of Focus can operate at different levels depending, on the intention of the person i.e., ones use or misuse of power and/or force.

> You will never reach your destination if you stop and throw stones at every dog that barks.
>
> — WINSTON S, CHURCHILL

---

7. The Law of Truth, "Always Be True To Yourself" - Say no to the things that don't support your spiritual path and values.

The Law of Truth is simply asking the soul to be true to yourself and saying NO, to the things that don't support your spiritual path and values.

> He who would accomplish little must sacrifice little; he who would achieve much must sacrifice much; he who would attain highly must sacrifice greatly.

— JAMES ALLEN

Roman Ruins, Amman Jordan.

8. The Law of Attraction, "Like Attracts Like" - Let go of the people and situations that no longer serve your purpose.

The Law of Attraction speaks to the concept that **"like always attracts like"**. As we evolve, we also attract different types of people in our life. Sometimes this means that we need to move away from people who no longer provide the "value added" qualities we need e.g., we may mix in different circles, encounter new teachers and people who inspire us. In other situations, it might be necessary to remove dysfunctional types of energy out of our lives i..e, selfish, negative and toxic people who thrive on manipulation and control. We only become the victim if we allow it to happen.

> The only way to avoid pissing people off is to do nothing important.

— OLIVER EMBERTON

We are made up of a complex array of energy, and as such, we mostly seek those who resonate with our vibrational energy and qualities. In other words, the energetic resonance of people is not the same. There may be some Older souls, and there are many Younger souls, but we are always drawn to whom we feel most comfortable "like always attracts like". There are people who are more selfless, and there are people who are more self-serving. There are people who are less ambitious, and there are people who are more ambitious. If we spend time with people, who don't provide something "value added" our vibrational energy or vitality can become drained and distorted. If we spend time with people who are more positive and provide some-thing "value added" our energy transforms.

If you spend time with people more evolved or enlightened than you; you'll find these people more emotionally intelligent, sensitive and caring, individuals. They're also more positive and value the wisdom of learning; surround themselves with other positive people and are often more forward-thinking and ahead of their time. They've well and indeed given up any need to be liked and have the courage to challenge others and speak out when needed.

No matter how distant or foreign they may appear at first, they often provide the challenges in life that you need. Do you need to make any changes?

9. The Law of Receiving, "Ask, and You Shall Receive" - Ask the Universe for What You Want.

The Law of Receiving reminds us to, "Ask the Universe for What You Want", however, it is imperative that you need to understand what you are seeking or wanting out of life. To enable this to happen, you need to reflect on what you want (vision) and how you want to achieve it (a plan). Basically, the Universe expects you to do some homework first. Give some thought to what your goals, dreams, and aspirations are and then create a plan for yourself. The plan should cover actions or strategies that you will need to undertake to make it work.

When you ask the Universe for something, you're activating The Law of Attraction but operating on another level which requires intense mental focus and commitment for it to work effectively i.e, also activating, The Law of Focus.

Ask and You Shall Receive.

There are three levels of "Ask, and You Shall Receive" that I use.

My 3 level approach is:

1. Ask your Angels - I use this technique on a day to day basis for practical and simple requests. Don't be afraid to ask your Angels.

There are angels for practically everything, its only limited by your imagination.

Tips: be humble, specific and offer thanks. A little humour helps too!!!

2. Ask your Management Team - I use this technique periodically only for a major issue or something I am struggling with in life, even searching for guidance. It's best to meditate and use any technique you like - just find a quiet, reflective space and sit in a comfortable position or posture. Focus on your breathing, just relax and imagine that you have a team of guides (everyone has guides, and they're your own team of spiritual helpers). How many? It's really up to you.

I usually just have a conversation with mine, sometimes I see faces and get names and other times I've tried to visualise faces and given them individual names. I like to believe that our Guides change over the course of our lifetime. Maybe some stay with us forever, for various karmic reasons. Try it!

Tips: be humble, use reflective practice, open conversation and always offer thanks. Your guides are spiritual entities you've known before or have karmic agreements with, so just be relaxed and enjoy their company or presence. A number of sessions are helpful over a short period of time.

3. Going to Counsel- is useful if infrequently used, possibly once a year if that. I only go to counsel for a major life event or crisis that is impacting on my ability to stay centred on my life path. On the other hand, I could be at a major crossroad in life or just want the Universe's support with something significant in my life e.g., self-publishing my book.

I usually imagine I am surrounded by a lush, overgrown, tropical forest with a nearby stream. When I turn around, I see a massive quartz stone Pyramid. I find the entrance and walk inside and usually all I see is darkness but somewhere towards the geographic centre of the pyramid; I see a beam of bright, white light. I walk up to the light, and sometimes the distance and time vary. Once I enter the beam of light, I suddenly see hundreds of ghost-like entities of various form, shapes, and sizes; floating high up above and all around me.

Going to counsel - spiritual beings of the highest order

These entities are evolved beings of the highest order, and it's equivalent to drawing on your Universal Armoury that's so powerful, it has the potential to be your greatest gift and change your life.

Tips: be in awe with wonder, be humble, be specific with what you are asking them as it's a treasured moment to cherish when going to counsel. But always come with the right intention (spiritually motivated), not from a selfish intention.

10. The Law of Wisdom, "Our Forgiveness and Understanding" - Seek knowledge in order to understand and forgive.

The Law of Wisdom is the spiritual warrior who always seeks knowledge with a sense of higher purpose i.e., the right intention to have a broader understanding and view of everything in life.

"Any resentment you hold onto is a wall in front of your heart. No technique other than forgiveness can remove it, and no one but you can do it." - Marianne Williamson

"Any resentment you hold onto is a wall in front of your heart. No technique other than forgiveness can remove it, and no one but you can do it." Marianne Williamson.

Knowledge is the source of our Universal Power, and Universal Power is the source our Knowledge. They are synergistically connected like Yin/Yang. This is not about intelligence, to the contrary. The spiritual warrior always understands that it's what you do with the gift of Knowledge that most counts. I believe knowledge used with the right intention is what enables and gives us the power to forgive.

11. The Law of Service, "Our Compassionate Nature" - Work to alleviate the suffering of others.

The Law of Service is the embodiment of the compassionate soul who understands nourishing their destiny, can only be achieved by alleviating the suffering of others. They understand their compassionate nature and work within their abilities to care, show mercy and empathise with others. Much like a Bodhisattva, they are ordinary people compelled to direct their actions to practice the way of life of a Buddha. If there is no compassion for our fellow man how can Humanity claim to be anything but just self-serving for its own misery?

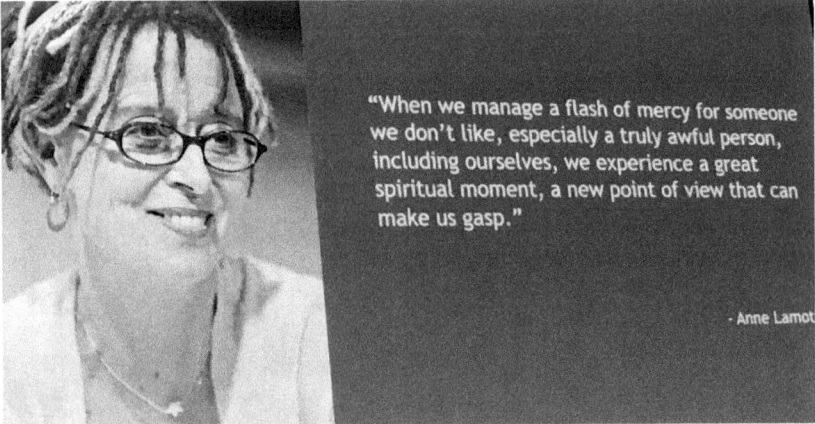

"When we manage a flash of mercy for someone we don't like, especially a truly awful person, including ourselves, we experience a great spiritual moment, a new point of view that can make us gasp."

- Anne Lamot

Anne Lamott, American novelist, and non-fiction writer.

> When we manage a flash of mercy for someone we don't like, especially a truly awful person, including ourselves, we experience a great spiritual moment, a new point of view that can make us gasp.
>
> — ANN LAMOTT

12. The Law of Selflessness, "Our Gratitude and Kindness" - Have an Open Heart and Love Unconditionally.

The Law of Selflessness is the art of living the sacred or Spiritual Way. No matter what our beliefs, culture or language, we are all capable of living the Spiritual Way. It's Universal.

- "La Voie Spirituelle", is French for the spiritual way.
- "El Camino Espiritual" is Spanish for the spiritual way.
- "神道; Shéndào" is Chinese for the sacred way.

With our heart open there is only gratitude and kindness; and selfless compassion for everything in the world. Our inner, intuitive voice of reason knows this; it knows all about the impermanence of life.

When we live in fear or show hate toward others; we don't do justice to our spirituality or ourselves.

> If we become ignorant of something so simple such as the fragility of our existence; how can we possibly evolve or transcend as humankind.
>
> Life affords us many opportunities to develop insight and growth, yet so many of us, are blinded to these joyful moments in life.
>
> If we are not receptive to the kind forces of change, the shackles of despair and misery overtake. Our hearts become closed, and we never discover the essential meaning of gratitude and loving kindness.

— DAVID SHAUN LARSEN

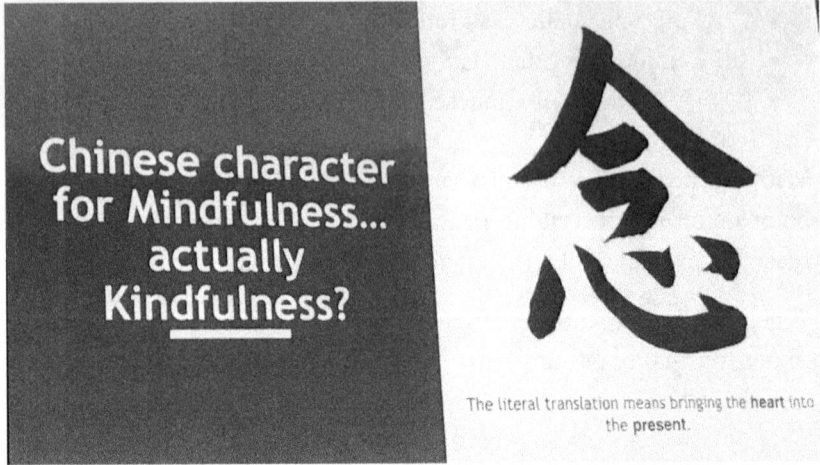

Chinese character for Mindfulness... actually Kindfulness?

The literal translation means bringing the **heart** into the **present**.

> When we add kindness to mindfulness we get "kindfulness," a new approach to meditation. Kindfulness is the cause of relaxation. It brings ease to the body, to the mind, and to the world. Kindfulness allows healing to happen. So don't just be mindful, be kindful!
>
> — AJAHN BRAHM

See it on YOUTUBE: Kindfulness by Ajahn Brahm

A photo of Angel Eyes, Dingo Puppy, K'gari (Fraser Island), near Hervey Bay Australia. He's been one my guiding Angles....

Bless you, Angel Eyes, your eyes are mesmerising and speak to nothing but unconditional love and understanding; how could we ever hurt you.

ABOUT THE AUTHOR

I like to see myself as someone who has always been ahead of my time and a facilitator of many destinies, which includes being a writer, concept developer, innovator, health professional, healer, and teacher. I am a qualified Registered Nurse and experienced Manager with a Master's in Public Health and Health Administration.

David Shaun Larsen

For the past 25 years, my professional career has primarily focused on managing and implementing health and humanitarian projects. This has afforded me with an invaluable insight into the operational and strategic management of quality orientated medical and humanitarian projects; working in a range of challenging and extraordinary situations.

A writer at heart, and Author of *'Beyond The Black Stump of Eternity'*. I am also someone who is an introvert but has always been a high-achiever with an ambition to create transformational change in the world. Although I value my solitude, having the gift of the gab, enables me to constantly explore opportunities to express my insights and share what I've learned with others. As a healer, I am a trained remedial therapist, spiritual astrologer, and reiki channeler.

Creating the space to have conversations and telling stories that truly matter is powerful. My purpose in life is to improve the quality of people's lives through alleviating the suffering of others. This drives my keen interest and passion in everything; whether from ideas generation to addressing health inequities or writing about a range of social justice and global issues.

What I have realised most about life, is that intention is everything, as long as it is with the right intention! We all have a valuable gift to ensure that those around us thrive because it's ultimately about advancing the welfare of Humanity and making a difference in the world. In saying this, I also provide an exceptional toolkit of services; with a wealth of practical ideas, therapies, and strategies for personal health, wellbeing and empowering others. Whether living a life with exceptional purpose, achieving personal aspiration or striving to reach your full potential; it's important that we work towards the things that matter and are essential for maximising our spiritual fulfilment and success.

Visit me at www.davidshaunlarsen.com

Email: davidsdm@yahoo.com

David Shaun Larsen

Photograph taken at the Honour Awards, Sydney 2016. Nominated for Health and Wellbeing category.

PERSONAL AND SOCIAL RESPONSIBILITY

I occasionally volunteer at the Hervey Bay Pet Adoption Centre – just love the work plus the dedicated group of volunteers who work there.

Ideally, I would like to promote the idea of having a writing group for older people in Hervey Bay.

Encouraging older people to tell their stories is so powerful, especially in this day and age when you can purchase an e-book program such as Vellum (or an equivalent program) for a minimal fee. The power of telling your story, developing your self-esteem as a writer and potentially generating an income source, far exceeds the cost.

Most people have varying abilities to write, therefore I see it as our societal responsibility to encourage our older people to tell their stories; possibly self-publish and become the beholders of their stories.

"Much like Elders do in our Aboriginal culture".

Please note 20% of all proceeds from the sale of my book are donated to: –

- **Doctors Without Borders** (Medicines Sans Frontières)
- **Animal Welfare Organisations on the Fraser City Coast**

BIBLIOGRAPHY

1. BBC, Religions, 2004. **Tibetan Buddhism**. http://www.bbc.co.uk/religion/religions/buddhism/subdivisions/tibetan_1.shtml. Publication date unavailable. Updated 14 January, 2004. Accessed 10 January, 2017.

2. Wikipedia, 2017. **Triratna Buddhist Community**. https://en.wikipedia.org/wiki/Triratna_Buddhist_Community. Updated 2 July, 2017. Accessed 14 January, 2017.

3. Academy of Classical Oriental Sciences, 2017. **The Chinese Medicine Meridian System | Academy of Classical Oriental Sciences.** http://www.acos.org/articles/the-chinese-medicine-meridian-system/. Accessed 19 June, 2017.

4. Wikipedia, 2017. **Chakra (**sometimes spelled **Cakra** or **Cakka).** https://en.wikipedia.org/wiki/Chakra. Accessed 21 January, 2017.

5. Wikipedia, 2017. **World War II Casualties**. https://en.wikipedia.org/wiki/World_War_II_casualties. Accessed 22 January, 2017.

6. WHO, 2015. **Global Health Observatory (GHO) data HIV/AIDS.** Accessed 23 January, 2017.

7. Wikipedia, 2017. **Rwandan Genocide**. Accessed 24 January, 2017.

8. Wikipedia, 2017. **Gender Equality**. https://en.wikipedia.org/wiki/Gender_equality. Accessed 28 January, 2017.

9. UNICEF, Operational Guidance Overview in Brief, 2017. **PROMOTING GENDER EQUALITY: AN EQUITY-FOCUSED**

APPROACH TO PROGRAMMING. https://www.unicef.org/gender/files/Overarching_2Pager_Web.pdf. Accessed February 27, 2017.

10. UNAIDS, 2016. **GLOBAL AIDS UPDATE**. http://www.unaids.org/sites/default/files/media_asset/global-AIDS-update-2016_en.pdf. Accessed 28 February, 2017.

11. Man UP, 2017. **One Bloke's Mission to Save Aussie Men**. http://manup.org.au/the-facts/the-stats/. Accessed 10 March, 2017.

12. World Economic Forum, 2017. **Global Gender Gap Report 2016.** Accessed through the WEF, http://reports.weforum.org/global-gender-gap-report-2016/. Accessed 12 March, 2017.

13. United Nations, 2017. **World Happiness Report 2017**. UN World Happiness Report. http://worldhappiness.report. Accessed 13 March, 2017.

14. Wikipedia, 2017. **King Hit Culture**. https://en.wikipedia.org/wiki/Sucker_punch. Accessed 13 March, 2017.

15. Australian Marriage Equality, 2017. **Australian Marriage Equality is a national organisation working to ensure all adult Australians can marry**. http://www.equalitycampaign.org.au. Accessed 14 March, 2017.

16. BUZZ FEED News. **The Typical Australian Politician Is A 51-Year-Old White Man Who Owns Two Homes.** https://www.buzzfeed.com/aliceworkman/meet-andrew?utm_term=.eadNn1826#.vjRkYelxo. Accessed 31 March, 2017.

17. Wikipedia, 2017, **Men's sheds** or community **sheds.** https://en.wikipedia.org/wiki/Men%27s_shed. Accessed 14 March, 2017.

18. Hillsong. https://hillsong.com/vision/. Accessed 16 March, 2017.

19. ONWARD TOGETHER, 2017. **ONWARD TOGETHER.** https://www.onwardtogether.org. Publication date 19 January 2017. Accessed 19 April, 2017.

20. Australian Dictionary of Biography, 2017. **Parkes, Sir Henry (1815–1896)** by A. W. Martin. Australian Dictionary of Biography, Australian National University. http://adb.anu.edu.au/biography/parkes-sir-henry-4366. Accessed 18 April, 2017.

21. Centennial Trust Parklands, 2017. **7 reasons why Sir Henry Parkes matters**. History and Heritage, Centennial Trust Parklands, http://blog.centennialparklands.com.au/sir-henry-parkes/. Accessed 19 April, 2017.

22. NSW Government, 2017. Office of Environment and Heritage, **"Centennial Park, Moore Park, Queens Park"**. http://www.environ ment.nsw.gov.au/heritageapp/ViewHeritageItemDetails.aspx?ID= 504539720. Accessed 20 April, 2017.

23. Trove: Digital Newspapers, 2017. December 1919, *Sydney Morning Herald*, **"Personal Notices"**. http://nla.gov.au/nla.news-page1252317?zoomLevel=3&searchTerm=mary%20edith%20mur ray&searchLimits=l-decade=191. Publication date 19 January 2017. Updated 9 March, 2017. Accessed 13 April, 2017.

24. National Centre of Biography, Australian National University, 2017. Murray, George 1832–1898. **Obituaries Australia.** http://oa. anu.edu.au/obituary/murray-george-16594/text28506. Publication date 19 January 2017. Accessed 13 April, 2017.

25. Peter Leyden, 2017. **Why Trump's Inauguration is Not the Beginning of an Era—but the Ends.** https://shift.newco.co/https-medium-com-peteleyden-why-trumps-inauguration-is-not-the-begin ning-of-an-era-but-the-end-72a86833f0a3. Publication date 19 January 2017. Accessed 19 April, 2017.

26. Fortune International, 2016. **California Passes France As World's 6th-Largest Economy.** http://fortune.com/2016/06/17/california-france-6th-largest-economy/. Publication date 18 June, 2016. Accessed 11 July, 2017.

27. Investors Business Daily, 2017. **It's Official: Clinton's Popular Vote Win Came Entirely From California.** http://www.investors.com/politics/commentary/its-official-clintons-popular-vote-win-came-entirely-from-california/. Publication date unavailable. Updated 2 July, 2017. Accessed 9 July, 2017.

27. BBC, 2017. **What our descendants will deplore about us.** http://www.bbc.com/future/story/20140627-how-our-descendants-will-hate-us. Tom Hatfield. Publication date unavailable. Updated 2 July, 2017. Accessed July 9, 2017.

28. ActUp, 2017. **AIDS Coalition to Unleash Power**. https://en.wikipedia.org/wiki/ACT_UP Publication date unavailable. Updated 6 July, 2017. Accessed 10 July, 2017

29. GetUp, 2017. **JOIN THE MOVEMENT OF 1,079,803 AUSTRALIANS.** https://www.getup.org.au. Publication date unavailable. Updated 2 July, 2017. Accessed 9 July, 2017.

30. Australian Conservation Foundation, 2017. **Stop Adani's mega polluting coal mine. Take the #StopAdani Challenge.** https://www.acf.org.au/stop_adani?utm_campaign=1707_stpadach2&utm_medium=email&utm_source=auscon. Publication date unavailable. Updated 10 July, 2017. Accessed 10 July, 2017

31. The Guardian, 2017. **Abbot Point coal port spill causes 'massive contamination' of Queensland wetland.** https://www.theguardian.com/business/2017/apr/10/abbot-point-coal-port-spill-causes-massive-contamination-of-queensland-wetland. Publication date 10th April 2017. Updated 10 July, 2017. Accessed 10 July,2017.

32. The Guardian, 2017. **Great Barrier Reef at 'terminal stage': scientists despair at latest coral bleaching data.** https://www.theguardian.com/environment/2017/apr/10/great-barrier-reef-terminal-stage-australia-scientists-despair-latest-coral-bleaching-data. Publication date 10th April 2017. Accessed 10 July, 2017.

33. Wikipedia, 2017. https://en.wikipedia.org/wiki/Kalkadoon. Publication date 10th April 2017. Updated 2nd February, 2017. Accessed 12th July 2017.

34. Chern'ee Sutton, 2017. **Contemporary Aboriginal Art.** http://www.cherneesutton.com.au/index.php?_a=document&doc_id=8. Publication date unknown. Accessed 12 July, 2017.

35. Australian Indigenous HealthInfoNet, 2005. **Social Determinants of Indigenous Health.** http://www.coop.com.au/social-determinants-of-indigenous-health/9781741751420. Publication date 2007. Accessed 12 July, 2017.

36. Amnesty International, 2016. **5 Things about indigenous history that you probably didn't learn about in school.** https://www.amnesty.org.au/5-things-about-indigenous-history-you-probably-didnt-learn-in-school/. Publication date 1st July, 2016. Accessed 12 July, 2017.

37. Australian National Museum, 2014. **Collaborating for our Indigenous Rights.** http://indigenousrights.net.au/civil_rights/the_referendum,_1957-67. Publication date unknown. Accessed 10 July, 2017.

38. Sydney Morning Herald, 2010. **Aussie slang? She'll be right, mate.** http://www.smh.com.au/lifestyle/aussie-slang-shell-be-right-mate-20100125-muaa.html. Publication date 25 January, 2010. Accessed 12 July, 2017.

39. The International Fund for Animal Welfare, 2017. **12 Aug 2017: Paddle out for Whales.** http://ww.whalewatch.com.au/paddle-out-for-whales.html. Publication date unknown. Accessed 11 July, 2017.

40. Médecins Sans Frontières. **Doctors Without Borders.** https://www.msf.org.au. Accessed 14 July, 2017.

41. Wikipedia, 2017. **Lake Mweru.** https://en.wikipedia.org/wiki/Lake_Mweru. Publication date 2017. Last updated 12 July, 2017. Accessed 14 July, 2017.

42. UNAIDS, 2016. **GLOBAL AIDS UPDATE.** http://www.unaids.org/sites/default/files/media_asset/global-AIDS-update-2016_en.pdf. Publication 2016. Accessed 29 May, 2017.

43. The Guardian, 2017. **Australia should bring Manus and Nauru refugees to immediate safety, UN says.** https://www.theguardian.com/australia-news/2017/nov/10/australia-should-bring-manus-and-nauru-refugees-to-immediate-safety-un-says?utm_source=esp&utm_medium=Email&utm_campaign=GU+Today+AUS+v1+-+AUS+morning+mail+callout&utm_term=251656&subid=15927438&CMP=ema_632. Publication date 10 November, 2017. Accessed 10 November, 2017.

44. Creswell Eastman (Cres), 2017. **How Creswell Eastman saved a million brains.** http://www.abc.net.au/local/stories/2015/12/02/4364236.htm. Accessed 25 May, 2017

45. DW Made for Minds, 2017. **Anti-gay sentiment on the rise in Africa.** http://www.dw.com/en/anti-gay-sentiment-on-the-rise-in-africa/a-19338620. Accessed 27 May, 2017

46. LGBT Denmark, 2017, http://lgbt.dk/english-2/. Publication date 2017. Accessed 7 June, 2017.

47. SBS, 2017. **The Vietnamese refugees who changed white Australia.** http://www.sbs.com.au/news/article/2015/04/14/vietnamese-refugees-who-changed-white-australia. Publication date 14 April, 2015. Accessed 16 June, 2017.

48. The Australian, 2017. **Australia is world's most successful immigrant nation.** http://www.theaustralian.com.au/business/opinion/bernard-salt-demographer/australia-is-worlds-most-successful-immigrant-nation/news-story/1b07d0d672e5eb6ba5e8b6630e5e55af. Publication date 20th March 2017. Accessed 13 June, 2017.

49. SBS, 2017. **2017 - 2018 Skilled migration intake announced.** http://www.sbs.com.au/yourlanguage/hindi/en/article/2017/05/10/

2017-2018-skilled-migration-intake-announced. Publication date 10th May, 2017. Accessed 14 June, 2017.

50. Migration Policy Institute, 2017. **Frequently Requested Statistics on Immigrants and Immigration in the United States.** http://www.migrationpolicy.org/article/frequently-requested-statistics-immigrants-and-immigration-united-states. Publication date 8 March, 2017. Accessed 15 June, 2017

51. Sane Australia, 2016. **Fact vs myth: mental illness basics.** https://www.sane.org/mental-health-and-illness/facts-and-guides/fvm-mental-illness-basics. Publication date 16 October, 2016. Accessed 15 July, 2017.

52. mindhealthconnect, 2017. **mindhealthconnect.** https://www.sane.org/mental-health-and-illness/facts-and-guides/fvm-mental-illness-basics. Publication date 16 October, 2016. Accessed 17 July, 2017.

53. Australian Network on Disability, 2017. **DISABILITY STATISTICS.** https://www.and.org.au/pages/disability-statistics.html. Accessed 9 October, 2017.

54. Jan Daisley, 2017. **BOOKS.** https://jandaisley.com/books/. Accessed 9 October, 2017.

55. The Conversation, 2016. **Understanding the NDIS: many eligible people with disabilities are likely to miss out.** http://theconversation.com/understanding-the-ndis-many-eligible-people-with-disabilities-are-likely-to-miss-out-61016. Published 7 July, 2016. Accessed 9 October, 2017.

56. **NDIS' virtual assistant Nadia, voiced by Cate Blanchett, stalls after recent census, robo-debt bungles.** http://www.abc.net.au/news/2017-09-21/government-stalls-ndis-virtual-assistant-voiced-by-cate-blanchet/8968074. Published 21 September, 2017. Accessed 27 October, 2017

57. Robina Courtin, 2017. **RobinaCourtin.com.** http://www.robinacourtin.com/. Accessed 12 September, 2017.

58. United Nations, 2017. **World Happiness Report 2017**. UN World Happiness Report. http://worldhappiness.report. Accessed 13 March, 2017.

59. ABC News, 2017. **What happens when a country strives for happiness — at any cost?** http://www.abc.net.au/news/2017-06-23/bhutan-strives-for-happiness-but-at-what-cost/8633424. Posted 23 June, 2017. Accessed 14 October, 2017.

60. Maria Rodale, 2017. **Top Ten "Micro Moments" of Happiness.** http://www.huffingtonpost.com/maria-rodale/top-ten-micro-moments-of_b_237567.html. Updated 17 Nov, 2011. Accessed 14 October, 2017.

61. THOUGHT CATALOG, 2016. **12 Reasons Why Old Souls Have Such A Hard Time Finding Love.** https://thoughtcatalog.com/brianna-wiest/2016/10/12-reasons-why-old-souls-have-such-a-hard-time-finding-love/. Published 19 October, 2016, Accessed 18 July, 2017.

62. ACON, 2017. **LOVE Project.** http://loveproject.org.au/. Accessed 15 October, 2017.

63. NCBI, 2015. **Neurosurgical patties: adhesion and damage mitigation.** https://www.ncbi.nlm.nih.gov/pubmed/25699413. Published July 2015. Accessed 15 October, 2017.

64. George Kinder, 2000. **The Seven Stages of Money Maturity**. https://www.penguinrandomhouse.com/books/92653/the-seven-stages-of-money-maturity-by-george-kinder/9780440508335/. Published 11 April 2000. Accessed 14 October, 2017.

65. Niall Conway, GiS 2017. **Australia - A Nation Embracing its Geospatial Future.** https://www.gis-professional.com/content/article/australia-a-nation-embracing-its-geospatial-future-2. Published 7 August, 2017. Accessed 28 October, 2017

66. Soul Emotions 2017, **Kiwi startup Soul Machines reveals latest artificial intelligence creation, Rachel.** http://www.newshub.co.nz/home/money/2017/07/kiwi-startup-soul-machines-reveals-latest-artifi

cial-intelligence-creation-rachel.html. Published 9 July, 2017. Accessed 27 October 2017.

67. Robert Virtue, ABC News Central, 2017. **Remembering Australia's role in man landing on the moon.** http://www.abc.net.au/local/stories/2014/07/21/4050043.htm. Published 21 July, 2014. Accessed 29 October, 2017.

---

www.ingramcontent.com/pod-product-compliance
Lightning Source LLC
LaVergne TN
LVHW051621080426
835511LV00016B/2099